The Evolution of Social Systems

MONOGRAPHS IN PSYCHOBIOLOGY:
An Integrated Approach

Edited by Samuel A. Corson

Ohio State University
Department of Educational Theory and Practice
Columbus, Ohio, U.S.A.

VOLUME 1 PSYCHOPHYSIOLOGICAL ASPECTS OF READING AND LEARNING

edited by Victor M. Rentel, Samuel A. Corson and Bruce R. Dunn

VOLUME 2 CRITICAL ISSUES IN PSYCHOLOGY, PSYCHIATRY, AND PHYSIOLOGY

edited by F.J. McGuigan and Thomas A. Ban

VOLUME 3 THE EVOLUTION OF SOCIAL SYSTEMS

by John Paul Scott

This book is part of a series. The publisher will accept continuation orders which may be cancelled at any time and which provide for automatic billing and shipping of each title in the series upon publication. Please write for details.

THE EVOLUTION OF SOCIAL SYSTEMS

by

John Paul Scott

Department of Psychology
Bowling Green State University
Ohio, USA

GORDON AND BREACH SCIENCE PUBLISHERS
New York • London • Paris • Montreux • Tokyo • Melbourne

Gordon and Breach Science Publishers S.A.

Post Office Box 786
Cooper Station
New York, New York 10276
United States of America

Post Office Box 197
London WC2E 9PX
England

58, rue Lhomond
75005 Paris
France

Post Office Box 161
1820 Montreux 2
Switzerland

3-14-9, Okubo
Shinjuku-ku, Tokyo
Japan

Private Bag 8
Camberwell, Victoria 3124
Australia

Library of Congress Cataloging-in-Publication Data

Scott, John Paul, 1909–
    The evolution of social systems.

    (Monographs in psychobiology ISSN 0749-1190; v. 3)
    Bibliography: p.
    Includes indexes.
    1. Evolution.   2. Social evolution.   3. Behavior evolution.
4. Behavior genetics.   5. Sociobiology.   I. Title.   II. Series.
QH371.S3984   1989   575.01   88-24546
ISBN 2-88124-317-7 (cloth)   ISBN 2-88124-358-4 (paper)

This book is dedicated to the memory of

Sarah Fisher Scott, who helped write the first version,

John Paul Scott, Jr., Ph.D., whose early and tragic death forestalled a promising career in psychobiology and

Sewall Wright, master architect of the genetic theory of evolution.

Contents

Preface

This book had its beginnings in a seminar on the evolution of social organization that I attended while on sabbatical leave at Stanford University. At that time, Dr. David Hamburg and his colleagues were doing some fascinating research on chimpanzee social organization, both at Stanford and in Africa, and the participants in the seminar were tremendously excited by the results. As I listened to their presentations and added one of my own, I soon realized that while their data were excellent, their theoretical explanations were incomplete in two important respects, and I began the task of remedying these deficiencies.

In these pages, I have explored the implications for evolutionary theory arising from two important sets of ideas, neither of which is adequately expressed in most contemporary thinking about the evolution of social organization. The more general of these is the systems concept, an idea long current among biologists but first extended to other phenomena by von Bertalanffy (1968). A major part of this concept is the universality of two-way causation or feedback among the entities composing a living system. Seen in this light, the one-way causation postulated by mechanistic theories of evolution becomes untenable. All evolutionary processes are therefore interrelated, directly or indirectly, and to greater or lesser degrees. In this conceptual framework, evolution can be defined as change in the organization of living systems, and I have used this general model to review all evolutionary processes.

The second set of concepts employed here is a more limited one, that of the genetic bases of biological evolution. While these foundations and the theories arising from them are well understood by geneticists, they are often inadequately appreciated by theorists who attempt to explain the evolution of social organization. Nor do genetical theorists always appreciate the effects of social organization on changes in genetic systems, neglecting the principle of feedback.

In the course of integrating genetical theories of evolution with the systems concept, I point out that there are at least three workable theories of biological evolution, none of which is universal and each of which is useful if applied to appropriate species and conditions.

In applying these theories to the evolution of behavior and social organization, I show that each of these phenomena has major feedback effects on genetic change. Behavior strongly modifies natural selection because behavioral adaptation takes place within the life span of the individual expressing it, often within a few seconds, instead of awaiting generations of genetically modified physiological adaptations. Social organization not only alters the evolutionary process of natural selection by creating new sources of selection but may facilitate genetic change through social interaction. For those species that possess it, social organization becomes a part of evolutionary theory.

Finally, I discuss two processes of evolutionary change other than those involved in changes of genetic systems. Both are especially important to the human species, and while both are interrelated with the processes of genetic change, neither one is directly controlled by biological evolution. These changes include cultural evolution largely based on communication through language in the human case, and ecosystem change, or eco-evolution, strongly related to biological evolution through co-evolution among species having ecological relationships (another example of feed-back in biological systems), but also to some extent independent of it through ecological succession.

There are no final answers here. Evolutionary theory will itself evolve as new discoveries are made. What I have done in this book is to point out some new directions.

John Paul Scott

Acknowledgments

I wish to thank those persons who have helped me write this book in its final form, particularly Dr.'s N. E. Collias, Loring Brace, Benson Ginsburg and George Barlow, who read portions of the manuscript and made helpful suggestions; to dozens of students who discussed its issues in graduate seminars; to the secretaries who typed innumerable versions and especially Ms. Barbara Sharp; and to my wife, Dr. Mary-'Vesta Marston Scott, who served as an editor.

I also wish to thank Dr. Luis Lara Tapia and the Instituto de Investigaciones Antropológicas of the Universidad Nacional Autónoma de México for permission to reprint as part of Chapter IX a portion of my paper, "Ethology and Aggression" from the volume *Para conocer al hombre. Homenaje a Santiago Genovés* (in press); also the Elsevier/North Holland Press for permission to reprint Table 10.2 from my article "The evolution of function in agonistic behavior" (Scott, 1981).

Chapter I

Evolution and Systems Theory

The value of a scientific theory lies in its potential for stimulating further thought and research. Ideally, a theory should be experimentally testable. If not, as is the case with historical theories such as biological evolution, it should at least explain the observable facts in a logical and consistent fashion. In so doing it will perform another sort of function, that of indicating which facts are missing and should be discovered. The theory of biological evolution has served this function on an enormous scale by providing the stimulus during the latter half of the 19th century and the first years of the 20th for collecting all the available facts concerning the comparative anatomy of living and extinct forms of life as well as the description of embryonic development in living plants and animals.

Will theories of the evolution of social behavior and social organization provide a similar stimulus for research in the social sciences in our own times? Here we are faced with a particularly difficult problem of developing testable historical theories, in that *all* the observable phenomena of behavior and social organization are contemporary, with the exception of tracks and constructions that may have persisted from remote periods. Experimenters are therefore reduced either to gathering information that supports or denies certain theories or to observing ongoing evolutionary change processes and experimenting with these insofar as this is possible. It does not necessarily follow that these processes are the same as they were in bygone eras. Indeed, it would deny the whole basis of the concept of evolution if one were to assume that evolutionary processes themselves could not change.

But evolutionary theory is more than a useful motivator for the ongoing scientific enterprise of which it is a part. Every known human culture has some mythological or divine explanation of how life began and where people came from. These beliefs are woven into their respective cultures and used to support and justify cultural practices. Our own culture is no exception.

The theory of biological evolution as developed in the 19th century was the first attempt to produce a scientific rather than a mystical theory of origins. It immediately became a center of conflict and very soon was misused to justify existing cultural practices. Thus the practices of many early industrial employers of paying starvation wages and requiring their employees to work under hazardous and unhealthy conditions was said to be a good thing because it resulted in the survival of the fittest. Because the early theories of biological evolution implied competition, they were used to excuse the destructive competitive practices of the culture in which the theories arose.

The principal advocates of this misapplied theory were two early sociologists, Herbert Spencer (1884) in England and William Graham Sumner (1883) in the United States. "Social Darwinism" was founded on bad science and is no longer taken seriously by sociologists, but it still appeals to some unsophisticated people.

A second misapplication of evolutionary theory was fathered by Galton (1869) in his studies of hereditary genius. He assumed that persons of wealth and power achieved this through biologically inherited talent, which led to the Eugenics Movement and the notion that the unfit should not be allowed to reproduce. This resulted in numerous sterilization laws in the United States in the 1920's, and the mass exterminations practiced by Hitler's Nazis in the 1930's and 40's.

It is therefore important that we develop as true a picture of evolution as possible, culture free and bias free. The following essays are a contribution to this effort. I shall begin with an important biological concept that many evolutionary theorists have overlooked, namely that all living things are organized into systems. Evolutionary theory must, therefore, explain changes in the organization of systems.

I shall therefore begin by examining evolutionary theory in the light of the systems concept. The use of this concept is inherent in the thinking of all workers in this field but is not always clearly expressed nor understood in all its complexity.

Definition of Evolution

In the context of systems, evolution may be defined as a process of change in the organization of a system or systems that persists and continues for more than one generation. This includes three broad classes of change processes: biological evolution, cultural evolution, and ecosystem change. The same definition might be applied to the development of an individual, except that developmental organization of such a system continues and persists for only one generation. Evolutionary change ordinarily extends over many generations and, unless there are factors which bring the process to a standstill, it should go on indefinitely.

THE NATURE OF LIVING SYSTEMS

Definition

A system is generally defined as a group of interacting entities. This definition applies to nonliving as well as living systems, but there is a clear line of demarcation between the two. Nonliving systems obey the second law of thermodynamics; that is, their organization decreases over time. On the contrary, the distinctive characteristic of living systems is that they tend to change in the direction of increasing complexity of organization. In a word, living systems are *negentropic*. This does not mean that living systems escape entropy entirely; organisms die and species become extinct, and as they do so they become disorganized and their constituents rejoin non-living systems.

The Organization of Living Systems

Living systems are organized as sets of nested systems and subsystems as indicated in Figure 1.1. The most inclusive system is the ecosystem, and the central and least inclusive one is the genotypic system. However, every system is made up of interacting entities, and a system may act as an entity itself on a higher level of organization.

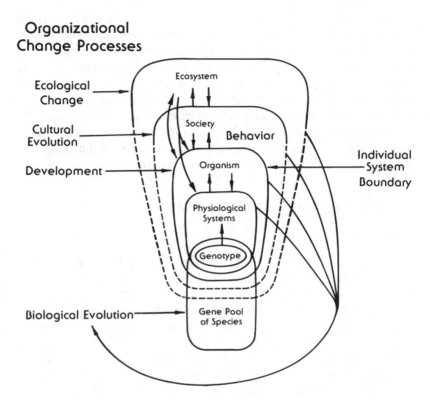

Figure 1.1. Polysystemic organization: major systems and subsystems of animal organisms. Living systems are organized in a set of nested systems and subsystems. Note that organization is inclusive; the parts cannot operate separately. Solid lines indicate structural or anatomical organization; dotted lines indicate that animal organisms are capable of movement and that behavior rather than structure is the predominant mode of organization on the more inclusive levels. A similar diagram for plants, whose powers of movement are non-existent or limited, would omit the social organization. Not shown on the diagram are the facts that societies include many organisms and that ecosystems include many species each of which may include many societies. (Modified from Scott, 1975, by permission of the University of Chicago Press.) (See also Figure 1.3.)

Interaction within and among Living Systems

The sort of interaction that occurs within a living system is not the same as the concept used in a statistical sense, where it implies two or more independent factors acting simultaneously on a third. Rather, the entities within the systems act directly on each other (see Figure 1.2).

This definition of interaction implies two-way causation: the principle of *feedback*. Such interaction occurs between lower and higher levels of organization as well as between entities on the same level, and in all directions simultaneously. Further, interactions on higher levels produce phenomena that do not occur on lower levels – the principle of *creativity*. As an example, genes do not "think" but brains can.

System Interaction   Statistical Interaction

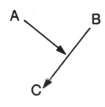

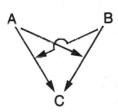

Figure 1.2. Interaction between entities within a system contrasted with statistical interaction, in which two or more independent factors modify each other's actions on a dependent variable but do not affect each other through feedback. The statistical type of interaction also can occur with a system, but the possibility of the feedback relationship must always be considered.

Development

The phenomenon of negentropy has a special application at the level of the organism. As an organism grows it becomes increasingly complexly organized, a process that we ordinarily call development. The same concept can be applied at higher levels without distortion, as long as there is an increase in the complexity of organization. Thus a social relationship can "develop", as can ecological relationships when a new species enters an area.

Stability

As they develop, living systems tend to become increasingly stable and resistant to change. The maintenance of stability becomes a special function at the level of physiological organization, where it is called *homeostasis*. Internal stability arises presumably because stable conditions lead to more efficient interactive functions of the component parts. This implies that living systems, by becoming stable, have some tendency to resist further changes in organization, a process that would, of course, work against evolutionary change. It also suggests a basic hypothesis: *Change in the direction of increasing complexity goes on because more complex organization permits greater internal stability in the system.*

Evolutionary Change

Contrary to the principle of stability, living systems possess organized processes of change that result in evolution. Such change, however, need not necessarily proceed toward increasing complexity. In many parasites, evolution has proceeded in the direction of simplified body structure and physiology, probably because, particularly in internal parasites, so many of the functions of living are carried on by the host. At the same time, ecological relationships of a parasite may become quite complex, as in the case of parasites that live within two or more host species. This suggests that evolutionary changes toward complexity must be evaluated on all levels of organization simultaneously.

Adaptivity

Living systems tend to protect their constituent entities and thus to prolong their own existence. This is a major principle of evolutionary theory, as well as systems theory; it predicts adaptation, which is a verifiable phenomenon.

EVOLUTION IN RELATION TO LEVELS OF ORGANIZATION

The major levels of biological organization as generally recognized are pictured in Table 1.1. Historically, the biological sciences have developed around each of these major levels. Although each level is included in the level above it (as shown also in Figure 1.1), scientists concentrating on one level often assume an independence of phenomena on lower levels that does not actually exist. Another common error of the past has been to assume one-way causation between levels, leading to reductionism and attempts to explain all phenomena on the basis of genetics, as if genotype and phenotype were completely congruent.

The limitation of the levels concept is that drawing a line between one level and another is almost always a somewhat arbitrary process, because one level is never completely separated from another. That is, there is reciprocal interaction between levels as well as within them. A level has meaning, therefore, only where there is significantly more interaction among entities at a given level than between the same entities and those in the inclusive sys-

Table 1.1
MAJOR LEVELS OF BIOLOGICAL ORGANIZATION

Level	System	Constituent Entities
Ecological	Ecosystem	Species (Animal & Plant)
Social	Society	Organism (Animal)
Organismic	Organism ("individual")	Physiological Systems
Physiological	Organ System	Organs
	Organ	Tissues
	Tissue	Cells
Genetic	Genotype	Genes

Note that social organization, and hence the social level, is found only in animal species, whereas all other levels are present in both plants and animals.

tem above it. Such a line is particularly hard to draw between organismic systems and their constituent physiological systems. The activities of neither can proceed without the other.

Evolutionary Organizational Change Can Occur at any Level of Biological Organization

The implications of this hypothesis will be discussed in detail later. However, such organizational changes may be only secondary. By definition, primary evolutionary change can occur only withinsystems whose organization persists longer than one generation. Thus, evolutionary changes within a system are impossible both at the physiological level and at the level of the individual organism, because of the death of the individual. Changes of organization within these systems are primarily developmental in nature. Developmental processes can evolve, but only in conjunction with changes on other levels.

Limitations of Evolutionary Change

To repeat, evolutionary change is limited to those systems in which organizational change proceeds for more than one generation. These systems are: 1) the gene pool of a species (biological evolution), 2) a society or persistent social group (cultural evolution), and 3) an ecosystem (ecosystem change or ecoevolution).

These three kinds of systems are not independent but are related to each other as systems which include subsystems; consequently the three kinds of evolutionary change must be related to each other. The nature of these interrelationships must depend on the reciprocal causal relationships between the systems involved.

Causal Relationships between Living Systems and Subsystems

As Figure 1.1 illustrates, the most inclusive living system is an ecosystem, made up of a large number of plant and animal species. Within an ecosystem, each species may be considered a subsystem of the whole. Within animal species, individual organisms may be organized into social groups, within a social group or society there are organisms, and within each organism there are physiological systems.

Finally, at the lowest level there is the genotype of each organism.

Drawing such a diagram brings out an obvious fact concerning both social and ecological organization. In contrast to organization at lower levels, units of both societies and ecosystems do not remain in constant contact, a phenomenon that makes for a great deal more freedom of action between the component parts and results in greater flexibility of the systems involved.

Here we have a great divide, a naturally occurring discontinuity in organization (Figure 1.3). At the level of the organism and below, organization is based upon constant anatomical contact, or structure. Above it, contact is only sporadic, interaction is behavioral, and the concept of structure becomes only a weak metaphor. Similarly, at the ecosystem level organization is only partially dependent on spatial relationships.

The diagram also includes arrows which indicate the direction of causation. The simplest hypothesis is that of one-way causation, proceeding from the lowest level of organization through intermediate levels to the highest. This hypothesis, that of reductionism, holds true only with respect to individual genotypes, as such systems are extremely resistant to change factors from any source at higher levels. As far as is known, once individual genotypes are formed at conception, they do not change in response to external factors, with the possible exception of radiation which may produce somatic mutation. Such mutations may produce a minor local change such as a white spot or, commonly in the case of induced tumors, they may totally disrupt the system.

While the structure of a gene ordinarily does not change within an organism, its expressed *action* is not independent of external factors. There are numerous cases of genes whose action varies under different environmental conditions, such as the gene that produces black hair pigment in the Siamese cat only in the colder regions of the cat's body, and other genes whose action appears only late in development, such as the gene involved in Huntington's Disease of humans, a degenerative disorder of the nervous system. Genotypes are always part of the total systems matrix.

Above the level of the genotype, whose action can be expressed only through physiology, the situation changes. Physiology affects the organism's behavior, but behavior can also affect physiology, as anyone can demonstrate to himself by running up a flight of stairs.

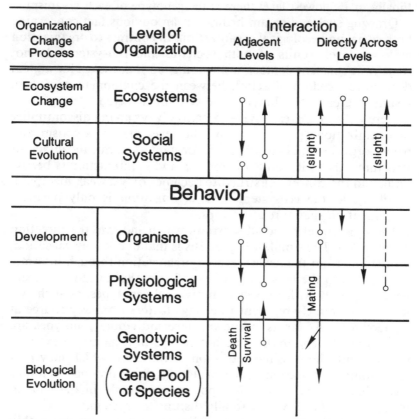

Figure 1.3. Feedback relationships between animal systems of different levels of organization. Note that within upper-level systems (Ecosystems, Social Systems), entities are related to each other by behavioral interaction; in lower level systems (Organisms, Physiological Systems, Genotypic Systems) entities are related to each other through fixed structure. All systems show reciprocal causation with those on adjacent levels except for genotypic systems, which comprise the most stable biological systems known and affect other levels only through physiological systems and are not directly affected in return. Indirect effects, however, are produced by differential death and survival and other processes of biological evolution, modifying the gene pool available to the next generation. Across levels, only organismic and ecological systems directly affect non-adjacent levels. The effects of organisms are relatively slight, except for mating behavior, which can affect the gene pool. The important point is that systems on any level of organization can affect and are affected by systems on every level, directly or indirectly. (From Scott, 1982, by permission of Sage Publications, Inc.)

Likewise, physiology can be affected more or less directly by factors in the ecosystem and in social systems (Figure 1.3). The behavior of an individual can also affect a social system or even an ecosystem, although effects are usually much more drastic in the reverse direction, from the higher levels downward.

A very important implication of these diagrams is that ecosystems and social systems can change with or without prior genetic changes, although, by changing, they may produce subsequent changes in genetic systems through processes of selection. Consequently, biological evolution is defined as persistent and continuing change in the organization of genetic systems. The problem then is to discover the processes that produce such change.

Systems Theory is Anti-Reductionistic and Anti-Mechanistic

Reductionistic theory and mechanistic theory have often been employed by biologists in the past, and such assumptions have frequently produced valuable empirical results. Applied universally, however, they are inadequate. Mechanistic theory implies one-way causation, and this rarely occurs within a living system. One must always assume two-way causation, unless demonstrated otherwise, between any two entities within a system, and between systems at different levels.

The almost universal phenomenon of feedback (between systems as well as within and between systems on different levels), conflicts with the assumption of reductionism: that phenomena on lower levels of organization can completely explain phenomena on higher levels. In the past, some naive scientists have hoped to explain everything on the basis of the biochemistry of genes, but this cannot be the case if there is feedback at any level of organization.

Furthermore, interaction between systems at higher levels produces phenomena that are impossible at lower levels and therefore cannot be deduced from the properties of lower level systems. An example is the non-additive interaction of genes. From a reductionistic-mechanistic viewpoint, it ought to be possible to predict from the knowledge of the enzymes produced by the genes of an organism what kind of organism would be produced by them in development, but the nature of interaction between these enzymes can only be ascertained by observing the results. In contrast to reductionistic theory, systems theory states that there is no hope of explaining anatomy, behavior, social organization, or any other higher order phenomena, on a purely genetic basis, an empirical fact well known to geneticists.

Since genetic material is the basis of biological evolution, it follows that evolutionary processes never can give more than partial explanations of higher order phenomena, important though such processes may be.

I should add that the phenomenon of feedback is not completely universal in living systems, a notable exception being the lack of direct feedback between genes and physiological phenomena, as pointed out above. A satisfactory systems theory must include the possibility of simultaneous one-way and two-way causation, although placing emphasis on the latter. It is perhaps fair to say that neither rigid mechanistic theory nor oversimplified systems theory can be universally applied.

CONCLUSIONS

1) Any complete theory of living systems must include all levels of organization. Many systems theories are deficient in this respect. Even von Bertalanffy (1968), who pioneered the attempt to develop a general systems theory, paid scant attention to the genetic level and even less to ecosystems. Authors who have been primarily interested in human organization have usually omitted the ecosystem level (Lazlo, 1972; Berke, 1977). Miller (1978) omitted both the genetic and ecosystem levels, starting with the cell on the lowest level and placing above all others the supra-national system. The latter is a human political organization and by its nature cannot include all living phenomena.

For consideration of biological evolution all levels are essential. The genetic and ecosystem levels are especially important. Biological evolution is based on change in genetic systems, and a large proportion of the factors that produce differential survival (Natural Selection) proceed from surrounding ecosystems. The things that are changed by biological evolution include all kinds of living systems on all levels of organization. Any complete theory of evolution must therefore consider organizational processes on all levels. It is the purpose of this book to outline such a theory, or set of theories, with special attention to the evolution of animals, including their behavior and social organization.

2) The concept of living systems as a set of nested systems and subsystems places the concept of hierarchical organization into a different perspective. When we talk of higher and lower levels of organization we need to remember that this is shorthand for more or less *inclusive* forms of organization. Which end is up, genetic systems or ecosystems, is purely arbitrary.

We should also remember that the concept of hierarchy is a metaphor borrowed from human social organization, where it meant a group of people organized into ranks graded according to the degree of power exercised by each rank. While the concept may have limited applicability in some other levels of organization (as, for example, in the brain and nervous system), and may be similar to social dominance organization found in some non-human animals, it conflicts with certain fundamental and general characteristics of system organization. The top ranks of a human hierarchy are exclusive, not inclusive. Further, the concept usually assumes 1-way causation, conflicting with the basic system principle of interaction and 2-way causation. Therefore, contrary to assumptions made by many systems theorists, the concept of hierarchical organization is not a general principle applying to all living systems.

3) The basic general characteristics of living systems are: interaction and 2-way causation between component entities and between systems on the same and different levels; organization as a set of nested systems and subsystems; development or negentropy (the tendency for organization to become increasingly complex); maintenance of stability; adaptivity; and emergence or creativity (phenomena that do not exist on lower levels of organization become possible at higher levels).

These characteristics do not comprise a theory. They can be stated as general principles, and anyone can work out their consequences or derive hypotheses that explain them. It is not the purpose of this book to develop such a body of systems theory, but rather to reconcile biological evolutionary theories with these principles.

4) Most importantly, genes can act only in conjunction with

other genes, as interacting entities within genotypic systems. No gene can act independently. Even viruses, which are the equivalents of single genes, can only function in conjunction with the genes of other organisms.

In addition to the general properties of living systems outlined above, systems on each level of organization have certain special characteristics of their own. Because changes in the organization of genetic systems are the basis of biological evolution, it is especially important to know the nature of genetic systems and recognize their unique qualities.

Chapter II

The Nature of Genetic Systems

THE GENE POOL AS A SYSTEM

The gene pool is defined as those genes that are available to a continuously interbreeding group of animals, human or nonhuman. Considered as a system, the entities composing the gene pool are individual genotypes (gene combinations). The ultimate units, of course, are the genes themselves, but they are able to interact with each other only as genotypes, which can be considered as subsystems of the whole. The concept of the gene pool is thus a somewhat artificial abstraction because genotypes can interact with each other only through higher levels of organization, particularly as genetic factors affect behavior. Thus, the basic genetic system is the genotype, and the gene pool is really the sum of all potential genotypes that can be derived by the reassortment of genes in a population of interbreeding individuals.

THE GENOTYPE AS A SYSTEM

A genotype is the assembly of genes belonging to a particular organism. These genes interact with each other as a system, the entities of which are the genes themselves. The basic problem of biological evolution is to understand how such systems may be changed, and this rests on the nature of genes and their interactions with each other.

The Nature of the Gene

The gene itself is a large organic molecule composed of DNA (deoxyribonucleic acid), and is a very large and complex protein molecule, double stranded, with the two strands connected in a ladder-like fashion by four amino acids (adenine, cytosine, guanine and thymine), which are regularly paired (adenine with thymine and cytosine with guanine). These pairs are repeated in differing orders which give each gene its unique chemical structure. Since the strands can be very long, an enormous number of combinations is possible.

Genes have three major organizing functions: 1) to reproduce themselves by organizing external substances into duplicates, 2) to organize material from living and non-living sources into substances that maintain the organismic systems of which the gene is a part, and 3) to organize systems on a higher level through developmental processes. All these functions are involved in the general process of evolution, which I have defined as persistent and continuing change in the organization of living systems, but the last has paramount importance, involving as it does the interactive functioning of genes.

Gene Interaction at the Genotypic Level

The nature of interaction between genes at the genotypic level has been discovered through studies of molecular genetics. Summarized, a gene acts by producing single-stranded RNA (ribonucleic acid). *Messenger RNA*, a molecule complementary to the DNA of the gene that produced it, is formed against a DNA template. Essentially it corresponds to a single strand of DNA. It leaves the nucleus (hence the name, "messenger") and joins a body in the cytoplasm called a ribosome. Here it forms a protein in conjunction with *ribosomal RNA* (a form of RNA bonded to a protein). The third form of RNA, *transfer RNA*, transfers a specific amino acid to a growing polypeptide chain which becomes a complex protein. Thus, messenger RNA directs a group of transfer RNA's to form a specific protein outside the nucleus and at a distance from the parent DNA (Ayala, 1976).

In this way, each gene synthesizes a specific protein which is usually an enzyme. These enzymes can interact on higher levels of organization outside the cell through the chemical reactions that they induce. The development of an organized living system on a still higher level (the organism) can therefore be thought of as a chain of enzymatic interactions.

Genes are customarily divided into two classes: *structural genes* that produce proteins, and *regulator genes* that turn on protein synthesis in other genes, or turn it off. The division is not clear cut; in some cases, the same gene may have both functions, protein-synthesis and regulation of other genes. If a gene were discovered that regulated another and was in turn regulated by it, we would have a true case of 2-way interaction and feedback.

As far as known, gene interaction does not change the structure of the genes themselves but operates by modifying the production of RNA. Such modification could be mutual. Being directly chemical in nature, such interactions are different from those, say, on the social level, where 2-way interactions with feedback may continue over long periods before stability is reached.

Can genes act directly on each other? Cases of so-called position effects have long been known. A gene moved from one location on a chromosome to another lies next to a different gene or genes, and its action may be different from what it was in the original position. Presumably, close contact produces alterations in the RNA produced by the genes concerned. New evidence from research with movable genetic elements should throw light on the exact nature of the process. A gene can also modify the action of another gene or even an interactive gene complex at a distance as do regulator genes.

Does 2-way causation occur between genes? In the case of position effects, the adjacent genes could modify each other's synthesis of RNA, or only one could be affected. In any case, 2-way interaction between genes appears to be simple and direct, not occurring repeatedly as it does with entities at higher levels. Also, when we look at the results of gene interaction upon the development of higher levels of organization, the entities appear to interact in the formation of a final product rather than on each other. Such interaction would be similar to the concept as it is employed in statistical methods such as analysis of variance.

The outstanding peculiarity of the genotypic system is its ability to replicate itself in a precise fashion during development through the process of mitosis. No living system on a higher level can achieve this except through the replication of genetic systems.

Finally, the nature of primary gene action and interaction is such that genes do not and cannot act by themselves but only as components of an ongoing system.

Gene Interaction between Members of an Allelic Pair

The simplest form of gene interaction is that between an allelic pair, two genes at the same locus. In the case of albinism, the gene c has no effect if the dominant gene C is present. From this viewpoint, the allelic pair is a subsystem within the total genotype.

Complete dominance is not the only way in which a gene pair can interact. The heterozygote may be intermediate between the two homozygotes as it is with some rare cases such as that of thalassemia in humans. A single mutant gene produces deformed red blood corpuscles, while two of such genes produce corpuscles that are so badly deformed that they are non-functional, often leading to severe anemia and death. In this particular case, the gene interaction is roughly additive in nature.

The case of polydactylism in the guinea pig is quite different. The semi-dominant gene Px produces an extra digit, restoring the missing thumb on the front paw of a guinea pig. But $PxPx$ produces not an animal with two thumbs but one with literally dozens of extra digits on both front and hind feet. Furthermore, almost every part of the body is affected, including the central nervous system as well as bones and muscles. The resulting monster dies either before birth or immediately afterwards. The results of the $PxPx$ combination could not have been predicted from a knowledge of the Px effect alone (Scott, 1938). The results of the interaction between these two alleles is thus non-additive.

In general, the effect of two identical mutant genes at the same locus is often, though not necessarily, greater than one alone, and this is the source of the hypothesis of additive effects of genes. When one considers the effects of two unlike genes from different loci, however, the effects are usually non-additive and often unpredictable.

Interaction between Non-allelic Genes at the Intracellular Level

Wright (1968) summarized the results of years of research by himself and his students on the genetics of coat color in the guinea pig, in the course of which the effects of combining genes at nine major loci and their numerous alleles were measured. As a result of this and extensive studies of gene interaction by other authors, he stated seven general principles, five of which are directly pertinent to the concept of the genotype as a system.

1) *Multiple factors*. Many genic loci affect any phenotypic characteristic.

2) *Universal pleiotropy*. Conversely, any one gene affects many characters. In an earlier work, Dobzhansky (1927) had found that 10 out of 12 genes selected at random had some effect on the shape of the spermatheca of male fruit flies (*Drosophila*), a trait which was not the one through which the mutant genes were first noticed. The combination of pleitropy and the multiple factor phenomenon ensures that any given characteristic of an organism is the result of the particular combination of genes in its genotype, plus its interaction with living systems at other levels.

3) *Uniqueness of alleles*. Each allele at any one locus has a unique array of effects, thus extending principles 1) and 2).

4) *Relativity of dominance*. The dominance-recessiveness relationship between two alleles is dependent upon the whole genome of which they are a part and upon the environment.

5) *Universality of interaction effects*. The combined effects of multiple loci on a character involve much non-additive interaction.

These principles are entirely consistent with the concept of the genotype as a system whose interacting entities are the genes, but their implications have not always been appreciated by evolutionary theorists. In particular, they raise serious doubts about theories based on assumptions of independent action of genes, additive interaction of genes, and single gene replacement.

Following Wright's pioneering work the detailed genetic analysis of coat color inheritance has been carried out in even greater detail in the house mouse. I shall therefore use the latter species to provide detailed illustrations of gene interaction. Silvers (1979) listed 56 known gene loci having a total of 147 alleles (many genes have multiple mutations), again supporting Wright's principle of multiple factors. Some of these mutants have effects on characteristics other than color (small eyes, motor defects, lethality) and so are pleiotropic. But there are at least several dozen loci whose primary effects are on pigment formation, which takes place within cells. Thus they are ideal for the study of gene interaction within the cell, presumably involving the interaction of enzymes produced by genes.

We can infer that the growth of normally colored hair (i.e., similar to that of a wild mouse) is dependent on a combination of several dozen genes. Wild type genes are dominant over the mutants in the majority of cases. In short, a mouse must have all these genes in order to develop normal coat color.

How are the actions of these genes related to each other? They could be additive, duplicative, complementary, or multiplicative. The only way that we can infer the nature of interaction of the wild type genes is by observing the actions of the mutants. One of the basic techniques for analyzing the operation of a system is to examine the function of each entity in the system, first by itself, and then in every possible combination with the other entities. In a genotypic system the method is usually modified to studying a variation in a gene (a mutation), first in combination with the total array of wild-type genes, and then in combination with variants from each of these gene loci.

Thus Russell (1949a,b) studied the effects of certain mutant genes and their combinations on the pigment granules in mouse hair. These granules varied in color, size, shape, position in the hair cells and along the hair shaft, and sometimes by clumping together. All these characteristics had effects on hair appearance, but the primary effects took place either within cells or between adjacent cells.

The embryological development of hair pigment is well known (Wolfe & Coleman, 1966). Certain cells (melanoblasts) arise from the crest of the embryonic neural tube and migrate out into what will become the skin of the embryo. There they become melanocytes, one-celled glands that produce pigment. Those that surround a hair bulb develop projections through which they inject pigment into the hair cells, where it takes various granular forms. In the ordinary wild mouse hair, pigment is present in two colors, phaeomelanin (yellowish) and eumelanin (black). As the hair grows, these are produced alternately, the result being a black-shafted hair with a yellow band near its tip.

In one experiment Russell measured the effect of 6 different gene loci upon the maximum number of pigment granules counted in any microscopic section through a hair. Singly, each gene had a predictable major effect on hair appearance. Thus, *aa* produces a solid black hair, *bb* changes black to brown, *c^{ch} c^{ch}* removes yellow pigment and so produces a chinchilla colored mouse, *dd* produces a light colored mouse (dilute) by concentrating pigment in the center of the hair, pp produces a similar colored mouse with lighter pigment and pink eyes, and A^Y, a gene which is lethal as a homozygote, produces a yellow mouse with no dark pigment in the A^Ya combination.

As seen in Table 2.1, the combinations of these genes produce effects that are far from additive. Neither brown nor chinchilla separately has any effect on the granule count in combination with black, but together they reduce it. In combination with black, dilute and pink-eye reduce counts approximately equally, but in combination with brown, one is more effective than the other.

In combination with black, yellow reduces the granule count by half, but its effect is enhanced by chinchilla, which has no effect by itself. In combination with dilute and pink-eye, both of which produce strong effects by themselves, the effect of yellow is only slightly greater than with black alone.

In the second part of the table, the granule counts from more complex combinations are compared with those predicted by simple additive effects of each gene in combination with black. Two of the cases agree, but the rest do not, and two of them are widely different. We can conclude that the additive hypothesis is not necessarily wrong, but it certainly should not be trusted without a detailed examination of the actual physiology of the gene action as well as its final result.

Table 2.1
HIGHEST COUNTS OF PIGMENT GRANULES IN
MOUSE HAIR (AFTER RUSSELL, 1949A)

Phenotype	Genotype	Alone	Counts	
			With bb (Brown)	With A^Yabb (Yellow)
Black	$aaBBCCDDPP$	95	95	47
Chinchilla	$aaBBc^{ch}c^{ch}DDPP$	98	88	30
Dilute	$aaBBCCddPP$	73	53	41
Pink-eye, Dilute Hair	$aaBBCCDDpp$	71	60	45

	Actual	Predicted by Additive Effect	With A^Ya (Yellow)	Predicted by Additive Effect
$aaBBc^{ch}c^{ch}ddPP$	73	77	15	30
$aaBBc^{ch}c^{ch}DDpp$	55	74	23	27
$aaBBCCddpp$	59	49	44	2

Table 2.2
COUNTS OF RADIOACTIVE TYROSINE
INCORPORATED INTO MOUSE SKIN (AFTER COLEMAN, 1962)

Phenotype	Genotype	Counts		With A^Ya	
		Actual	Predicted	Actual	Predicted
Black	*aaBBCC*	1200		460	
Brown	*aabbCC*	2660		1060	1920
Chinchilla	*aaBBc^{ch}c^{ch}*	442		140	0
Brown-Chinchilla	*aabbc^{ch}c^{ch}*	482	1902	157	1162

A more direct measure of gene action and interaction is given by Coleman's (1962) study of the enzyme tyrosinase which converts tyrosine into eumelanin. Presumably this enzyme is the result of primary gene action, and in any case its action takes place within the cell. Table 2.2 shows some of his results, using black (*aa*) as a standard. Brown, which if anything produces a somewhat lighter colored mouse than black, more than doubles enzyme activity, and chinchilla which had no effect on granule number, reduces enzyme activity by about 2/3. But in combination the count is little more than chinchilla alone; the two effects do not add.

Yellow by itself reduces enzyme activity by approximately the same amount as chinchilla (2/3), but together they do not reduce the count to zero. A similar effect is seen with the three factor yellow-brown-chinchilla combination. Yellow reduces the count in any combination, and a multiplicative function might be deduced. With black, yellow reduces the count by 62%. Applying this figure gives predicted counts that are not grossly inconsistent (168 vs. 140, 1018 vs. 1060, and 183 vs. 157), so the multiplicative hypothesis is at least tenable. But the effect is still not a simple additive one.

These data (and innumerable similar sets of supporting data could be added) therefore agree with Wright's principle that much of the effects of gene interaction are non-additive. Additive interaction is possible, but it cannot be assumed in the absence of data, nor as a general case.

Exceptions

Is there any exception to the rule of gene action through gene combinations? There are a few situations where there are 1:1 relationships between a gene and the enzyme that it produces. The "one gene one enzyme" rule means that if a particular enzyme is identified in an individual one can assume that it carries the corresponding gene.

Since the maintenance processes of organisms are dependent upon enzymes, the presence or absence of a gene producing an essential enzyme may mean life or death to the organism. Thus, there may be a 1:1 relationship between a particular gene and life of the organism. But even in this case, there are many essential enzymes in any complex organism, which means that its life is dependent upon a combination of genes.

Another apparent exception is that of a dominant gene such as Huntington's Disease which produces the same identifiable effect (degenerative changes in the nervous system) in any gene combination. But even such dominant genes are modified in their expression, if carefully studied, as in the *Px* gene, where there is considerable variation in expression of the gene in both the heterozygous and homozygous conditions (Scott, 1938).

Likewise, there is a 1:1 relationship between a gene and a daughter gene that it produces in the process of replication. But even this is dependent upon the presence of other genes; no gene can reproduce by itself. Even a virus consisting of one gene can only reproduce in the presence of the genes of its host species. The consequence of these findings is that any genetic theory of evolution must deal primarily with the evolution of gene combinations or, in broader terms, the evolution of genotypic systems. It follows also that any theory based on independent action by individual genes is, at the best, quite limited, and at the worst badly in error.

Stability of the Genotypic System

The lifetime of a genotypic system is as long as the life of the organism that it organizes through developmental processes. In a multicellular organism it reproduces itself through the general process of cell division which includes a special process that reproduces the genotype itself.

Mitosis involves the duplication of each chromosome together with the genes that it carries, and the transfer of one of each daughter chromosome to each of the two daughter cells. As it occurs in the early stages of development, mitosis should result in the exact duplication of the genotype in each of the millions of cells that comprise a large multicellular organism. The genotype is, therefore, one of the most stable of living systems.

It is not, however, completely stable. Mitosis occasionally malfunctions, as in non-disjunction of chromosomes, and in chromosome breakage and translocation. This may result in abnormal development, as it does with individuals bearing more than the usual number of chromosomes. In humans, abnormal numbers of the sex chromosomes are fairly common, and most such cases are sterile and show some defects of intelligence. The earlier the chromosomal accidents occur the more serious the consequences; if these accidents occur in the sex cells every cell in the organism will be affected. If they occur late in development the consequences are probably minor, resulting only in the death of the cells immediately concerned.

Another cause of instability is gene mutations; if a gene is chemically transformed, mitosis will reproduce the new form rather than the old. If a mutation occurs early in development it may affect the organism in only a minor way, or it may cause serious disability or death. Later in development, it may produce only a local defect or aberration, such as the white spots produced by somatic mutations.

A basic problem of embryology is how a single genotype, passed along unaltered to all cells can cause these cells to be differentiated into various tissues and organs. One answer, long ago offered by Child (1921), is that the cell is a preorganized system with respect to its cytoplasm and hence the daughter genotypes work in different environments. Another suggestion is that genes do not work uniformly at all periods in development: that regulatory genes may turn certain genes on or off at different times, thus producing differential development. An example is the regulation of growth through hormones, as occurs in puberty.

Still another possibility is that the genotype itself becomes altered, despite the apparently uniform action of mitosis. The giant salivary gland chromosomes of *Drosophila* have long been known and also that they display their constituent genes in different arrangements from those found in other cells.

Gorovsky (1980) has reviewed the evidence concerning gene changes during development. In various species of animals there is some evidence that originally single genes may be replicated in certain tissues, while repeated sequences may be underreplicated in others. This of course suggests that the genotypic system may itself be modified during development. Less direct evidence arises from transferring nuclei from differentiated cells into an enucleate egg; such nuclei are unable to reproduce an entire organism.

There are also extra-chromosomal genes in cytoplasmic bodies such as mitochondria and (in plants) chloroplasts. These are not involved in mitosis and hence may not be divided equally between daughter cells, another possible source of differentiation in development, or, alternatively, instability.

The concept of stability applied to genotypic systems leads to several conclusions. The general concept is that living systems become increasingly stable as a result of their tendency to become increasingly complexly organized. The primary function of a genotype, however, is to produce organizational change on a higher level, and not to change its own organization. It starts off in development as a completely organized system and, with the exceptions noted above, tends to maintain its organization throughout its existence.

Change in the direction of increasingly complex organizations and stability of the genotype is therefore an evolutionary process, occurring over generations rather than within a generation. The processes through which these changes are achieved will be the subject of later chapters.

Organisms are customarily divided into two classes according to the complexity of their genotypes. *Prokaryotes* (bacteria and blue green algae) have only single chromosomes and their constituent genes. *Eukaryotes* (all other cellular organisms) have two or more chromosomes in pairs and are distinguished by the processes of duplicating these chromosomes (mitosis and meiosis). Eukaryotes also have extra-chromosomal genes in the mitochondria and (in plants) chloroplasts. Thus there is good evidence that complex organisms have complex genotypes, and that more simply organized species have simple genotypes. Even more simple are the acellular viruses, which are essentially single genes.

Negentropy

This fundamental characteristic of living systems, the tendency toward increasing complexity of organization, is found both in developmental processes and in evolutionary processes. Genotypic systems induce negentropic developmental processes and are themselves changed by the negentropic evolutionary processes.

Adaptivity

In addition to developmental organization, the genotypic system has the function of regulating ongoing maintenance processes throughout life. It has been suggested that one of the processes of aging involves the deterioration of genes. Other studies indicate that damage to genes in active cells may be relatively frequent, but that the genotype has some capacity to repair or replace them. In this case the genotype displays a certain amount of adaptivity.

Emergence and Creativity

This is a phenomenon which necessarily involves comparisons between two levels of organization, and the processes existing on each. One of the fundamental functions of genotypic systems is development of a higher level organization, the physiological, with all its numerous functions that go beyond those of the genotype. For example, organisms move, but genotypes cannot, except as they are carried by the organisms that they produced.

In a complex organism, some of its functions are carried on at the genic level, as for example, the production of enzymes such as insulin whose functions facilitate physiological maintenance. Others, such as the circulation of the blood are possible only at the physiological level. Except for enzymes and daughter genes, there are no "genes for" particular characteristics. If there were, the result would be consistent with the hypothesis of preformation, a concept abandoned by biologists soon after the invention of the microscope some centuries ago.

THE EFFECT OF SEXUAL REPRODUCTION ON GENOTYPIC SYSTEMS

With any genetic theory, evolution is dependent upon genic change, since its variation underlies phenotypic variation. There are two principal sources of such variation, sexual reproduction and mutation, of which only the first will be considered here.

Meiosis

In this process the diploid number of chromosomes in the parent individual is reduced to the haploid number in the germ cells, with the result that only one member of each gene pair is passed along to each germ cell. If the parents are both homozygous for a gene pair, as is the case for all such pairs in a highly inbred strain, this process will have no effect. But if the members of the original gene pair are unlike, or heterozygous, the resulting germ cells will vary.

Which member of a particular pair of chromosomes goes to a given germ cell is completely a matter of chance. Furthermore, because of the process of crossing over, or exchange of material between homologous pairs of chromosomes, genes that exist on the same chromosome in the parent do not remain together, although they are more likely to stay together if they are close to one another. Again, this process is purely a matter of chance.

The result depends upon the degree of homozygosity. If the gene pairs are all homozygous, as in completely inbred strains, there will be no change from generation to generation, except that resulting from mutation. But if any considerable number of gene pairs are heterozygous, the result will be to produce germ cells variable in proportion to the number of variable gene pairs. Since the process of fertilization is also a random process, the resulting offspring will vary as a function of genetic variation in both parents.

The Effect of Meiosis on Genotypic Organization

From the viewpoint of the genotype as a system, the process of sexual reproduction disorganizes the gene combinations of the parents and reorganizes them in a random fashion among the offspring, the resulting variation being proportional to the amount of variation present in the gene pairs. The degree of reorganization is therefore dependent on genic variation.

The Effect of Sexual Reproduction on Variation

Except for special cases such as the limitation of crossing-over between X and Y sex determining chromosomes, the process of sexual reproduction therefore produces a maximum amount of variation in the available gene combinations in the population. Since the vast majority of plant and animal species reproduce sexually, it may be assumed that maximum variation of gene combinations is advantageous for survival of the species.

This contrasts with the situation in which there is no sexual reproduction, In an asexually reproducing species, an individual *must* pass along all its genes to each of its offspring, and there is no genic variation except that produced by mutation. In a multicellular organism reproducing by budding or fission, such a mutation is likely to affect only a small part of the body. In a species that reproduces through parthenogensis (the development of unfertilized eggs) there is a possibility of mutation in the germ cells that can be passed along to the whole body, but in an organism that reproduces by means of fission, as do some sea anemones, the result is a clone of genetically identical individuals.

Thus, without sexual reproduction, a species can utilize variation through mutation very ineffectively. A species that magnifies the variation produced by mutation should be much more variable, hence be able to adapt more quickly to changed conditions and hence to be more likely to survive in the long run. Such a species is continually trying out all of the available combinations of genes.

Another consequence of sexual reproduction is that there is no way that a parent can pass along "his" or "her" particular combinations of genes to his or her offspring. All that he or she can do is to offer variable halves of a particular combination to a partner who offers another set of variable halves. The resulting combinations are similar only to the extent that those of the parents may be similar and always reflect the combinations found in both parents.

CONCLUSIONS

The gene pool, the sum of all genetic material available to a species, is an abstract concept and does not function as a system. The genotype, the genes and other genetic material within a particular individual, is therefore the fundamental genetic system.

Considered as a system, the genotype has all the general attributes of living systems, but expressed in special ways. Its function is unusual in that it is primarily concerned with organizing materials from outside itself into living systems, and especially to organize such systems on higher levels. Looked at in another way, its functions include one of the essential functions of living systems, reproduction. This includes the reproduction of genes, and the reproduction of physiological systems and organisms. Reproduction at higher levels of organization is always dependent on the reproduction of genotypes.

The interacting entities composing the genotypic system are the genes. Studies of their interaction demonstrate that they indeed function as a unitary system. Dozens of genes affect any one characteristic of an organism, and any one gene affects numerous characteristics. Much of gene interaction is non-additive. Therefore, biological evolution is predominantly a process of change in gene combinations, including changes in individual genes. It follows that any theory of evolution based solely on change in individual genes, or upon additive effects of genes, is at best limited. What these limitations are will be discussed in future chapters.

The nature of feedback between pairs of genes at different loci has still not been completely determined, but the function of regulator genes is well known. A gene may affect the action of another either at a distance or by being adjacent to it. In any case, interaction is chemical, not behavioral as it is in social interaction.

Other general systems characteristics are also present at the genotypic level. Negentropy is seen as the genotype produces an organism, through developmental processes. The same processes illustrate emergence and creativity as new processes appear that are impossible at the genotypic level.

Finally, stability of the genotype is maintained through the process of mitosis accompanying growth and cell division. Thus the genotype is one of the most stable of living systems.

How, then, can it change? The solution, in sexually reproducing organisms, is meiosis and fertilization. In this form of reproduction, the genotype is broken down into random combinations which are reassembled in conjunction with similar random combinations from other genotypes. In such species, the genotype is subject to a built-in process of self-destruction and reorganization.

Nothing that I have so far described concerning the nature of genetic systems would result in evolutionary change, that is, change that would persist for more than one generation. The gene pool is an abstraction derived from genotypic systems, and consists of a population of genotpyes, complex interaction systems that have no inherent qualities or processes that would lead to change. Indeed, a basic characteristic of complex living systems is stability, and the genotype is one of the most stable systems known. Further, mitosis, the chromosomal process for the transmission of genotypes from one cell to a daughter cell is normally one that results in exact duplication.

Even the process of sexual reproduction, which regularly destroys and recreates genotypic systems in each generation, does nothing to change the gene pool of the species, which must be altered if evolution is to occur. In an infinitely large population with completely random mating between individuals (it is important to remember these assumptions) each gene reappears in the same frequency in each generation. This is the law of *constancy of gene frequency*, usually called the Hardy-Weinberg law after its discoverers. Gene combinations are constantly shifting in such a population, but not gene frequencies. The essential problem of genetic evolutionary theory is to demonstrate how the change process inherent in sexual reproduction can be transformed into population change, and this is the subject of the next chapter.

Chapter III

Processes of Change in Genetic Systems

The most basic change processes are those that result in individual variations that are genetically transmitted, a condition first recognized by Darwin as essential to evolutionary change, although he, in common with other biologists of his time, had no knowledge of the what the processes might be. One of these is the process of meiosis in sexual reproduction, which is a powerful and constant producer of variation in genotypic systems. It in turn is dependent upon another change process, that of gene mutation, which has a double role, that of producing variation among the genes, the entities composing genotypic systems, and less importantly, of producing changes in populations of genes.

MUTATION

Naturally Occurring Mutations

Geneticists have found that in any particular species, such as the fruit fly, *Drosophila melanogaster*, most individuals carry much the same combinations of genes. These particular combinations are called the "wild type" genes, and most of them show clear cut dominance in breeding tests with individuals whose appearances depart from the wild type. Also, any wild population will carry numerous hidden recessive genes, or mutations. Occasionally, a dominant mutation will appear. Whether dominant or recessive, major mutations often, but not always, have deleterious effects in the majority of gene combinations, and many of them are lethal.

The Mutation Process is a Random One

Mutations have been produced experimentally in a variety of ways: radiation, chemicals and heat, for example. Of these, radiation is probably the most important natural cause, but no matter how induced, the nature of the mutation bears no relation to the inducing agent. While some mutations occur more frequently than others, they are not a response to a biological need.

Mobile Genetic Elements

In addition to chemical changes at particular loci, other sources of variation are mobile genetic elements whose effects depend on their location on the chromosome to which they become attached (McClintock, 1951, 1956; Rubin, 1983). The demonstrated effects for most of these elements, including the oncogenes that produce cancer, are deleterious. Whether or not these elements contribute anything to adaptively positive change is still to be determined, but they probably do contribute a large fraction of spontaneous mutations and chromosomal rearrangments, perhaps as much as 10% (Rubin, 1983). Still another source of variation is the incorporation of viruses into the normal genome of a species, involving the modification of gene combinations such that the viruses no longer produce injurious effects (Varmus, 1983). This is primarily a case of evolutionary adaptation to the virus, but it does have the effect of increasing genic variation. Since the effect of these processes is to increase variation, they should not otherwise alter the general process of mutation.

   Mutations and allied processes provide the raw material of variation and thus the basis of evolutionary change. How can we reconcile this with their commonly deleterious effects, i.e., how can they lead to adaptive evolutionary change? In the first place it is not unexpected that random change in a complex system should be more likely to interfere with its functioning than to improve it. To use an analogy, it is unlikely that shooting a rifle bullet into a complex machine such as an automobile engine would improve its functioning.

Interaction of Mutation with Sexual Reproduction

Here we observe a counterbalancing function of sexual reproduction, whose genetic effect is to try out variant genes in all sorts of possible combinations, in some of which a new mutation may result in an improvement of function. Furthermore, not all mutations are deleterious. Dobzhansky (1937), in writing of *Drosophila*, observed that mutations fall into a broad spectrum ranging from lethal through neutral to mildly favorable effects on viability. Also, the same mutation may have deleterious effects if the flies are reared in one environment, but a favorable effect in another.

Mutation as a Cause of Change in Populations

What are the theoretically expected effects of the process of gene mutation on genetic change? It is necessary for such changes, but can it bring about change independently of other evolutionary processes?

Mutations occur relatively commonly in some genes and relatively rarely in others, but the average rate in germ cells has been estimated as something in the nature of 1 per million per generation at any given gene locus. However, because of the large total number of genes, estimated as approximately 100,000 in complex organisms such as man, the chance of *some* mutation occurring in a given individual is relatively large, approximately 1 in 10.

Nevertheless, a specific genetic change throughout a population in one locus produced solely by gene mutation is likely to be extremely slow. Even when the million to one event occurs in one individual, the chance of its being passed along to the next generation is only 1/2 for each offspring, and there is a good chance that the mutation will be lost entirely unless the animal has a large number of descendants. Further more, many mutations can be reversed; i.e., mutate back to the original condition. In such a case, mutation and reverse mutation should eventually reach an equilibrium. The point at which stability is reached depends on the relative rates of each, so that the gene frequency of the total population should therefore approach stability. If there is no reverse mutation, and other factors do not interfere, gene mutation could produce a very slow irreversible change. For example, in a population of a million individuals there are 2 million genes at a given locus. At a rate of 1 mutation per million in a generation, it would take 2 million generations to change all of these genes, except that, as the mutation process proceeded, there would be fewer and fewer unmutated genes available in each generation, with the result that the process would go on more and more slowly. In short, while mutation is essential for the production of genetic change, without which evolution could not occur, by itself it produces changes in large populations extremely slowly, and other processes must be considered.

The chance of producing complete changes in a small population is considerably better. If we take the smallest possible population in a sexually reproducing species, one male and one female per generation, evolutionary change by mutation should proceed much more rapidly. Such populations do not exist in nature, but the inbred strains produced in the geneticist's laboratory by brother-sister matings form such populations. If there are 50,000 gene pairs in each individual, the chance of *some* mutation occurring, assuming a mutation rate of 1 per million per generation is one in 10 or, in two individuals, one in 5. But the chance of the same mutation occurring in both members of the pair is 1 in a million squared, which means that change occurring in this fashion has such a small probability that for all practical purposes it never occurs.

However, a given mutation in one parent may spread rapidly through the small population through the random processes of meiosis and fertilization. Given that a parent carries a mutation in one member of a gene pair, it will pass this along to 1/2 of its offspring. The chance that the experimenter will select two of the individuals carrying the mutation for the next generation is therefore 1/4 and they in turn will produce offspring 1/4th of which will be homozygous for the mutation. The chance that the experimenter will select two of these homozygous individuals for parents in the next generation is 1/16. The chance that the gene will spread throughout the whole population in this fashion is thus 1/64. If we consider the other mating combinations by which this could occur over a somewhat longer period of time, the total probability is somewhat larger and in any case is not an impossibly small figure.

Since the probability that similar mutations will occur in different sublines of an inbred strain is very small, one would expect that different sublines of the same inbred strain would gradually diverge from each other. As a matter of practice, geneticists ordinarily agree that it is unsafe to assume that two strains will remain genetically identical for more than 5 generations, and it is customary to assume that after 20 generations they will be distinct sublines.

Empirical evidence supports this reasoning. At the time of the Bar Harbor fire of 1947, I was maintaining a strain of C57BL/10 mice and donated breeding pairs to the Jackson Laboratory to replace their destroyed stock, while still maintaining my own. Some years later Denenberg (1959, 1965) learned of these strains and tested them on a classical conditioning learning task and showed that they were significantly different. The mice had been separated into different strains for 32 generations of brother-sister mating in one strain and 25 in the other making a total of 64 generations in which divergence could occur. This is an experimental demonstration of the fact that evolutionary changes through mutation can occur with relative rapidity among small inbred populations. Ginsburg (private communication) found that the incidence of audiogenic seizures had diverged in these populations also.

Change would of course occur much more slowly in inbred populations that were larger than two per generation, and the rate of change becomes very slow indeed in very large populations. We can conclude that mutation, if independent of other change processes, is a relatively unimportant source of evolutionary change, important as it is as the essential basis of genetic variation. Its primary effect on change, or probability of occurrence, is directly related to large numbers, which however, have the counterbalancing effect of slowing the rate of population changes. We must now consider the possibility that inbreeding itself may produce changes in a variable population.

INBREEDING

Most of the insights relating to evolutionary processes came from the practical problems of agriculture. Darwin's theory of Natural Selection (1859) came directly from the artificial selection that he saw practiced by farmers. Similarly, Wright's (1922) discovery of the effects of inbreeding on evolutionary change came from his research on the inbreeding of animals at the Department of Agriculture in Washington, D.C. As he studied the pedigrees of short-horn cattle (Wright, 1978), which have been maintained in England since 1780, he observed that breeders tended to make matings within their own herds, and that they combined selection with inbreeding through what they called line breeding, i.e., repeated matings to especially favored animals and their offspring. Once a breeder developed a good line, neighboring farmers sought matings or purchased the better animals, thus producing a flow of gene combinations into other herd populations. Combining inbreeding and selection in this way produced rapid genetic changes, even in a relatively slow breeding species such as cattle. And as Wright (1922) maintained and observed inbred strains of guinea pigs, he saw them change and diverge before his eyes, even though the matings were made at random.

Genetic Changes Produced by Inbreeding

The principal genetic consequence of inbreeding is the reduction of heterozygosity, at the rate of 18.75% per generation in brother-sister matings. By the 10th generation of such matings, approximately 95% of the original genetic variation is gone, and by the 20th generation the figure approaches 100%. This process not only reduces variation, but also eliminates certain genes from the gene pool of the population concerned, and thus brings about evolutionary change.

Where the rate of genetic change due to repeated inbreeding of a standard sort such as brother-sister mating remains constant over generations, the amount of change becomes smaller and smaller as homozygosity is achieved. Furthermore, the degree of inbreeding is inversely proportional to the size of the breeding population. A breeding population of 8 produces a much slower rate of inbreeding than one of 2 individuals.

Random Drift

In the absence of processes other than mutation the genetic change produced by inbreeding is random in nature, i.e., which of a pair of alleles becomes homozygous is purely a matter of chance. Therefore, genetic change of this sort has been called "random drift" or, in honor of the person who first noticed it, the "Sewall Wright effect" (Huxley, 1942).

Inbreeding and Genetic Systems

From the viewpoint of genetic systems, the result of inbreeding is to increase the frequency of certain gene combinations and, in the case of highly inbred laboratory stocks, to ensure that all individuals carry the same combination. We should remember that inbreeding functions on the level of the gene pairs themselves, not on the level of gene combinations. Therefore, its effect may be to destroy or break up combinations that have desirable or superior effects.

Interaction with Mutation

As pointed out above, inbreeding also facilitates the entrance of new genes into the gene pool via mutation. Since both mutation and inbreeding are random processes, many of the new genes so brought into the population are likely to be deleterious in nature. As Wright (1980 and earlier) himself stated, inbreeding in the absence of selection will result in degeneration and extinction of a population.

Here we begin to see that evolutionary processes operate as a system, each one affecting the others, and so involving reciprocal causation. But to use this theoretical formulation we must distinguish between the entities that comprise the system and the means through which they interact; i.e., processes. This concept will be developed further in a later integrating chapter.

Occurrence in Natural Populations

Obviously inbreeding will have little significance as an evolutionary process if it occurs only within the artificial populations of the laboratory. A brother-sister mating plan produces a very rigid and

stable genetic system. Every animal in the strain has identical genotypic systems. Such a situation negates the effect of sexual reproduction in producing variation. Such a plan does not occur in any
known wild species of animals, and its sole counterpart exists in
certain plant species such as the sweet peas studied by Mendel,
that are self-fertilizing and hence genetically constant generation
after generation except for mutations.

Does inbreeding occur in milder degrees among wild animals?
J. W. Scott (1942) found that on the mating grounds of the sage
grouse, 85% of all matings were done by one male. Selander and
Johnson (1973) found in their studies of the distribution of variable enzymes in wild rodent populations that these were not scattered at random but concentrated in local populations. The degree
of inbreeding in any one population depends on its mating system,
this in turn on behavior, and this in turn upon the species
involved.

Inbreeding will occur when a population is constantly small, and
also in one that fluctuates in a cyclical fashion. Elton (1930) in his
studies of animal populations pointed out that in many rodent and
other animal species populations are periodically reduced to small
numbers, with the consequent elimination of certain gene combinations. This produces genetic change in a population, the so-called
"founder effect." But the surviving combinations are not totally
dependent on chance and may be the result of differential survival.

Importance of Inbreeding

Is inbreeding an important evolutionary process? The degree of
inbreeding in a species depends first on its mode of reproduction.
If it only reproduces asexually, inbreeding cannot occur, as no
breeding takes place. The same thing is true in species that reproduce parthenogenetically. In the case of reproduction through self-
fertilization inbreeding is absolute; the individual mates with
itself. The latter two sorts of reproduction facilitate change
through mutation to an extreme degree, as any mutation that
occurs in the germ line is automatically transmitted directly to the
next generation. This also has the effect of enhancing the role of
natural selection, as the only two evolutionary processes in such
species are mutation and natural selection.

Among sexually reproducing species, which comprise the vast majority of animals, the degree of inbreeding depends on the mating system, which in turn depends on the social organization of the species and its consequent organization into subpopulations, as in packs of wolves or troops of primates. Geography may also result in the subdivision of a population.

A key dimension is the size of the subpopulation so produced, as size determines the degree of inbreeding. The pertinent dimension is the size of the breeding population, as the nonbreeding members of a population have no effect.

Overall, the importance of inbreeding is an empirical question that must be determined specifically for each species. In a species composed of large, random breeding populations, it would obviously have no effect. At the opposite extreme, in a self-fertilizing species, each individual forms a breeding population of 1, and inbreeding likewise has no effect. In between are species that are divided, by whatever means and whether continually or intermittently, into small or moderately sized breeding populations. It is such species that should exhibit the maximum effect of evolutionary change produced by inbreeding.

NATURAL SELECTION

Definition

Natural Selection is the most misunderstood and misused of all concepts relating to evolutionary processes, albeit a major one. As originally used by Darwin, it rested on an analogy with the activities of animal and plant breeders, who selected for parents those individuals whose characteristics appeared most desirable to their human owners. Darwin suggested that animals and plants were undergoing a similar process of selection by "Nature", meaning the whole array of physical, ecological, and social factors that affected each species. To 19th century scientists, Nature (with a capital N) was a comfortable concept, implying as it does some degree of personification. Today we may define the process less personally, more accurately, and more generally as *differential survival*, which may be brought about in limitless numbers of ways.

The definition of differential survival clearly implies that "Natural Selection" is not a single monolithic process but an inclusive category for numerous processes that may act additively or interactively to produce differential survival. Also, it is not necessarily dependent on competition, which is only one of the many processes that lead to differential survival. One group of individuals may simply out-reproduce another, without ever coming into contact. Consequently, the metaphor of Natural Selection as a force exerting pressure is inappropriate, although it has been used by many evolutionary theoreticians.

The factors that lead to differential survival are almost innumerable and vary from season to season. A deermouse living in the Middle West may struggle with intense cold in winter and intense heat and drought in summer. Factors may differ from one location to another, such as the presence or absence of predators and parasites, and even at different times in the life cycle. Consequently, Natural Selection is not a monolithic, unchangeable force but rather an omnipresent process of differential survival. It, in conjunction with the other processes discussed above, may bring about change in the organization of genetic systems.

Adaptation and Fitness

An essential part of the theory of Natural Selection is that genetic change goes in the direction of increasing adaptation; i.e., a species should, in the long run, be increasingly able to survive.

The concept of adaptation implies directional changes, and these may take place on any level of organization: genetic, physiological, behavioral (organismic) or social. This, in turn, implies the potential modification of all organizational processes: growth, maintenance processes, developmental processes, behavioral processes, and social processes. Therefore, *differential survival may affect any level of organization.*

From the viewpoint of systems, the converse of the above statement is also true: *processes at any level or organization (including ecological levels) may influence differential survival.*

The concept of *fitness to survive,* usually shortened to fitness, represents an attempt to measure the degree to which an organism is adapted for survival in its environment. As the above discussion indicates, an accurate estimate of fitness could only be determined for a given instant in time. The only overall measure of fitness is survival itself, which can be measured as length of life. And, as Hamilton (1964) pointed out, fitness has evolutionary significance only as the number of surviving offspring relative to those produced by other individuals in the population. Since in a sexually reproducing species the number of surviving offspring also represents the fitness of another individual or individuals, this figure of "inclusive fitness" becomes very difficult to calculate.

Thus the concept of fitness, while an attractive one based on the assumption of independent individuals in a population, becomes relatively useless when applied to a system. Whenever two or more individuals interact, as they do in biparental reproduction, a system is present.

To restate the above, variation in processes at any level of organization may bring about differential survival, which will then feed back on these processes and shift their occurrence in one direction or another. Biological evolutionary change can occur only if the variation in the processes is genetically determined, either directly or indirectly. Since genetically determined variation is involved in all living systems, biological evolutionary change should be universal. At the same time, the processes of evolutionary change should differ from one level of organization to another.

Levels of Organization and Differential Survival

As shown in Table 3.1, processes leading to differential survival can operate on any level of organization. To begin on the lowest level, any gene that fails to duplicate itself will not survive. Since a gene is known only by its activity, this phenomenon is purely theoretical, but it is highly likely that it does take place, and that myriads of defective genes simply disappear.

On the next highest level, a genotypic system can fail in another basic function, that of initiating and carrying out the processes of development. Differential survival of fertilized eggs (zygotes) can take place at this level. Even before this, either eggs or sperm can fail in the function of fertilization, leading to differential survival of the germ cells themselves.

Table 3.1
DIFFERENTIAL SURVIVAL IN RELATION TO LEVELS
OF ORGANIZATION

Level of Organization	Example	Unit of Change
Gene	Failure to reproduce	Gene
Germ Cell	Failure of fertilization	Germ Cell
Genotype	Failure to develop	Zygote
Physiological	Maladaptive function	Organism
Organismic	Maladaptive behavior	Organism
Social	Maladaptive social organization	Social Group (local population)
Ecological	Extinction of a species	Species

Development, defined as the processes whereby an organism is produced, can result in differential functioning on the physiological level of maintenance processes such as the regulation of sugar metabolism by insulin and so lead to differential survival. Behind this, of course, is failure of some developmental organizing process.

Developmental processes can indirectly lead to differential behavior of the organism as a whole, as in the case of Huntington's Disease, and so to differential survival by a different route. On both the physiological and organismic levels, it is the organism and its genotypic system as a whole which does or does not survive.

On the two highest levels, a malfunctioning social system may lead to differential survival of social groups. Similar differentials on the ecosystem level lead to the phenomenon of extinction, or differential survival of species.

From this reasoning, it is clear that differential survival can occur on at least five levels of organization, and to this list may be added the deme or local population that might or might not be organized into a social system or systems.

In the past, various theorists have argued that differential survival (selection) can only take place on one level of organization, usually the organism (Lack, 1966) or the gene (Williams, 1966; Dawkins, 1976). Logically, on the other hand, processes leading to differential survival can exist on every level, excluding none, and this is what I am emphasizing.

The level that is affected then depends on the nature of the function of the process that is involved. This, in turn, raises the question of the level of genetic organization that is affected by differential survival: gene, genic subsystem, genotypic system, multiple genotypic systems, and the gene pools (Table 3.2). For example, a major deleterious gene such as that associated with Huntington's Disease may function on the organismic level and so affect differential survival on that level. In this special case, it is a single gene rather than a genotypic system that operates. But one cannot generalize from this case to those involving gene interaction within genotypic systems and subsystems, as is the case with the great majority of variations. Such a gene, which has deleterious effects in every gene combination, can only be selected against and cannot be a model for positive selection, which must be based on improved survival in at least one gene combination.

EFFECTS OF DIFFERENTIAL SURVIVAL ON THE EVOLUTION OF GENOTYPIC SYSTEMS

Assuming a population in which variation of a characteristic related to differential survival is principally caused by variation among genotypes, those individuals will survive that have the more favorable combinations of genes, and in the long run the numbers of individuals carrying such combinations will increase, eventually bringing about the situation in which all or at least the great majority of individuals carry the same combination of "wild type" genes.

Table 3.2
LEVELS OF ORGANIZATION IN RELATION TO
GENETIC ORGANIZATION

Level of Organization	Genetic Level of Organization
Gene	Gene
Germ cell	Haploid set of chromosomes
Zygote (fertilized egg)	Genotype
Physiological (including cells, tissues, organs, organ systems)	Genotype
Organismic	Genotype
Social	Groups of genotypes (frequently related)
Deme (local population)	Groups of genotypes (not necessarily related)
Species Population	Gene pool (including all genotypes in species)
Ecosystem	Groups of gene pools

Formation of New Gene Combinations

In order for this to occur, there must first of all be new genes in the population. These are, of course, produced by mutation. Second, sexual reproduction results in constantly trying out all possible combinations of variable genes in the population. If there are new genes, new combinations will result automatically, and differential survival will favor certain combinations over others.

This general process can be analyzed in more detail on the basis of probability, taking the simplest possible case, that of two mutant genes that have never before been in combination. The chance that a particular combination of this sort will be formed depends on the following factors:

1) Relative survival value of the mutant genes in existing combinations

2) The size of the population

3) The frequency of the mutant genes in the population

4) Dominance and recessiveness

5) The number of genes in the new combination

The chances of a new combination being formed are better if each new gene in the combination has neutral or positive survival value in some of the pre-existing gene combinations, i.e., if they have minor effects. From the viewpoint of the systems model, this is equivalent to selection of a new gene by the genotypic system. If a mutant gene produces strongly unfavorable effects in existing combinations, it will either disappear entirely or be extremely rare.

In any case, a new mutation will be rare when it first appears. If we assume that only one each of two mutant genes exist in the population, the chance that individuals carrying these genes will meet is 1/n-1, n being the size of the population, and assuming strictly random mating by the organisms involved. Obviously, the chance of the two genes meeting is much better in a small population, being certain in a population of two, and one in a million minus one in a population of that size. This again illustrates the advantage of small inbreeding subpopulations in evolution.

The chance of individuals who carry the two genes meeting is improved as the frequency of the genes in the population increases, thus enlarging the denominator of the above fraction. Frequency can be increased either by repeated mutations or by differential survival value.

Dominance and recessiveness affect the probability of expression of the new combination. If two individuals mate, each carrying a different recessive gene, the probability of expression in the F1 generation is zero, and the probability of the new combination being formed is 1/4. The chance of two such individuals mating is again 1/n-1 in a random breeding population, and the probability of expression of the two genes in the same offspring in an F2 generation will be 1/16. The combined probability of expression in the two generations is thus 1/64.

In contrast, the probability of expression of a combination of two dominant genes is 1/4 in the first generation and 9/16 in the second. Thus the probability of an expressed effect affecting differential survival is many times greater for two dominant genes than two recessive ones. This itself might explain the prevalence of dominant wild-type genes.

The difference in expressivity is a two-edged sword. Because a dominant gene is always expressed, it is always exposed to selection. Consequently, dominant genes with strongly unfavorable effects are extremely rare outside the geneticist's laboratory, one of these being Huntington's Disease, where the dominant gene has its effect in later life, after the individual has had an opportunity to reproduce. On the other hand, a recessive gene with unfavorable effects is always protected against selection in the heterozygous condition; under these conditions recessive genes survive better than dominant ones.

Thus, recessiveness is an advantage only if the gene's effects are unfavorable, again indicating that dominance should be favored over recessiveness in evolutionary change. The other alternative is one of no dominance, in which two alleles are both expressed in the heterozygote. In this case, such genes would have the same advantages and disadvantages as dominants and should react in the same way to selection.

The final factor affecting the probability of a new combination being formed is the number of loci in the combination. Obviously, the greater the number of genes in the combination, the less probable that the combination will occur by chance. Since sexual reproduction can only occur in pairs, three or more individuals each bearing a new gene cannot combine, and the simplest assumption is that one individual already bearing a combination of two new genes mates with another bearing a third mutant, thus multiplying the original probability by $1/n-1$, or $1/(n-1)^2$.

Therefore, the probability of combining larger numbers of genes in combinations becomes $1/n-1$, $1/(n-1)^2$, $1/(n-1)^3$, etc. Since this fraction becomes exceedingly small with a large population, it is important both that the size of the population be reasonably small, and that the numbers of mutants in the population (the denominator of this fraction) be reasonably large (see factor 3, above). Against this, the chance that a mutant will occur at all is better in a large population than a small one. Thus, the ideal situation is one in which a large population is divided up into several semi-isolated small breeding populations (see Wright's model below).

In conclusion, the ideal conditions producing rapid evolution of gene combinations following the introduction of a new gene are: favorable or at least neutral effects in most pre-existing combinations, moderately small population size, dominance, and relatively high frequency of the new gene.

Wright's Shifting Balance Theory

The only author who has seriously addressed the problem of evolution of gene combinations is Wright (1977 and earlier papers). His shifting balance theory is based on four assumptions: 1) A population with a large amount of *heteroallelism* with respect to minor factors, 2) *pleiotropy* in the effects of most allelic differences, 3) *multiple fitness peaks* in the field of genotypic variation (i.e., that there are several different combinations of genes that have superior survival value; this involves the assumption of *extensive interaction effects*) and 4) a population divided into multiple *partially isolated demes*, (such a division might be either geographic or produced by social organization).

Wright considered that the evolutionary process is divided into three phases: 1) *Random drift*, producing random variation of genotypic combinations in different demes, followed by 2) *mass selection* (i.e., of the whole population) *under shifting conditions* (i.e., the conditions producing differential survival are variable), resulting in a demic population shifting across a saddle or valley to a new peak; and 3) *interdeme selection*, which Wright envisioned as happening by excess individuals produced by a favorable combination in one deme emigrating into others and transforming them, rather than direct competition between demes as wholes.

Wright then developed a mathematical model for a population with 6 homoallelic peaks (based on combinations between 4 loci) and another for 6 heteroallelic peaks (based on combinations between 3 loci), both with pleiotropic effects. He concluded that such models would indeed lead to relatively rapid evolutionary changes.

Actually, the number of gene combinations in a population could be virtually limitless, depending only on the number of variable genes in the population. But if conditions affecting mass selection were constant, the result would be the maintenance of the one most favorable combination for those conditions, with very slow change dependent on mutations producing favorable new combinations (essentially the single gene substitution model.)

Seen in perspective, the Wright model involves three random factors, two of which, mutation and meiosis, increase variation, and one of which, sampling drift based on small populations, produces a random change in variation. In addition, the model postulates one directive factor, differential survival (or selection), which is most effective if it, too, is variable. He also concluded that any one of these factors acting by itself would be either ineffective or deleterious.

Compared with my own presentation above, Wright did not address the problem of what happens to new genes in a population and how totally new combinations are formed, but attacked the problem of a population where large numbers of heteroallelic loci are already established. My own line of reasoning which is an extension of this more general case based on simple reasoning, leads to a somewhat different emphasis but to similar conclusions.

Selection for Favorable Gene Combinations

Most of the theories of evolution have been either directly or indirectly derived from empirical results obtained by plant and animal breeders attempting to improve their products. As stated above, Darwin's concept of Natural Selection was suggested by Artificial Selection as he assumed it was practiced by plant and animal breeders, essentially a process of mass selection applied to the whole species. Wright's theories of inbreeding, on the other hand, arose from his studies of the actual breeding practices of animal breeders as recorded in pedigrees, which were a combination of selection plus inbreeding in local semi-isolated populations.

In addition, there are two commonly used techniques whose evolutionary implications have not hitherto been emphasized. The first of these is the use of a mated pair as the unit of selection. Dog breeders, in attempting to select for the complex characteristics demanded by breed standards, frequently employ what they call "nicking". If a given pair are not producing particularly good puppies, each may be mated with a different animal until a particularly good litter is obtained. The breeder then repeats this successful mating as many times as possible.

From the viewpoint of genetic systems, they are selecting for a pair that has a high probability of producing desirable gene combinations. This suggests that the same sort of selection may be occurring under natural conditions.

This technique involves a second, that of "progeny testing". The breeders are primarily looking not at the parent animals but their offspring. This technique is used most often in cases where the desired characteristic is not observable in a parent, as with a bull in the selection of dairy cows for milk production. In this special case, the unit of selection is the bull plus his female offspring.

In either case, selection involves more than one generation and more than one individual. This reminds one of Hamilton's (1964) concept of "inclusive fitness", which he defined as the capacity of an individual to transmit "his" genes to the next generation, measured by the phenotypic characteristics of that generation. From the viewpoint of genetic systems and gene combinations, this would have to be modified to read "the capacity (in combination with another individual) to produce favorable gene combinations in the next generation".

Hamilton's formulation nevertheless has some merit, in that if an individual does not or cannot reproduce, its own survival has little impact. The case of infertility is one of individual selection, which supports the general proposition that I have stated, that selection can take place on any level of organization. But even here, individual selection involves the selection of the parents, who have one less surviving offspring.

If the above is considered in more detail, the probability of a particular individual achieving a mating that produces a more adaptive combination of genes is greater in proportion to the number of prospective mates. Also, a given population may include many, or only a few prospective partners that give such results. The effect of differential survival should be to increase the proportion of individuals in a population carrying such combinations until it approaches 100%. At this point, differential survival could only occur relative to other populations, which would amount to selection on the level of groups.

Within a population, is random mating or non-random mating with the same individual more favorable to change? If a given individual mates with several others, the chance of producing some favorable combinations is better than with only one, but the chance of producing a large proportion of such combinations is better with a repeated mating with one individual, and the two tendencies must be balanced against each other. Or, the two tendencies can be combined as they are in certain polygynous mating systems. This might account for the fact that polygyny is a relatively common type of mating system among some but not all taxonomic categories of birds and mammals.

Finally, we need to consider selection as a trans-generational phenomenon; i.e., differential survival is simultaneously affecting many generations. Hitherto, most theorists have concentrated on a given individual in one generation, and there is some logic behind this, as hereditary causation proceeds in only one direction, from parent to offspring, and not the reverse. But this omits the feedback function implicit in systems organization; differential survival affects heredity in the preceding generation, and so on back up the line, although with a rapidly diminishing effect in accordance with the law of genetic correlation, based on the fact that the chance of a parent's passing on a particular gene to a particular offspring is .5 and thus only .25 to a particular grandchild. Actually, the effect on remote generations will be much less than that, because of the fact that the important phenomenon is gene combinations, which are broken up in every generation.

If selection can take place both on the level of an individual and of a mated pair and their offspring, can it also take place on lower levels, including that of the gene itself? The answer is obviously, yes, at least under certain special circumstances, those of major gene effects. If one takes a gene that has a major effect little modified by other genes, such as albinism in mammals, this can be readily selected by an experimenter, either for or against, and it obviously has a poor survival value in a wild population. Thus, differential survival can take place with respect to a single gene, and it is on this basis that many theoreticians such as Williams (1966) have generalized.

The difficulty with such generalizations is that they are derived from a special case. The whole history of the investigation of mutations demonstrates that genes with major effects are almost always deleterious, and such genes cannot be the basis of positive evolutionary change. The gene for albinism is one which knocks out the whole system of pigment formation, without which an animal is poorly equipped for survival. It is the genes with minor or moderate effects modifiable in different combinations that must be important in positive evolution. We must conclude that selection on the genic level is important chiefly in a negative fashion, although one cannot completely negate the possibility that some day a major gene having only a positive effect will be discovered.

What Natural Selection is Not

Before proceeding to the synthesis of the genetic theory of evolution through systems theory, it is important to list some of the erroneous concepts of Natural Selection (differential survival).

1. It is not a force but a process of differential survival.

2. It is not dependent upon competition. Differential survival can occur without the concerned organisms ever coming into contact or having a direct effect on each other. The emphasis on competition among many evolutionary theorists is probably an artifact based on Anglo-American culture which strongly emphasizes competition between individuals. In actual observation, animals rarely get into competitive situations, usually avoid them if they arise, and frequently employ a non-harmful solution such as the dominance-subordination relationship. Perhaps the best illustration of a strictly competitive situation is that between two trees growing close together and attempting to utilize the same space and resources. Two animals in the same situation can move apart and so avoid competition.

It is probably no accident that the great majority of evolutionary theorists after Darwin were either English or American. Living in a culture that emphasizes competition, scientists seized on the possibility that differential survival could be explained by competition, neglecting other possibilities. Such reasoning led to the excesses of Social Darwinism and still leads many theoreticians to reject any evolutionary process other than Natural Selection. Prince Kropotkin's (1902) book on mutual aid, written by a person who came from a culture that emphasized cooperation, is still a wholesome antidote to evolutionary ethnocentrism.

3. Natural Selection is not invariable, but a process that continually varies in both degree and direction. The same population of deermice in the Middle West may be selected for those who survive intense heat in the summer, intense cold in the winter, and neither one in spring and fall, all in the same year.

4. Natural Selection is not a single monolithic process but a final pathway through which the outcomes of a great variety of processes are expressed. Mathematically, this makes it a dependent rather than an independent variable, one which reflects an almost infinite number of factors.

CONCLUSIONS

Functions of Genes

While genes are the basic constituent entities of genotypic systems, their functions are expressed only as they interact with each other within such systems. Geneticists have long been aware of this fact on the level of phenotypic expression of genes. In multicellular organisms, such interactions involve activities outside the cells in which genes carry on their primary activities. At the present time molecular geneticists are exploring the intra-cellular interactions of genes, and this in the long run may lead to further modification of the genetic systems theory of evolution. Since much molecular genetics is done with micro-organisms, we already know that gene interaction occurs in the simplest organisms such as bacteria.

Geneticists have also known for generations that a single gene by itself does not produce an organ or a behavior but produces variation in some (and usually many) characteristics. Therefore, any theory of evolution based solely on changes in single genes is based on erroneous assumptions.

Mutation and Systems Theory

Gene mutations bring about changes in the entities composing a system, and only indirectly on the functioning of the genotypic systems in which they are included. Since mutation is a random change, it is unlikely that alteration of an entity which is part of a complex and stable system will improve the functioning of that system. It is much more likely to destabilize or disorganize the system. This, or course, is nothing new, merely a restatement of the long-established fact that most mutations reduce viability.

Systems Theory and Reproduction

The mode of reproduction has a profound effect on the process of genetic change. Asexual reproduction maintains the stability of genotypic systems and protects them against the effects of mutation, as there is no way in which a mutation in a single cell can spread to all other cells in the daughter individuals.

On the other hand, reproduction by parthenogenesis, which involves the development of an individual from a single unfertilized egg cell, opens the door to the effects of mutation. A mutation in the egg or in the preceding line of germ cells can affect the entire body. But since the mutation is tried out in only one gene combination, it will persist only in the unlikely event that its effect is favorable in that particular genotypic system.

Finally, sexual reproduction and meiosis break down all genotypic systems in a population and reorganize them in new systems in each generation. This is in accordance with a general axiom of systems theory – "no reorganization without disorganization". The result is to maximize variation among gene combinations, but to produce no permanent change (the Hardy-Weinberg law).

In this situation, a new mutation, unless its effect is strongly unfavorable as in the case of a lethal gene, has a much better chance of falling into a combination in which its effect may be favorable. A species that reproduces sexually is therefore much more capable of evolutionary change that one which reproduces by any other method.

Systems Theory and Inbreeding

Like mutation, inbreeding produces random changes in the entities composing the genotypic system, without reference to the functioning of the system as a whole. Change through inbreeding reduces the total number of gene combinations or genotypic systems possible in a population, fixing some and eliminating others. Since the process of inbreeding is a random one, it is likely in the absence of other processes to result in dysfunctional changes in genotypic systems.

Systems Theory and Natural Selection

Natural Selection is an inclusive category of processes that have in common the effect of Differential Survival. These processes can bring about differential survival of living systems on any level of organization. Unlike other change processes, differential survival is directly related to the functioning of these systems. In turn, the survival or non-survival of these systems produces changes on the corresponding levels of genetic systems: gene pools, genotypes, and even genes.

Conversely, the functioning of systems at every level can bring about changes in the constituent sub-systems at any level. In contrast, to mechanistic-reductionistic theory, systems theory emphasizes two-way interaction and feedback. Natural selection is not a mysterious outside force acting on organisms but an inclusive category of processes, many if not most of which have their origin in living systems. Systems theory emphasizes the fact, implicit in Darwin's theory of natural selection, that differential survival not only alters genotypic systems, but that the latter, through the process of adaptation, alter the process of differential survival. Thus, the most general trend in evolutionary change is to negate natural selection.

Finally, differential survival is the only non-random process that brings about genetic change. To this should be added that it is not completely correlated with function. To take an extreme example, the people who died in the eruption of the volcano Krakatoa did not do so because they were any more poorly adapted for survival than those living in other parts of the world. Also, differential survival can bring about its effect only through interacting with processes that are inherently random. The nature of these interactions is the subject of the next chapter.

Chapter IV

Genetic Evolutionary Theories and the Use of Appropriate Models

One of the most general phenomena exhibited by living systems is interaction, involving reciprocal and mutual causation. Therefore, a basic technique of systems analysis is to examine the components of the system in every possible combination, first alone, then two at a time, then three at a time and so on to a consideration of the total system.

In the last chapter I considered the four major evolutionary processes singly, and the results are summarized diagrammatically in Figure 4.1. The three major levels of genetic organization are indicated by circles in the center of the diagram. The genes are actually the entities composing the genotypic system, which is a combination of genes including many genic subsystems. The gene pool is an abstraction and is primarily useful for providing a method of measuring the total evolutionary change in a species through changes in gene frequencies. But gene frequencies are only partial measures, as they merely reflect changes in individual genes and say nothing about changes in genotypes, which are the only paths through which gene action can be expressed as phenotypes, which in turn are the visible expressions of evolutionary change.

The four processes are pictured as rectangles to emphasize the distinction between them and the living systems that they affect. As pointed out in the last chapter, mutation and inbreeding directly affect the genes. Sexual reproduction, including meiosis and fertilization, primarily affects genotypes, affects genes only by rearranging their combinations, and has no effect on the gene pool. Finally, differential survival, which is a category reflecting the activity of innumerable processes, has effects on all three levels of genetic organization.

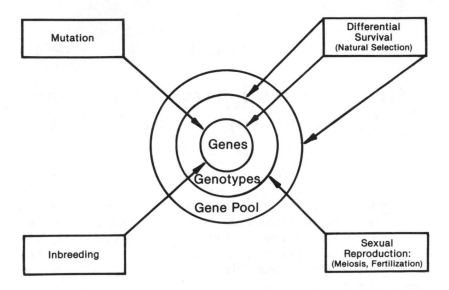

Figure 4.1. The four major processes that bring about genetic change. Note that Mutation and Inbreeding affect genes directly and only indirectly affect other levels of genetic organization; Sexual Reproduction (meiosis and fertilization) changes only genotypes; Differential Survival affects all three levels directly and indirectly. Note also that the genetic material (genes and genotypes) is organized into systems; of the four change processes, Sexual Reproduction is organized as part of organismic and social systems, whereas Natural Selection may or may not originate within living systems.

ORIGIN AND LOCATION OF CHANGE PROCESSES

We may now ask the question: What is the origin of these change processes, and where do they take place? The answers to these questions should in part determine the limits of interaction between processes.

Mutation

The major factor that brings about gene mutation is radiation, and this has its origin outside living systems, but some chemical mutagens may be produced by living systems. In addition, genes that increase the frequency of mutation in other genes are well known, including the mobile genetic elements.

The actual process of mutation takes place wherever the genes are located. In higher organisms this is within the cell nuclei, but it can occur also in certain cytoplasmic organelles such as plastids and mitochondria. The mutations that are significant in evolution are those that occur in the germ line, but it is now suspected that degenerative genic changes frequently take place within somatic cells, but that the cells are somehow able to repair them.

Inbreeding

This is defined as non-random breeding resulting from the limitation of population size, and has three principal origins. One is the division of a population into demes through accidents of physical geography such as islands or valleys, or by historical geological processes such as glaciation. The same thing may be brought about by ecological factors such as the distribution of a food source. Whatever their causes, such divisions have great evolutionary import for the origin of new species. In this connection, the phenomenon is usually called isolation. This latter term has no connotations of population size, as it may occur in either large or small populations, but the same imposition of limits on breeding combinations is involved.

A second source is cyclical or accidental reductions of population sizes, such as frequently occurs in populations of small rodents, which may achieve enormous numbers for a few years only to be almost wiped out by combinations of unfavorable circumstances. In some animal species such reductions of breeding populations may occur every winter, only to be built up again the next summer.

A third important factor is the occurrence of social organization which determines the identity and numbers of possible mates. For example, in certain herd mammals, mating takes place only within organized social groups rather than between them. In any case, inbreeding is a phenomenon that takes place as a part of sexual reproduction, the union of male and female germ cells. Mating behavior is often but not necessarily involved.

Sexual Reproduction

No one knows the origin of sexual reproduction; we only know that it occurs widely though not universally in living organisms. From the evolutionary viewpoint, its essential processes are those of meiosis, which occurs during the formation of germ cells, and fertilization, the union of germ cells. Sexual behavior merely facilitates the latter process.

Differential Survival

This is essentially differential reproduction (an activity of a living organism) which may or may not be caused by differential mortality. The causes of differential reproduction are innumerable and may arise anywhere in the living or nonliving universe.

ISOLATION AND THE SPECIES PROBLEM

So far, I have considered the genetic-systems theory of evolution only as such changes take place within a species. I have not taken up the special problem of how new species arise.

The plant and animal geographers, including Darwin, early came to the conclusion that oceanic islands were favorable places for the evolution of new species and eventually came to the conclusion: *no speciation without isolation*. From the viewpoint of genetic systems, it is obvious this must be so; if all individuals share access to a common store of genes there is no way that one group can change genetically without involving the whole species. But if the species is divided in some way, the two groups can begin to evolve independently. As has been pointed out many times, geographical isolation is not the only way a species may be divided – other possibilities include reproductive isolation by a variety of factors such as differences in sexual behavior, chromosomal incompatibility, choice of habitats, etc.

Also, isolation brings about inbreeding in the broadest sense, that breeding takes place only within each separate population. This is different from inbreeding within a species only in degree and amplitude. The division of a population into demes leads to the same divergence, and the possible extinction of a local deme has the same if less drastic consequences as the extinction of a species.

Thus the same genetic-systems processes go on between species as within them. The difference is that, unlike changes within a species, those between species become independent. If they evolve at all, related species diverge, a general principle that is not always appreciated, especially by those who attempt to find animal models for human conditions.

A chimpanzee, for example, is not a speechless human in a fur coat, nor does it represent a primitive human ancestor that somehow got delayed along the route. Rather, chimpanzees are evolving into chimpanzees and have been for millions of years. If allowed to survive, they will continue to change, but whatever the result, interesting though it may be, it will not be a human.

INTERACTIONS BETWEEN PROCESSES

In a group of four items, there are six possible interactions taken two at a time, four taken three at a time, and one with all four together. Each item appears in three combinations of two, and in three combinations of three. This reasoning, which simply reflects the mathematical formula for the number of combinations in a group, has a very general application to systems of all sorts and provides a guide for the analysis of interaction between the four major evolutionary processes (Figure 4.2).

Mutation can only act directly on genes, but the variation so produced can through gene action affect all other processes: sexual reproduction, inbreeding insofar as choice of mates is influenced by genetic variation, and differential survival. Reflecting the fact that the causes of mutation for the most part originate outside living systems, the other three processes have essentially no effect on mutation, with the exceptions noted above and, of course, modern man's ability to control radiation and other mutagenic agents.

Inbreeding also acts directly on genes. It counteracts the effect of mutation by eliminating genes from a population and so reducing variation. It can only act in conjunction with sexual reproduction, i.e., inbreeding is only possible in conjunction with sexual reproduction but has no effect on it. Inbreeding also alters differential survival by reducing the numbers of genes.

In return, inbreeding is affected by mutation, is not affected by sexual reproduction other than it is dependent on it, and is indirectly affected by differential survival through genetic effects on mating systems.

Sexual Reproduction and Meiosis have no effect on mutation, no effect on inbreeding except to make it possible, but have an effect on differential survival by producing effects on the survival or extinction of a species, i.e., species having sexual reproduction appear to be favored in evolution.

In return, sexual reproduction is affected by mutation, not affected by inbreeding, and is associated with differential survival in that it has adaptive qualities and, most importantly, that it magnifies variation that is the basis of differential survival. Thus sexual reproduction has much more limited capabilities of interaction than do the other three processes.

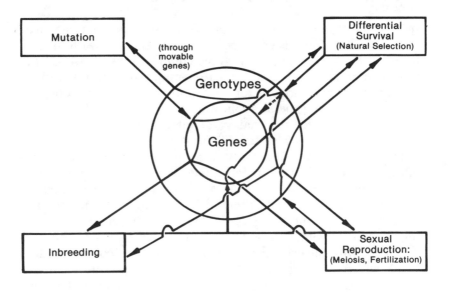

Figure 4.2. Interaction of evolutionary change processes. No process is completely exempt from feedback; even Mutation (in the sense of variation produced by movable genes) may be affected by Differential Survival, whose primary affects are on genotypes and through these to all other processes. Inbreeding, acting only in conjunction with Sexual Reproduction, acts directly on the genes, as does mutation. Differential Survival both affects and is affected by all three other processes. In summary, evolutionary change processes do not act independently of each other.

Differential Survival is affected by all three of the other processes and reciprocally affects two of them, inbreeding and sexual reproduction.

To summarize, feedback relationships are minimal with respect to mutation, which is essentially a 1-way causal agent affecting all three other processes. Inbreeding is unusual in that it has counteractive effects on the outcome of mutation, is dependent on sexual reproduction although neither affects the other, and has a reciprocal relationship only with differential survival. Sexual reproduction has only one reciprocal relationship, that with differential survival, which itself has two such relationships and is affected by 1-way causation from the third.

THEORIES OF EVOLUTION

One-Process Theories of Evolution

Since evolution is defined as genetic change, and since mutation is the source of genetic change, there is only one conceivable one-process theory. The Mutation Theory was proposed in the early days of evolutionary theorizing, but even then referred to sudden phenotypic changes in plant species rather than gene mutations. It is now generally agreed to be too simple to describe what goes on in any natural situation, and the theory has only historical significance.

As I pointed out above, mutation by itself could bring about slow changes in a population, but in any actual situation these changes would inevitably be modified by differential survival, resulting in a two-process theory.

Two-Process Theories

Since mutation is essential, there are only three possible theories involving two processes. Of these, Mutation plus Sexual Reproduction would maximize variation, but since mutation is the only change factor, it would be subject to the same limitations as the one-factor mutation theory. Mutation plus Inbreeding would be impossible, since inbreeding cannot take place without sexual reproduction.

This leaves Mutation plus Differential Survival, which is the same as Darwin's original two-process theory of Variation plus Natural Selection (Differential Survival) except that Darwin, living in the days before Mendel's work had been rediscovered, had no knowledge of what produced variation. Today, variation must include both gene mutation and variation on the genotypic level produced by meiosis and sexual reproduction.

This theory is appropriate in species that lack sexual reproduction. If applied to bisexual species, however, it neglects two phenomena. One is the variation among genotypes as wholes and their corresponding phenotypes, and the other is the interactions between genes and genic subsystems within the genotypic systems. The Mutation-Differential Survival theory is therefore inappropriate in sexually reproducing species, which comprise the vast majority of all animals and plants.

This does not mean that it is unimportant. While there are no vertebrate species that reproduce asexually, and only a few unisexual (parthenogenetic) Arthropods or Mollusks, asexual reproduction is the rule in the acellular organisms such as bacteria and is the only method possible in viruses, which consist of single genes. A bacterial species, existing in almost infinite numbers, having generation times of a few hours, and including a relatively simple genotypic system, represents an enormous target for mutation. Changes can occur relatively rapidly, as the development of drug-resistant strains of bacteria attests.

Three-Process Theories

Again, mutation is essential to any theory, and the only possible combinations are the three which include it. Mutation-Inbreeding-Differential Survival is impossible, since inbreeding is dependent on sexual reproduction. Of the other two, Mutation-Inbreeding-Sexual Reproduction is possible, as both mutation and inbreeding would bring about random genic change. However, it is very unlikely that this would not involve differential survival, even in the geneticist's laboratory. In the development of inbred strains, some strains survive and others do not. As Wright (1980 and earlier) pointed out, inbreeding in the absence of differential survival (Natural Selection) should lead to degeneration and extinction.

The final combination, Mutation-Sexual Reproduction-Differential Survival, is a workable theory. Not every population is divided into subpopulations, some being very large. Such populations should evolve through differential survival of genes and gene combinations. But if mating is really random in a large population, the difficulty would be that reproducing a given combination would have a very low probability, especially if – as would be true in the beginning – the genes involved were rare. Under such conditions, the evolution of gene combinations would be very slow, and indeed this may explain the stability of species that exist in large homogeneous populations.

The only process that could go rapidly in such a population would be the differential survival of a major gene that would produce favorable, if variable, effects in a large number of combinations. The occurrence of such a gene in a complex system is, as I have pointed out, very unlikely.

The Four-Process Theory

Such a theory will apply only to species that reproduce sexually and are subdivided, by whatever means, into subpopulations. These conditions being met, the four processes acting together should provide the opportunity for the most rapid evolutionary change (Wright, 1977). A test of this theory would be to see if these conditions are in fact met in those species that have evolved farthest and most rapidly as measured by fossil evidence, or appear to be changing most rapidly at the present time.

This is not the only possible theory of evolution. As pointed out above, there are at least two other possible combinations that are workable, given appropriate conditions.

A systems-interaction analysis of the four basic processes of genetic change thus leads to the formulation of three theories, each of which has validity under appropriate conditions. There is no intrinsic conflict between these theories, and most of the past arguments concerning them have been based on the assumption that there can be only one correct theory. Such is not the case; there is no one true way in evolution. Another assumption that has caused trouble is that the simplest theory must be the best, and so it may be for the convenience of the thinker. But one of the basic characteristics of living systems is the tendency toward increasing complexity of organization, and it is unlikely that simple explanations will suffice. And while the genetic change processes outlined above differ in complexity, none of them is simple, and this is especially true of Differential Survival.

Which one (or more than one) of the three theories is most appropriate will then depend on the conditions in which a species lives and the manner in which it is organized. This in turn points to ways in which these theories can be objectively tested, through actual observed changes in and among species, and their genetic nature.

Relationship to Non-Systems Theories

In the past, two major genetic theories of evolution have been proposed. The first, that of single-gene substitutions, first proposed by Fisher (1930) and followed by many authors since, is essentially identical with the two-process, Mutation-Differential Survival theory outlined here. It has held a prestigious advantage because it closely conforms to Darwin's original Variation-Natural Selection theory, and it also has the advantage of simplicity and being easy to understand.

As pointed out above, this is not an erroneous theory. It is appropriately applied to species in which asexual reproduction takes place, but such species are relatively rare among multicellular animals and plants. Also, its proponents have always had great difficulty in explaining the existence of sexual reproduction and its evolutionary function. The enormous magnification of variation resulting from meiosis and fertilization has often been treated as if it were irrelevant evolutionary noise, but this assumption runs counter to the basic evolutionary principle of adaptive function.

This difficulty disappears if the system concept is applied. First, genes never act individually but always interact in combinations as parts of complex genotypic systems. The evolutionary function of sexual reproduction is thus obvious: to facilitate and try out changes in genotypic systems.

The major competing genetic theory of evolution is Wright's

(1932, 1977) shifting balance theory, which is essentially the same as the four-process theory outlined above. It also has its limitations; it cannot apply to species that reproduce asexually, nor to species that are not subdivided into demes. Wright himself never claimed that it was universal, but only that under appropriate conditions it should lead to more rapid evolution.

Thus, these two theories do not conflict but each should be valid under appropriate conditions. Also, it is possible that the two-process theory has some application even in species that are affected by sexual reproduction. There are major mutant genes whose effects override those of modifying genes and thus have similar effects in all combinations. In these special cases, variation from other sources can be disregarded. The difficulty is that most if not all of such genes produce deleterious effects and lead to non-survival. I cannot think of any case of a major gene producing universally favorable effects, though some, like the gene for black pigment in mammals, are almost neutral.

Thus the Mutation-Differential Survival Theory has a limited but important role in a sexually reproducing species, that of counteracting the harmful effects of mutation. It could have a positive role in the unlikely event of a major beneficial mutation.

So far, the systems approach has not produced anything completely new, although it does make major contributions to understanding the limitations of current theories, and resolves some of their apparent contradictions. What is new is the one viable three-process theory, that of Mutation-Sexual Reproduction-Differential Survival, which should apply to the considerable number of species that are not subdivided into small populations and hence cannot be affected by inbreeding.

EXPERIMENTAL TESTS OF EVOLUTIONARY THEORIES

From the viewpoint of scientific research, a theory is important only if it can be experimentally tested. For the most part, evolutionary theories are historical in nature and hence cannot be tested except as they appear to be logical or illogical. This, of course, can lead to endless arguments.

With genetically based theories, the situation is somewhat different. One can never test what went on in the past, but it is possible to test what goes on today. For example, experimental laboratory populations can be set up, and processes such as mutation, inbreeding, and selection can be varied under controlled conditions. Such experiments are always subject to criticism that they are not natural; evolution does not go on under controlled conditions.

The best and most direct way to test genetic theories of evolution is to make crosses between related species that are different from each other with respect to characters of interest. Among mammals, the number of such crosses are limited because there are relatively few species that are interfertile, and even among these, the F_1 hybrids may be sterile, as in the cross between the horse and donkey. However, even such cases as these provide some evidence.

As stated above, the principal alternative theories of genetic evolution are the gene combination theory and that of single gene replacement, the latter including multiple additive factors. These should apply to any sort of variation, anatomical or behavioral.

There are two general conditions with respect to evolved differences in behavior patterns. The first is that both species have the pattern but in different forms, and the second is that the pattern is present in only one species, indicating either that it has evolved anew in one of them, or that it has dropped out in one but not the other.

In either case, there are two possible modes of inheritance with respect to the gene combination theory. The first of these is that the gene combination must be present in homozygous form in order to produce the pattern present in either parental species. The heterozygous combination or any other combination will not give the same result as seen in the parents. The second possibility is that the combination from one parent will be effective in the F_1 hybrid (the hypothesis of dominance). If the first hypothesis is correct (namely, that the parents' patterns only appear as a result of the homozygous condition), the F_1 hybrids should be like neither parent. Backcrosses of the F_1 to either parent should produce 1/4 of individuals like the parent (assuming that a combination of only two genes is necessary). The remaining three combinations should give variable expressions of the behavior pattern, but none like the parent. In an F_2 generation, 1/16 of the animals should be like one parent, 1/16 like the other, and 1/4 like the F_1. The six remaining combinations of genes should produce patterns unlike the parents and F_1.

If, on the other hand, the species differences are produced by a single gene or by multiple additive genes, the distribution of the various expressions of the character should be quite different from the above. The single gene hypothesis should give distributions corresponding to simple Mendelian ratios, and the additive hypothesis should give similar distributions based on cumulative effects. A few examples will illustrate the information now available from species crosses.

Bentley (1971; Bentley & Hoy, 1974) made crosses between two species of crickets, *Teleogryllus commodus* from Australia and a related species, *T. oceanicus* from Polynesia. These species have long been separate and the males show different patterns of courtship songs. The F_1 males sing in different patterns from either parent species, and among these, there are distinct differences in the reciprocal hybrids, indicating that some of the genes producing the species differences are carried on the X chromosome. The F_1 females are sterile, but the F_1 males can be backcrossed to the parent species. Bentley obtained considerable numbers of such backcross hybrids and measured their songs with respect to some 18 different characteristics. In none of these was there any indication of a bimodal distribution that would be consistent with a single gene hypothesis. Bentley did not present the complete data, and therefore it is impossible to distinguish between the gene combination and multiple additive gene theories. The results, however, definitely show that many genes are involved, and that these are found on several chromosomes. As presented, the data are consistent with the hypothesis of gene combinations, which are necessarily homozygous in order to express the parental characteristics. One interesting finding was that the F_1 females were more attracted by the songs of similar F_1's than by the songs of the parent species. Thus, the same genes apparently affect both the song and its reception, indicating the way in which the original differences were evolved.

Among birds, a female lovebird of the species *Agapornis roseicollis* builds her next by rapidly biting along the edges of leaves, tearing off the resulting saw-edged strips, tucking them under her feathers on the back and rump, and flying off to a hole in a tree, where she forms the strips into a nest. A female of the species *A. fischeri*, on the other hand, cuts the leaf strips in the same way, but carries them to her nest in her beak one at a time. Thus, the pattern of strip tucking is present in one species and absent in the other.

Dilger (1962) raised F_1 hybrid females between the two species. These birds cut strips as did both parents, but made ineffective tucking movements. As they flew to the nest, the strips fell on the ground. Occasionally, a female did carry a strip in her beak like the *fischeri* parent, and so got her nest built in an inefficient way. Such females gradually improved season after season, but never showed the full pattern of strip tucking.

This is a case where a pattern (strip tucking) is present in one species and absent in the other. Again, it is consistent with the hypothesis of gene combinations that must be present in the homozygous form, as the heterozygous F_1 is not like either parent.

A third case comes from the genus *Canis*. This group of animals is unusual in that fertile hybrids can be produced between all four of the major species: the wolf (*Canis lupus*), the dog (*C. familiaris*), the coyote (*C. latrans*), and the jackals (*C. aureus* and others). While many of the social behavior patterns such as barking are shared by all of these species, there is one distinct difference between coyotes on one hand and dogs and gray wolves (*C. lupus*) on the other (Ginsburg, 1976).

When threatened, a coyote will arch its back like a cat, open its mouth to the fullest extent, and hiss. The three components of the pattern are not necessarily expressed as a unit, the gaping being the easiest to elicit. In similar circumstances, a dog or gray wolf will never arch its back, but will retract its lips from its clenched teeth and growl, the whole pattern being called a snarl. The dog does not open its mouth except perhaps to snap at whatever is threatening it. The snarl is not an alternative pattern, as coyotes also show it. This species difference is another example of a pattern which is found in one species but not in another.

Ginsburg and Moon (1983; Moon & Ginsburg, 1983) have studied the behavior of gaping in crosses between coyotes and dogs. In the F_1 generation, in which all animals should have the same genotype except for varying genes present in the parents, the usual reaction was the snarl, but the coyote pattern could be elicited in extremely threatening situations, at least in some animals. Again, the gaping pattern was the easiest to elicit.

In the F_2 and F_3 generations, all of the animals could be induced to produce at least one of the three components of the coyote patterns, but there was a great deal of variation in the time of development at which the patterns could be produced and also considerable variation in the degree of social stress stimulation required.

The underlying genetic organization is obviously not that of a single gene. As the data now stand, the best working hypothesis is that both the dog and coyote possess gene combinations that permit the expressions of the coyote patterns, but that the dog possesses gene combinations that completely suppress them. Thus, the segregation that takes place in the hybrids should be that of the suppressor genes. The evidence presently available does not clearly distinguish between the gene combination and single gene replacement theories, but the case illustrates a common situation among mammals; namely, that complex sequences of behavior patterns are rare; rather, small patterns can either be expressed separately or combined in different sequences.

Fuller (1976) reviewed the evidence concerning the inheritance of communicatory behavior in interspecies hybrids and pointed out that this involves both a capacity to send signals and a capacity to receive them, which may be affected by the same genes, as seems to be the case in crickets, or may not. He concluded that components of behavior are inherited independently and that variation rests on multiple factors rather than segregation at a single locus. No master gene integrates the components of a complex pattern into an effective whole; rather, using Dobzhansky's terms, Fuller concluded that we are dealing in each case with a "coadaptive gene complex", or gene combination.

A method of interspecies genetic analysis that is not dependent on hybridization is to compare organic enzymes in two related species. The enzymes identify the genes that produce them and there is no need to crossbreed. Results with chimpanzees and humans (King & Wilson, 1975) indicate close similarity between the two species, far closer than between the observed phenotypes. This points to the importance of gene combinations in species differences and causes one to speculate that this may be an example of systems creativity – namely that genes in combinations produce variations impossible for single genes. The authors themselves concluded that regulator genes are more important in evolutionary change than are changes in the structural genes that produce enzymes. This in itself implies interaction among combinations of genes.

Finally, the genetic systems theories presented here are within themselves incomplete. The actions of genes and genotypic systems are expressed developmentally in various levels and sorts of organized systems, each of which may change in different ways and feedback to modify the genetic processes. What is missing from Figure 4.1 is the means through which adaptation for survival takes place, and this will be the subject of the following chapters.

Chapter V

The Evolution of Physiological Systems

So far in this book I have treated genetic evolutionary change as if it were a passive response to the four processes illustrated in Figure 4.1. Actually, any theory of Natural Selection implies that genetic evolutionary change feeds back and alters the process of Differential Survival. In Figure 5.1 I have illustrated the main ways in which this feedback is accomplished in animals. In plants, of course, behavioral and social change are omitted. All of these ways are interdependent to some extent, but it is appropriate to begin with the lowest level of organization, that of change in physiological systems, or organic evolution.

THE NATURE OF PHYSIOLOGICAL SYSTEMS

The scientific study of biological phenomena began with anatomy, or the science of form and structure. This soon led to the study of function, and the science of physiology was born. The older biologists, most of whom were mechanistically minded, assumed that form was the determining cause of function, and the nature of living structure was the major topic of biological research in the 19th century. It also became the major focus of research on evolution, both as evidence that evolutionary change had occurred and because evolutionary theory brought order to the resemblances and divergences observed in comparative anatomy.

Structure, however, brought understanding of function only where there was variation in structure, and was of little use in comprehending function within an individual or even within a species.

Physiology soon became a science in its own right, and as it did, came to occupy a central position in the development of biological theory. It has special significance for the subject matter of this book for three reasons.

First, physiology was the science within which the systems concept first appeared. It is so often used as a model for systems theory at other levels of organization that it is important to understand the limits of physiologically based theory as well as its extensions. Physiology has major relevance to systems theory.

Second, since genic combinations can act only through physiological processes, physiological genetics is equally relevant to genetical theories of evolution.

Third, physiological function is intimately related to behavior. An animal cannot move or behave in any way without activating physiological functions. The systems organization of behavior and physiology is a central topic in behavioral research and must be involved in its evolution.

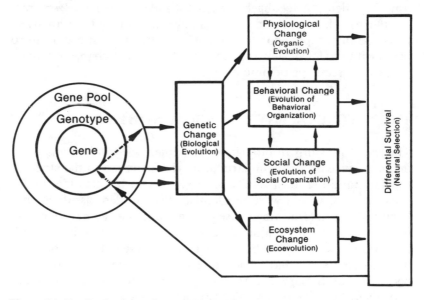

Figure 5.1. Feedback of genetic evolutionary change through systems organization. The process of Differential Survival is always modified by the results of its own operations. Note that changes in organization can act across systems as well as on adjacent systems (see Figure 1.3); also that system change at any level of systems organization may affect all levels.

Table 5.1
THE ORGAN SYSTEMS IN MAMMALS

System	Major Function	Immediate Adaptive Response
Digestive	Nutrition	Increase or decrease of nutritive materials
Respiratory	Supply oxygen, remove carbon dioxide	Increase or decrease of breathing rate
Excretory	Elimination of excess or harmful chemicals	Increase or decrease urine flow
Circulatory	Transportation of gases, liquids, dissolved solids	Increase or decrease of blood flow
Muscular	Movement, maintenance of body temperature (in warm blooded animals); breathing	Increase or decrease of contractions
Skeletal	Support, movement (with muscular system), protection	Growth, repair
Dermal System (skin and related tissues)	Protection, insulation, maintenance of temperature	Piloerection, growth
Neuro-endocrine	Coordination of biochemical functions; organization of behavior	Increase or decrease of glandular secretion; differential stimulation of muscles
Reproduction	Production of germ cells, fertilization; nutrition of egg or embryo	Decrease of function

The Organ Systems of Vertebrates

As the outcome of several centuries of study, anatomists and physiologists classified the parts of a human or other vertebrate body into some nine or ten organ systems, each with a major function (see Table 5.1). The first four of these are concerned with maintenance processes, and the combined result of these functions is to maintain the stability of the internal environment, or produce homeostasis.

The next two, which might be called the skeletal-muscular system because they are so intimately connected, include the bones and voluntary muscles. A major function is to produce movement, the basis of behavior. In warm-blooded animals, they are also concerned with the regulation of body temperature. In the case of bones, the major dynamic function is growth that has the effect of strengthening or repairing certain parts.

The skin is often considered to be a separate system because of its separate function, although it consists of a single organ. Closely related to it is the so-called adipose system, although it is still less complexly organized, consisting of a single class of tissues mixed with other organs, and whose function is food storage.

The neuro-endocrine system, once considered two separate systems, nervous and endocrine, stands alone in its function of coordination. Its general function is to be immediately responsive to change, either internal or external.

Finally, there is the reproductive system, dependent on all the others but unlike them in that it gives little in return. Its function depends on stability but contributes little to it.

From the viewpoint of logic, this scheme is all but perfect: a set of anatomically distinct systems, each with a separate function, and the whole integrated to form a system on a higher level, the organism. But, as always with living systems, function does not always follow logic. Muscular tissue (smooth muscle) forms a part of organs in the digestive, respiratory, circulatory and even the reproductive system. The skin, while it has a distinct function, can only be considered a single organ. Adipose tissue forms a part of many organs in different systems, although its function is most closely allied to the digestive system.

The overriding principle, then, is not logic but function on the higher level, which is accomplished predominately through organ systems but also through less elaborate means of organization. What then is the general nature of physiological systems as seen in the most highly organized animals?

GENERAL CHARACTERISTICS OF PHYSIOLOGICAL SYSTEMS

Hierarchical Organization

Systems on the physiological level are composed of a set of systems and sub-systems. At the highest level there are organ systems, whose entities are organs. As an example, the muscular system is composed of organs, muscles which are the entities that comprise the system. The organs are composed of tissues, or groups of similar cells. In the case of the muscular system the muscles are composed of muscular tissues which are groups of muscle cells, plus connective tissue. The cells themselves are in turn composed or organelles such as the nucleus and nuclear membrane. Thus the entities composing the system at each level and having different functions combine in a common function at the next higher level.

Structural Organization

The entities at each level are spatially related to each other in a fixed fashion, leading to the concept of structure. The structure in most cases cannot be altered without altering or destroying the function, which leads to the idea that structure is a cause of function. This is a mechanistic concept that has been widely held in the past. It was not until relatively recently that scientists began to recognize that the relationship between structure and function is reciprocal, as D'Arcy Thompson (1942) showed. Bones, for example, are shaped in accordance with the stresses that are laid upon them by muscle action and gravity.

Structural organization makes physiological organization quite different from social organization, in which the individual organisms are able to move about relatively freely and have no fixed spatial relationships to each other.

Interactions

At all levels, the interactions between physiological entities are physical and chemical in nature and usually depend on direct contact, again emphasizing the importance of structural organization. One organ system, the neuroendocrine, has the function of coordinating the function of all others. This results in a higher level of organization and new system, the organismic. The process of organization of physiological systems is that of development, again illustrating the general systems principle that living systems tend to become increasingly complexly organized.

Homeostasis

Once organized, physiological systems function to maintain internal stability, illustrating another principle of living systems. Homeostasis, however, is an overall organismic function involving several systems and not a separable function for each of the usually recognized physiological systems. For example, the kidneys (belonging to the excretory system) maintain constant levels of electrolytes in the body but can only do this in cooperation with the circulatory system.

Feedback

Homeostasis would be impossible without two-way interaction. Such two-way causation takes place not only between the entities at a given level of organization but also between different levels of organization. Consequently, the concept of hierarchical organization is strongly modified. Causation not only comes down from the nervous system, but the nervous system is also affected by activities on lower levels of organization, with an emphasis on structural organization and the maintenance of stability or homeostasis.

The Nature of Adaptation

Adaptation is one of the key concepts of evolutionary theory, and one that was developed in connection with the evolution of anatomical-physiological systems. An organism may adapt in two general ways. One, which we may called *immediate* or active change, occurs within the lifetime of the organism, and the other, *evolutionary* or passive change, occurs over generations. The effect in either case is to obviate or lessen the impact of differential survival.

Immediate Adaptation in Physiological Systems

The adaptive response of the digestive system is usually to increase or decrease food intake. Similarly, the respiratory system increases or decreases the intake and outflow of gases, the excretory system speeds up or slows down the flow of urine, and the circulatory system reduces or increases the flow of blood. The muscular system increases or decreases the strength and rapidity of muscle contraction. The skeleton and skin are more limited in their responses, responding only by growth, which is a slow process. Likewise, the immediate response of the reproductive system to unfavorable conditions is a negative one; by decreasing its function, energy is saved.

In general, the effect of the immediate adaptive responses of physiological systems, which are usually coordinated, is to maintain the constancy of the internal environment against any outside changes that might be deleterious. Thus, the major principle of physiological activity is homeostasis.

Evolutionary Adaptation in Physiological Systems

Evolutionary change might proceed in three directions: to improve physiological function, to worsen it, or to have no effect. Differential survival should work against the second possibility, leaving only the other two.

Since a major internal function of physiological systems is maintaining homeostasis, evolutionary change should move in this direction. A major breakthrough of this sort was the development of the capacity to maintain a nearly constant body temperature, or homoiothermy, in birds and mammals, which explains their dominance relative to other forms of vertebrate life in the aerial and terrestrial habitats. This is not so important to an aquatic animal, as the water temperature remains nearly constant, especially in the ocean, and the cold-blooded fish still dominate in that habitat, although some birds and mammals have exploited it also.

Another consequence of immediate physiological adaptation and the fact that evolutionary change must either be favorable or neutral toward it, is that the possibilities of evolutionary adaptive change become limited. In a complex set of integrated systems, any change is almost certain to affect part of the system unfavorably. Consequently, the most viable changes are those that have little or no effect on current function, but may have effects in a later situation.

In any case, the effect of both immediate and evolutionary adaptive change is to modify the process of differential survival so as to protect the organisms concerned. Thus evolutionary change operates to produce stability on two levels: through homeostasis on the immediate level and, by increasing capacities of this sort, to bring about evolutionary stability. The process of differential survival thus works against itself, as I noted above.

CONCLUSIONS

I have considered physiological evolution and its relationship to systems theory in detail for several reasons. One is that the systems concept chiefly arose from the study of anatomy and physiology and has been shaped by its history. It does not follow that all other living systems have the same characteristics. Physiological systems are chiefly organized according to spatial relationships, or anatomy, and their constituent entities interact biochemically. Freedom of movement and behavioral interaction are found only on the level of social systems. On the other hand, the homeostatic principle, so strongly emphasized in physiological systems, does seem to be represented in a general tendency to develop stability at all system levels.

Second, the evolutionary consequence of homeostasis is to protect the organism against environmental conditions that bring about differential survival. The animal organism, particularly in the most highly organized species, carries around its own internal environment.

Thus, the process of differential survival is, in a sense, self-defeating. Acting upon physiological processes, it brings about genetic changes that reduce differential survival. As a self-limiting process, it should tend to bring about evolutionary stability rather than continuous change. This is a conclusion also reached by Wright (1935) through a different line of reasoning. I should add that this is true only if environmental conditions and hence the factors that bring about differential survival remain stable.

Third, the study of physiological function leads to the concept of two kinds of adaptation, immediate adaptation of organisms to the changing environmental situations around them, and long-term or evolutionary adaptation that takes place over successive generations. Thus the processes of homeostasis are immediately adaptive, but the capacities for achieving homeostasis were evolved through long-term adaptation. The operation of these two kinds of adaptation are even more apparent in behavior.

Fourth, the skeletal system has special significance in organic evolution because in most fossils only the hard portions of the body are preserved. Since this system has relatively little capacity to make immediate adaptive responses it should reflect primarily long-term or evolutionary adaptation. The paleontologists could not have made a better choice had they done so deliberately.

On the other hand, the skeleton reflects change in other systems only indirectly, and much could be going on in the soft systems without leaving a fossil record. Consequently, the evolution of the skeletal system may give a false impression of evolutionary conservatism.

Fifth, the reproductive system is another special case, for different reasons. It has little to do with the survival of an adult organism, but everything to do with the survival of offspring. Consequently, evolutionary change should proceed in the direction of improved fertility and fecundity, a result that is achieved in many different ways. The simplest, and possibly one of the most primitive methods, is the production of enormous numbers of germ cells, a phenomenon that still exists in the males of mammals and birds. Then there is internal fertilization, which first appears in the flatworms and involves sexual behavior. The other main adaptive change is in the direction of protection of fertilized eggs, internally and externally, and behaviorally and physiologically. Thus, the mode of reproduction either exaggerates differential survival or minimizes it.

On the other hand, the reproductive system has little to do with homeostasis except that by ceasing its function it may conserve energy and maintain internal stability in this way.

Finally, genotypic systems are expressed only through the organization of physiological systems which thus provide the most direct expression of gene action and implicitly the most direct reflection of evolutionary change. In the following chapter I shall review the major evolutionary phenomena that have arisen out of the study of changes in anatomical-physiological systems, i.e., organic evolution.

Chapter VI

On Theories of Organic Evolution and their Relevance to Modern Genetic-Systems Theory

Biologists of the 19th Century centered their work around the evolution of structural organization. Their general method was to collect one or more specimens of new or unfamiliar plants and animals, kill and preserve them, describe them carefully both internally and externally and on the basis of this evidence, compare them with known species and group like with like. If the new specimens were unlike any known before, they assumed that they had found a new species. They next assumed that the more similar two species were in form and structure, the more closely related they were, and they tried to deduce how one could have changed into the other, and in what order.

In addition to the anatomical evidence from living plants and animals, they had two other lines of evidence. One was that of fossils, which in some cases could provide more direct evidence of descent but were often scarce and usually provided only skeletal remains for study. Among living species there are often differences in appearance and in the soft parts of the body that are not reflected in the skeleton. In addition, it is often difficult to distinguish between speciation (splitting into two or more species) and species change in the same line of descent. This has given rise to endless arguments.

A third line of research was that of embryonic development in living species, where changes in organization could be studied anatomically. Comparison of corresponding stages in development provided additional evidence of close or distant relationships.

On the basis of these three lines of study, biologists constructed phylogenetic trees showing how living species could be traced back to common ancestors. On close examination many of the branches of these trees turn out to be phantoms, as biologists often resorted to the device of a hypothetical common ancestor yet to be discovered in the fossil record. One of the greatest unsolved puzzles was that the major phyla of animals could be traced separately as far as the Cambrian Period, below which the fossil record shortly ended. Thus there were many hypotheses (and little direct evidence) as to the origin of Chordates, including Vertebrates, from some more primitive phylum. If the phylogenetic diagrams were drawn more realistically they would have looked more like a small grove than a single tree.

The concept that dominated this period of biological research was that of *descent*. Under its influence comparative anatomists and paleontologists described and named the majority of living species, discovered that there were much larger numbers of extinct species, and described the embryonic development of many living forms. Whatever the merits and validity of the concept involved, it did result in the collection of a large body of factual information that is still available and useful. And the prime mover in establishing the value of descent as an explanatory concept was Darwin.

In this chapter I shall examine the major theoretical ideas that arose from these studies in the light of genetic-systems theories of evolution that have since been developed. One would expect that the two lines of evolutionary theories should converge, and that if there are major discrepancies some explanation must be found. There have been several attempts at such synthesis, but, as I shall point out, there are still places where new insights are valuable.

DARWIN AND THE THEORY OF NATURAL SELECTION

Historical Importance

Darwin's work had a major effect because he provided the first workable theory of evolution. His studies were especially impressive because he was a tremendous scholar who read everything available at the time. Also, in order to give himself direct information regarding animal species, he worked out the anatomy and classification of the barnacles, or Cirrepedia. And he had personal experience in another field, geographical distribution, through his voyage on the *Beagle*. Personally a man of highest integrity, and with supreme good judgment, he was respected by all, even by those who disagreed with him. As a model for a biological scientist he is hard to excel. But this should not blind us to the fact that, because his information was limited, his theory is incomplete.

Limitations of Darwin's Work

Although Darwin was a careful scholar, some of the secondhand information upon which he relied is erroneous. For example, Darwin read and wrote that dogs bark but wolves only howl. This is simply not so; wolves and dogs share the same basic behavior patterns including howling and barking (Scott, 1950b).

Second, Darwin realized that his theory depended on biological inheritance, but genetic theory was yet to be developed. It is fascinating to speculate on what might have happened had Darwin read Mendel's paper (Barlow, 1988). Instead, Mendel sent his paper to the European biologist Nageli, whose response was negative. Mendel's chief paper was published in 1866, only seven years after Darwin published his *Origin of Species*. But it is quite possible that Darwin also might not have appreciated Mendel's work, since it is essentially an experimental test of the chromosomal theory of inheritance, and the existence and behavior of chromosomes was still to be worked out. These two bits of information were only finally integrated in 1900, long after Darwin's death, when Mendel's work was rediscovered.

So Darwin invented his own theory of inheritance, pangenesis. Unfortunately, it was completely wrong, based on the idea of blending inheritance, whereas chromosomal and genic inheritance is particulate. But blending inheritance has the effect of reducing variation and so negating one of the essential elements in Darwin's theory. So he concluded that domestic dogs, being so highly variable, must have originated from a cross between two different species, the wolf and the jackal, an error which is still perpetuated in some scientific literature.

A final limitation of Darwin's work is that he made little use of the concept of systems except in the general sense of the anatomical systems. The term system is not even found in the index of the *Origin of Species*. Even in the case of sexual selection, which obviously involves social behavior and social systems, Darwin thought only in terms of individual organisms.

The Theory of Natural Selection

As Darwin later reported, this idea came to him from two sources. One was the writings of Malthus, who argued that in human populations, reproductive capacities always outran food production, and hence death from starvation and disease was inevitable. From this Darwin abstracted the idea of differential survival.

The other source was that of the practice of plant and animal breeding, which at that time consisted chiefly of picking out certain desirable individuals as ancestors of the next generation, and repeating this generation after generation with the resulting changes in form and function.

Darwin put the two ideas together and argued that differential survival must occur under natural conditions, and that nature (meaning general environmental conditions), must determine which individuals survived. He called this process Natural Selection as opposed to the Artificial Selection practiced by animal and plant breeders. He realized that it was dependent upon the existence of variation, and he devoted a volume to collecting evidence regarding the *Variation of Animals and Plants in Nature*.

Darwin, of course, knew nothing of the genetic processes of mutation and random assortment of variable genes. Nor could he know of the variation of genic combinations produced by meiosis and sexual reproduction. Darwin's theory of Natural Selection then, is not so much erroneous as incomplete. As I showed in a previous chapter, it is essentially a two-process theory, and equivalent to the modern Mutation-Differential Survival Theory, which has limited but important applications.

ORGANIC EVOLUTION IN THE LIGHT OF THE SYSTEMS CONCEPT

J. S. Huxley (1942) made the first attempt to reconcile the genetical theories of evolution developed by Fisher, Haldane, and Wright with the older theories derived from comparative anatomy and paleontology. Fully conversant with comparative anatomy, he had also done extensive research on the comparative social behavior of birds.

Evolution, the Modern Synthesis

Huxley's book of this title was published in the middle of World War II on cheap paper, and few copies are available today. Though not himself a geneticist, Huxley made full use of the systems concept in his treatment of genetic phenomena. Thus he speaks of "the diploid meiotic system" and stresses its importance in the production of variations. One of his chapters was entitled "Genetic Systems and Evolution", and he states that it is "an advantage to an organism to have its normal constitution as harmonious as possible with its main genes buffered by modifiers to maximum efficiency... and mutually adapted to each others activity, and neighboring genes harmonized through an optimum position effect" (p. 134). He did not, however, make full use of systems theory in connection with some of the principles derived from comparative anatomy.

Adaptive Radiation

This concept was first enunciated by H. F. Osborn (1910), chiefly on the basis of the paleontological evidence that modern mammals in the Cretaceous period rapidly entered almost all terrestrial, aquatic and even aerial habitats, and as they did so changed, diverged, and became adapted to life in these habitats, producing animals as diverse as whales, lions, bats, and many others now living or extinct.

From the viewpoint of modern genetic and systems theory, the genetic system of a species living in a particular habitat becomes buffered against the effects of fluctuating conditions that vary from year to year, producing what Lerner (1954) called genetic homeostasis. But if a species penetrates a new habitat and encounters selective conditions against which its genetic system is not buffered, one would expect that rapid change would take place, limited only by the capacity of the species to vary.

A minor modern example is taking place in the Northeastern United States. Approximately a century and a half ago, timber wolves were eliminated from this area, leaving vacant an ecological niche of predation on the deer population. Many years later, coyotes began to penetrate the Adirondack area and have now spread into northern New England. They found a vacant ecological niche, and as they entered it they rapidly changed in both physique and behavior. In the western dry plains and deserts, coyotes are small, scrawny animals that chiefly hunt rodents singly or in pairs. As they came into New England as deer hunters, they have become much larger and rather magnificent animals that frequently hunt in packs. The point is that in this new niche they are free from the selection that kept them in a relatively narrow mold. This case suggests that the phenomenon of stability in living systems is in part the consequence of stable external conditions as well as genetic homeostasis.

Orthogenesis

Where abundant fossils were available, paleontologists frequently observed that a given species appeared to evolve in one direction, i.e., in a straight line, and that related species sometimes evolved in parallel straight lines. This they called orthogenesis, and some concluded that this showed that evolutionary change was independent of natural selection. J. S. Huxley concluded that orthogenesis was subsidiary to natural selection, providing limits within which natural selection provided the main guiding role. He did not, however, suggest what produced an orthogenetic limit.

From the viewpoint of systems theory, the explanation is obvious. In order to evolve, a system must survive, and changes that destroy or seriously interfere with the function of the system are therefore impossible. The evolution of the horse, often cited as a case of orthogenesis, is an example. There is no way that the hoof of a horse could evolve into a prehensile hand without destroying its function as an organ adapted for fast running. Once the horse had started on the road of specialization of hooves, there was no way that it could go except toward a single hoof and longer legs.

This implies that one determinant of the direction of evolutionary change is, in addition to natural selection, the nature of the preexisting system. Similar systems in similar environments will therefore evolve in similar ways, producing parallel evolution. But it is rare that a system completely lacks flexibility. As Simpson (1951) suggested, even the evolution of the horse is not completely orthogenetic, if one considers all the fossil evidence.

Huxley offered another explanation of certain cases of orthogenesis, that they are the result of heterogonic growth or allometry. That is, the growth patterns of certain organs such as the antlers of deer are related in power functions to the general growth of the body. For example, the increase in size of the antlers might be expressed as the size of the skull multiplied by a constant raised to some power, and he gathered a considerable amount of data to show that such heterogonic growth relationships actually existed in a variety of animal species. Assuming that this phenomenon exists, it implies the existence of stable underlying systems not subject to variation. This in turn requires a physiological explanation which is not immediately obvious and indeed might only be found in certain special cases.

Specialization

Another general principle that came out of the study of organic evolution was that ancestral or primitive forms appeared to be adapted for existence in a variety of habitats, whereas their descendants tended to become more and more specialized. This observation is closely related to that of adaptive radiation; i.e., as a generalized ancestral form spread into various new habitats its descendants became specially adapted in a variety of ways.

The comparative anatomists and paleontologists also observed that specialization leads to extinction; highly specialized forms are unable to change in an evolutionary fashion when their habitat changes. And so the whole process begins over again, with some surviving generalized species adapting to new conditions and eventually becoming specialized in new ways.

This phenomenon is, of course, related to the general tendencies of living systems to become more complexly organized, and as they do so, to become more stably organized. The more stable the organization, the less the possibility of evolutionary change. In order for reorganization to take place, the system must become temporarily disorganized. But an individual cannot become physiologically disorganized and survive. The changes which a highly organized (specialized) species can undergo are thus limited to those which will not disturb its previous organization.

Adaptation and Preadaptation

An essential concept that arouse out of Darwin's work was that of adaptation, meaning a change in an organism that made it better able to function or, in Darwin's terms, fitter to survive. Consequently, the students of organic evolution constantly searched for evidence that the changes that they found in fossils and the differences that they observed among living species were adaptive.

The concept is consistent with systems theory: an adaptation implies a change in the organization of a system or systems. In the case of biological evolution, these must be changes in the genetic systems involved and in the systems organized by them.

It does not follow, however, that any change in the organization of a system must be adaptive and therefore that all biological phenomena are adaptive. This is a common error among unsophisticated evolutionary biologists. From the viewpoint of the 4-process theory of evolution, three of the processes are random in nature. Therefore, in considering the function of any biological phenomenon, one must always start with the null hypothesis: that the phenomenon may have no function or actually be harmful. Phenomena can therefore be arranged on a scale ranging from highly adaptive through neutral to strongly maladaptive. Most would be expected to lie toward the more adaptive end of the scale, but not necessarily. After all, species do become extinct, presumably because they are not well adapted for survival.

Also, the degree of adaptation depends upon the nature of the ecosystem in which an organism lives. A structure or physiological activity might have little use in a particular environment but become useful if the organism moves into a new one. This has given rise to the concept of *preadaptation*, one which is consistent with the genetic theory of evolution. Variation should constantly occur, and if a particular variation has little or no negative impact, it may persist to become useful at a later date as a result of environmental change.

This brings up the possibility of negative preadaptation, that a phenomenon that has a neutral effect in one environment may become harmful if the environment changes. In this case, there should be strong selection against it.

TAXONOMY IN THE LIGHT OF GENETIC THEORY

The scientific study of taxonomy, the classification of animals and plants, began with Linnaeus, long before Darwin's day, with the result that a great deal of the biotic world had been explored and described at least superficially and provided some of the facts on which Darwin based his case. The early taxonomists used the typological method described in the beginning of this chapter, and one can still find "type specimens" preserved in some of the old natural history museum collections.

Taxonomic research went along parallel to the newer science of genetics for many years, but it was not until Mayr (1963; 1970) extended the evolutionary theory based on population genetics to animal taxonomy that any attempt was made to relate the two fields. A major finding was that the typological method, which consisted of trying to describe an entire species in terms of one or two "typical" specimens, was invalid. A species population can be realistically described only in terms of means and variances. Under the old method, two widely different individuals from the same breeding population could be described as separate species, and this often occurred. Anyone who has tried to classify an animal or plant using the old keys based on types, or has tried to follow the directions for anatomical dissection of a species that the author developed from one or two specimens, can appreciate the inadequacy of the typological method – no other individual was ever identical with the type specimen.

The genetically based population concept also led to the redefinition of a species. Originally based on the concept of non-overlapping morphological types, a species now became a population of interbreeding individuals having access to a common gene pool, a group that was often but not necessarily morphologically distinct from others. In fact, there are numerous cases where populations are morphologically indistinguishable (sibling species) but do not interbreed. Consequently, the concept of isolating mechanisms, which Mayr attributed to Dobzhansky (1937), becomes of major importance. Mayr considered that this was the major role of behavior in evolution: the prevention of crossbreeding between populations. This implies the existence of non-morphological differences that are genetically determined.

This still does not solve the problem of how the original separation could have occurred, and there may be no general answer. The idea of geographical distribution had long been appreciated, ever since the days of Darwin and Wallace, and their successors had formulated it as "no speciation without isolation." An economical hypothesis to explain the occurrence of two sibling sympatric species, i.e., morphologically indistinguishable but non-interbreeding species that occupy the same area, is that a population has become spatially separated into two parts, evolved isolating mechanisms of some sort, and has then come back together.

Mayr's general theory of evolution was essentially a two-factor one, similar to that which Darwin had advanced. However, Mayr included under variation both mutation and "random drift" based on inbreeding. The latter is dependent on sexual reproduction, but he made little use of the role of sexual reproduction in magnifying the variation of gene combinations. He also believed that inbreeding and random drift could have little importance because animal species were not commonly divided into small local populations or demes. Subsequent research on a variety of species has proved him wrong in this respect.

A final major contribution to the species concept came from ecology: the idea that a species is an ecological unit, that each species has functional relationships with other species with which it comes into contact. In terms of the systems concept, species are the interacting entities that compose an ecosystem.

Overall, Mayr brought about a revolution in taxonomic thinking. In addition, he had a clear idea of the genotype as a system, with every phenotypic character affected by all genes, and every gene affecting all characters. He stated the concept of gene combinations by asserting that a phenotype was the result of harmonious collaboration of genes, and called the process of accumulating genes that work well together "coadaptive selection." But he did not apply his ideas to the problems of the evolution of social behavior and organization, and did not develop the roles of these phenomena in modifying change processes.

PALEONTOLOGY AND GENETIC-SYSTEMS THEORY

Relating paleontology to the modern genetic theory of evolution was a much more difficult process, as fossils never breed nor retain traces of DNA. The leading paleontological evolutionist of the mid-20th century was G. G. Simpson of the American Museum of Natural History. As the title of his 1944 book, *Tempo and Mode in Evolution* implies, his primary concern was the rate of evolutionary processes. He found evidence in the fossil record that evolution could proceed at rates ranging from zero (as indicated by a succession of identical forms) to the abrupt changes from one form to another that he named tachytely, succession of one form by a quite different but obviously related one.

From the viewpoint of genetic-systems theory, these differences in rates are readily explained. Cases of slow or zero change rates should occur under conditions that nullify the basic evolutionary change processes: i.e., a uniform and unchanging environment such as that found in some parts of the ocean and which should produce strong selection for the particular combination of genes best suited for survival under these conditions, plus similar selection against all other combinations. Sexual reproduction can produce very little variation in such a situation. If in addition there are very large random breeding populations such as are commonly found in living marine invertebrates, there should be no inbreeding and hence no possibility of genetic drift. This leaves one change process, that of mutation. Even it may be reduced to low rates in environments shielded from radiation and, in any case, should eventually reach an equilibrium with reverse mutation. Also, living systems tend to evolve in the direction of increasing stability. In a stable complex system living in a stable environment, there may be no way that mutation can improve the function of the system. Finally, species that are either self-fertilizing or reproduce by budding should be slow to change.

Thus it is relatively easy to explain slow rates of change. At the opposite end of the scale, Wright had defined the conditions under which the most rapid changes take place for a sexually reproducing organism: moderate rates of both mutation and selection, and the division of the species population into small, partially isolated sub-populations or demes in which new gene combinations could be tried out and spread from one deme to another. Simpson (1944) originally could not see how this kind of population organization could occur often enough to be important, but later came to agree that Wright's view was correct, although there was no way to test it out on fossil material (Simpson, 1953). He himself was inclined to attribute rapid change to adaptive radiation which, as shown above, is consistent with genetic theory.

More recently, the paleontologists Gould and Eldredge (1977) have concerned themselves with the same problem and have suggested a process that they call "punctuated equilibrium." To reconcile this with genetic theory they suggest a small population isolated from the main group, leaving few if any fossils because of small numbers, changing rapidly, becoming well adapted, and then expanding rapidly to replace the main group, either competitively or because the main line has become extinct. Again, there is no way to test this hypothesis on fossil material, but it is consistent with what occurs in living forms. Needless to say, it is not instantaneous transformation.

Genetic theory does, however, provide at least one instance of instantaneous creation of a new species: that of allotetraploidy. Ordinarily, hybrids between two distantly related species are infertile because their chromosomes will not pair up during the process of meiosis. But if a very large number of crosses are made purposefully or by accident there may occur a hybrid with diploid sets of chromosomes from both parents, and if they can work together sufficiently well to produce a viable individual there is the potentiality of producing a new species in one generation. Of course, there has to be two such individuals if sexual reproduction is to take place, except in the case of species capable of self-fertilization, as in the case of some plants and one species of cyprodontid fishes, *Rivulus* (Barlow, personal communication). Such new plant species have been produced experimentally. In the case of the marine invertebrates, where millions of germs cells are broadcast into the water, there might be a similar chance – very small – of this occurring.

Most of the difficulties in reconciling paleontology with genetic theory lie in the incompleteness of the fossil record. It is rare that researchers can accumulate enough complete and similar specimens to constitute a population, and when they do they are never sure whether the observed variation represents one species or more than one. There is no way that sibling species could be distinguished by their fossils, and there may have been much variation in the soft parts of the body that is not reflected in skeletons. Consequently, paleontologists have still to escape from typological thinking, and this is particularly evident in work done with the rare humanoid fossils, where each new find of skeletal fragments tends to be given a new species name.

EMBRYOLOGY AND EVOLUTION

The process of embryonic development is the way in which genotypic organization brings about physiological organization. It is in this fashion that genotypic systems create physiological systems. As with anatomy and the study of organ systems, the study of development began long before the discovery of the genes, and had a considerable effect on the history of evolutionary theory.

Periods of Development in Mammals

The development of the fertilized egg into an embryo and eventually into a fetus and infant can be divided into several periods, according to the major organizing process which goes on in each. The periods here described are those which take place in a mammal. Certain of these processes obviously do not take place in vertebrates such as fishes, whose eggs usually develop in an aquatic environment. I prefer not to use the term "state" of development, as there is nothing static about the developmental process. A period is simply the age range within which the major part of a particular organizational process takes place.

The first period is that of *fertilization*, usually very brief. The sperm enters the egg, resulting in the formation of a new genotype, and the organizational processes within the egg, hitherto quiescent, become activated. At this point the egg begins to divide, initiating the period of *cell division*. The process of cell division is little affected by the genotype, it being a capacity preorganized within the egg. The result of repeated cell divisions is a ball of cells. Cell division is, of course, the primary process of growth. As the egg divides, it begins to grow.

The third period is that of *implantation*. A mammalian egg contains very little nutrient material and must soon begin to absorb food and liquids from the body of the mother. It does so by passing down the oviduct from the ovary to the uterus, where it becomes imbedded in the wall of the uterus and begins to absorb nutrients directly from the cells of the mother.

The fourth period is that of *germ layer formation*. The cells not only grow but grow differentially, and the result is first to produce a hollow ball or blastula and then to divide the wall of the blastula into three layers: the ectoderm which will eventually become the nervous system and skin; the mesoderm or middle layer which will eventually become the bone and the internal organs; and finally, the endoderm which forms the lining of the digestive tract and respiratory organs.

Next is the period of *embryonic organ formation*. The ectoderm grows differentially, and forms first a groove and then a neural tube, an embryonic organ which is the forerunner of the spinal cord, brain and the nervous system. Such an embryonic organ is not the equivalent of an adult organ; it does not have the adult functions of a brain. Its function is to organize a brain and nervous system. Similarly, embryonic organs appear in the other layers. The mesoderm becomes divided into somites, segments that will form the segmental structure of the backbone and the muscles that are connected with them. The endoderm develops a tube which will become the digestive system and the organs developed from it. Externally a tail bud and limb buds appear, embryonic organs that will eventually produce a tail and four limbs typical of an adult vertebrate.

The next period is usually called the fetal period, or period of *adult organ formation*. As this occurs, the organs first begin to develop their adult functions. For example, the limb buds develop bones, muscles and eventually separate digits. When these are integrated with the developing nervous system and are innvervated, the limb first becomes capable of movement.

Finally, there is the period of *postnatal development*. An infant mammal may emerge from the womb in varying degrees of organization. Young colts are able to stand on their feet almost immediately after birth and run after their mothers within a few hours. A human infant, on the other hand, is usually unable to walk until after it is a year of age. The period of postnatal development may be very short, as it is in small mammals like mice which become adults at the age of 60 days or so, or it can be very long as it is in human beings, who reach sexual maturity only after many years.

The organizational process of development has many evolutionary implications. In the first place, the study of gene action has shown that genetic variation can appear at any period in development, even going back as early as the formation of the germ cells (De Beer, 1958). Therefore, differential survival can take place at any time in development.

From the viewpoint of systems theory, the process of development results in the creation of new systems. The entities composing them take on new functions, illustrating the principle of creativity. Embryonic organs interact in ways in which genotypes cannot, and adult organs take on functions which are impossible for embryonic ones.

Since differential survival is based on function, the basis for such survival changes in each period of development. An embryo with a defective limb bud may survive perfectly well in the period of embryonic organ formation, but when this limb bud becomes a club foot, the locomotion and hence the survival of the animal is compromised.

Evolution and Embryology

The science of embryology developed rapidly during the years following Darwin's announcement of the theory of evolution. It resulted in the discovery of several phenomena that demanded explanation, and some of these are listed here.

Vestigial Organs

Certain organs, such as the human appendix, are much larger and more prominent in embryonic development. This particular organ has entirely lost its function in adult humans, although in certain other mammals such as rats it forms a pouch useful for bacterial digestion. Why has not the human appendix entirely disappeared, especially since it not only has no function in adult humans but is often a handicap? There should be strong selection against people having appendices, yet appendices appear generation after generation.

The explanation is that the appendix may have a necessary function as an embryonic organ, and without it the digestive system could not develop properly. Most vestigial organs probably have such essential organizational functions in early development.

Reorganization of Embryos Whose Organization Has Become Accidently Disturbed

In general, the earlier the period in which such disorganization takes place, the greater the power of the embryo to reorganize and form a perfect individual. An example is the process of twinning. If the first two daughter cells of a fertilized egg are separated, each can develop into a complete individual, but if an embryo is divided in the period of embryonic organ formation, the only result is death. Similar results are obtained with relatively minor injuries in later development. For example, an injury to the brain in early postnatal development is usually followed by complete recovery, but the same degree of damage in an adult may be permanent.

Some degree of reorganization is retained even by adults in the process of wound healing. This capacity varies a great deal from species to species. A planaria worm can be cut into small pieces, each of which will regenerate (reorganize) into a perfectly formed worm. At the opposite extreme, a mammal has limited powers of tissue regeneration, and cannot replace even an organ. The tissues that repair most easily are those that are constantly growing, such as the epithelial cells of the skin, and the lining of the intestinal tract. It is precisely these and other-constantly growing tissues that are most susceptible to cancer, or uncontrolled growth.

Evolutionary Change and Developmental Change

Both evolution and development are processes of organization, and both proceed in the direction of increasing complexity. This resemblance did not escape the attention of the 19th century biologists, and some of them, especially Haeckel, became fascinated with the possibility that the development of an individual might duplicate the evolution of its species and so supply all the missing evidence for evolution. Haeckel therefore enunciated the so-called "biogenetic law", that "ontogeny recapitulates phylogeny". One can still find pictures in old textbooks purporting to show that the human embryo goes through a fish stage, although the pictures themselves show that the human embryo is like no fish on the face of the earth.

Unfortunately for the theory, as more modern embryologists studied embryos in detail, they found differences among embryos as great as those in adults, that evolutionary changes could occur in any developmental process, early or late, and that the forms of early embryos might be more different than those of the corresponding adults. For example, the early guinea pig embryo shows a phenomenon of inversion of the germ layers, in which the endodermal layer is temporarily on the outside of the ectoderm, nothing like the embryos of most other mammals.

The importance of embryology is that this is where the organizational processes of genes take place, and if we are ever to understand the interactions within genotypic systems, this is where it must be studied.

From the viewpoint of evolutionary change processes, early development is only casually concerned with mutation (unless a mutation occurs very early, it is unlikely to affect the germ line), and inbreeding and sexual reproduction take place only among adults. But it is the time when Differential Survival produces its greatest effect. Among humans, at least 20% of pregnancies never come to term, and there are probably many more miscarriages and spontaneous abortions that are either unreported or pass unobserved. Among laboratory animals, where exact counts of fertilized eggs can be made, the early death rates are much higher, rising to about 40%. Similarly in postnatal development the highest mortality rates occur at birth or shortly after.

In general, one can say that the earlier a disruption of a developmental process occurs, the more drastic is its effect. At the same time, the power of reorganization in response to disruption is also greater earlier in development. But not all developmental processes are strongly related to survival, so that evolutionary change can occur at any period of development.

Short-term Adaptive Responses

An embryo or fetus can respond to a threatening environmental change only to the extent that its adult physiological response capacities are developed. For example, there is nothing that a chicken embryo can do if the temperature of the egg is lowered. Adaptive responses for the furthering of reproduction must come from adults, and such responses have evolved in various forms, from the production of enormous numbers of eggs with accompanying high death rates to the ultimate degree of physiological protection seen in mammals and other viviparous forms that develop internally and are protected by the mother's adult physiological function.

Thus the adaptive responses of embryos must largely be long-term and evolutionary. It follows that development is a good place to study evolutionary change and, to this extent, it has special significance.

However, the evolutionary study of prenatal development has largely gone out of fashion. At the present time the field is most active in connection with postnatal behavioral development, where initial responses can be indications of genetic variation. Also, postnatal behavioral adaptation is related to the evolution of parental care.

Transformation of Short-Term Adaptation into Long-Term Adaptation

Waddington (1975) is one of the few modern embryologists who have attempted to reconcile developmental theory with the modern genetic theory of evolution. He proposed a theory of *canalization*, by which he meant that as development proceeded it became increasingly probable that the process would follow a particular direction. He further proposed that these limits were set by the gene combinations peculiar to the species, and that these in turn were brought about by selection for combinations that were buffered against change. While this is consistent with the general tendency of systems to become stable, it is more a description in new terms than an explanatory hypothesis that can be tested.

Following Baldwin (1896) who had proposed that a behavioral adaptation, such as the employment of cactus spines by Darwin's finches to lever grubs out of their holes, could be transformed into a long term adaptation by selection for those birds who learned the trick most rapidly, Waddington suggested that this could be a more general phenomenon involving both physiological and behavioral short-term adaptations. Otherwise, it is difficult to explain how complex adaptations of a unitary sort could arise.

Superficially, this sounds like Lamarckian evolution, or the inheritance of acquired characters through use. But Lamarck had proposed evolution through use alone, and this modern theory added two of the basic processes of genetic theory: variation through mutation and selection.

Neotony

This is a condition in which the adults of one species resemble the immature forms of a closely related one. The classical example is the axolotl, a salamander that lives in lakes in the arid regions of Mexico and the Western United States (Raff & Kaufman, 1983). A similar form is the tiger salamander, *Ambystoma tigrinum*, that lives in moist woodland regions. It return to water to breed, and the aquatic larvae breathe by external gills. Later, the larvae lose their gills, develop lungs, and emerge from the water to live on land. An adult axolotl has gills, lives in water throughout life, and resembles an adult tiger salamander with gills. It is easy to see how this adaptive change might have taken place in dry western regions, where life on land would be impossible for a salamander. The hypothesis has been tested through hybridization, from which it appears that the homozygous condition of a single recessive gene prevents metamorphosis in the axolotl (Tompkins, 1978).

The importance of this evolutionary developmental process is that it can produce a major change with a minimal disturbance of the function of the organismic system. In a well-organized system, any change is likely to be disruptive, and neotony avoids this.

It is not, however, a universal explanation. For example, adult humans share several characteristics that are similar to those of immature or fetal great apes. Among these are the reduction of body hair and the curvature of the spinal cord in relation to the brain. However, the major human evolutionary changes, upright stature and the adult voice box, are *not* neotonous (Lieberman, 1984). Differential neotony of various organs assumes that the developmental processes involved are independent of each other.

The alternative hypothesis assumes that these unselected "neotonies" are the accidental by-products of overall change processes, such as the enlargement of the brain and upright posture in humans. Thus the reduction of body hair might well be neotonous, but the shape of the spinal cord is not.

Ginsburg (1978) has suggested that neotony has played a part in the domestication of dogs, which mature sexually in the first year instead of in the second as does the ancestral wolf. He says that the social behavior of adult dogs resembles that of yearling wolves.

Again, this process will not explain everything. We should remember that cases of apparent neotony are based on description and comparison, and that the evolutionary changes that produced them may not be so simple and obvious as in the axolotl. Such cases are potentially subject to experimental testing by artificially delaying or advancing the time of sexual maturity.

The evidence from organic evolution repeatedly emphasizes the importance of pre-existing systems as a guiding and limiting factor of evolutionary change. A system can be reorganized only in ways that do not seriously interfere with its essential functions. Reorganization of an organismic system must be achieved by change in the organizing processes of development.

The least drastic sorts of change are those in which developmental processes are either prolonged or shortened, either as a whole for the entire organism, or limited to one or a few processes. Prolonged development is called *paramorphosis* by embryologists and evolutionists, and shortening it is named *paedomorphosis*, or maintaining the form of a child or young organism. Variation in the speed of developmental processes is called *heterochrony*.

Wake and Larson (1987) reviewed the evidence for the existence of the above two developmental evolutionary phenomena among species of lungless salamanders of the family Plethodontidae, which are common species in many North American woods. They found numerous examples in the premaxillary bones of the skull, in the wrist and ankle bones and in various sorts of tongue structures useful for catching prey. The evolutionary changes in the organs are at least partially correlated, indicating general changes in developmental processes rather than special ones. The authors concluded that the changes were consistent with Piaget's (1970) theory of "structuralism", essentially that developmental processes are organized in accordance with the principles of "wholeness", "transformation", and "self-regulation", all of which are consistent with systems theory.

Developmental processes are also important in the evolution of behavior. Cairns (1988) found that in his selection experiments with fighting mice that the form of the patterns of behavior underwent little if any change, but that the speed of development was easily modified. He concluded that genetic variation in the *speed* of developmental processes, or heterochrony, could exist in a population without seriously disturbing the functioning of the system, although large changes could result later in the social interaction of the organisms involved.

These studies lead to two conclusions: (1) that the study of development is a major way of studying and understanding gene action, and (2) that change in the speed of development is an important explanatory theory for the evolution of both form and behavior, involving as it does a solution to the evolutionary problem of overcoming systems stability.

All biological evolution must involve development. Such change is produced through the organizing activities of gene combinations, and development is where these organizing activities take place. Development is one of the fundamental ways of studying gene action, and the evolutionists of the future should combine developmental study with their study of adult characters. All such differences, whether anatomical, physiological, or behavioral, must be developed.

SUMMARY

The descriptions of external and internal structure made by the comparative anatomists and paleontologists of the 19th Century provided the necessary supporting evidence to validate Darwin's theory of evolution. The same scientists produced a subset of evolutionary theories that still influence modern evolutionary thought. These theories: adaptive radiation, orthogenesis, specialization, and preadaptation, are consistent with the general concepts of systems organization and, in fact, are more easily understandable in the light of these latter concepts.

The concepts of the genetic theories of evolution, on the other hand, contradict the assumptions underlying the older methods of description and classification of species. Thus the genetical concept of a population of interbreeding but variable individuals has produced in the science of taxonomy a revolution that was chiefly engineered by Mayr. This revolution is not yet complete in the science of paleontology because of the difficulty in many cases of gathering adequate population samples. But there is no reason to assume that the evolutionary processes that go in living forms are different from those that went on in their now extinct ancestors.

The genetic-systems theories of evolution have affected every sub-science of biology, including that of embryology. Once thought (erroneously) to provide especially valid evidence of evolutionary history, embryology has turned toward the analysis of organizational processes carried on and modified by genes and gene combinations. Changes in organization such as those observed in evolution must be accompanied by changes in developmental organizational processes. In addition embryology has thrown some light on the problem of how a stable and complex organismic system can be changed without disrupting its function. Two important hypotheses have been suggested. One is the conversion of short-term adaptation into long-term or evolutionary adaptation (the Baldwin effect), and the other is neotony.

The Baldwin effect is primarily a behavioral one, and the next chapter will be concerned with the evolution of behavior, which chiefly involves changes in short-term adaptive responses, and how this in turn modifies the operation of the four basic processes of biological evolution.

Chapter VII

On the Evolution of Behavior

As shown in the previous chapter, behavior is one of four major processes through which both immediate and long-term adaptive changes are expressed. Although closely related to physiological processes, it is much more responsive to changes in the external environment.

Through behavior an organism is able to regulate and control its position in space. It thus represents an escape from anatomical and structural organization and makes possible a new form of organization on a higher level, that between organisms, or social organization.

Behavior itself may be defined as the activity of an entire organism. In its simplest form, behavior is movement. As such, it is adaptive in that it allows an animal to move out of an environment that is unfavorable to survival and into a more favorable one. Such behavior is probably the most primitive and basic of any. It is essentially what Schneirla (1959) called Approach-Withdrawal behavior, and it may easily evolve into shelter-seeking behavior. But most behavior is organized in a more elaborate fashion than simple movement.

THE ORGANIZATION OF BEHAVIOR

The Behavior Pattern

Each species of animal has characteristic ways of behaving, or organized movements, that are called behavior patterns. Each pattern is associated with a particular set of conditions to which it is adaptive. For example, a dog drinks water or takes liquid food by

lapping with its tongue, while a chicken will take a beak full of
water and then lift its head, allowing the water to run down its
throat. If one wishes to understand the behavior of a species, the
first task is to describe the form and function of its behavior patterns, or ethogram.

The next step is to take this list and look for further organization. I began (Scott, 1956) by classifying patterns of behavior
according to their functions in representative animal species and
eventually came up with the modified list seen in Table 7.1.

Table 7.1
BEHAVIOR PATTERNS CLASSIFIED ACCORDING TO FUNCTION

Category	Function	Examples
Shelter-Seeking	Moving into an environment more favorable for survival	Paramecium, aggregating as a slide dries
Investigatory	Making sensory contact with new environments or new features within an environment	Mouse nosing walls of pen; deer gazing at other animals
Ingestive	Intake of nutrient materials such as food, water	Dog lapping water
Defensive	Protection against injury usually against non-specifics, but also against injury by conspecifics	Stinging by jellyfish; defensive biting by mice
Sexual	Interaction potentially resulting in fertilization of eggs	Courtship and copulation
Shelter-Building	Protection against unfavorable conditions, physical or biotic	Nest of wasps; burrows of prairie dogs, beaver dams, etc.
Epimeletic	Giving of care or attention, usually but not exclusively to offspring	Grooming of mouse pups by mother; feeding of bee brood by workers
Et-epimeletic	Calling or signaling for care and attention	Baaing of young lambs; whining of puppies
Agonistic	Patterns adaptive in situations of conflict between species mates	Attack, running away, defensive posture (of mice)
Allelomimetic	Behavior of doing what other animals do, usually with some degree of mutual imitation. Function is cooperative; may provide safety or facilitate attack	Flocking in birds; schooling in fishes; flocking in mammals; group hunting by wolves
Eliminative	Disposal of urine and feces; sometimes takes on a signaling function in mammals	Leg lifting reaction of dog

The most primitive function of behavior is that of shelter seeking, seen in any animal that can move, as it leaves an unfavorable environment and moves until it finds a favorable one. Associated with this function is that of investigation, whereby the animal samples one environment after another, finally coming to rest in a favorable one. Then there is the function of taking in solid and liquid food, ingestive behavior. Still another function is that of defense against injury by another organism, seen in its simplest form as a pattern of flight behavior, but also including complicated patterns of defense and even threats and reciprocal attacks. Among sexually reproducing species, patterns of behavior may occur that facilitate contact between the sexes and subsequently fertilization. All of these five behavioral functions can be observed in one-celled organisms such as paramecium, and one can assume that they are the most primitive.

Then there is a set of behaviors with more specialized functions, derived in some cases from the more primitive ones. Agonistic behavior, defined as behavior that is adaptive in situations of conflict involving members of the same species, is obviously related to defensive behavior. Epimeletic (care-giving) and et-epimeletic (care-soliciting) behavior are extensions of the reproductive function seen in sexual behavior. Allelomimetic behavior, defined as behavior in which two or more animals simultaneously show the same behavior patterns with some degree of mutual imitation, is unique, but may have been derived from mutual shelter seeking. It is often associated with defensive flight. Finally, there is eliminative behavior, the disposal of urine and feces, which is important only in terrestrial and aerial animals.

Behavioral Systems

One can conceptualize these behavioral categories as systems (analogous to physiological systems), each of which has a special function, and the entities of each system as being behavioral patterns. If so, one must recognize that behavioral systems have features of organization distinctly different from physiological systems. Each behavior pattern has a different function, just as does each organ, but the behavior patterns in most cases cannot function simultaneously as organs do; at any one time the entire behavior of an individual may be devoted to one pattern. Also, unlike an organ, the function of a behavior pattern is usually not continuous; it will disappear and reappear. This is related to the fact that behavioral functions are usually not maintenance functions but adaptive ones, adaptive in response to changes in the external environment as well as to internal changes. Consequently, while behavior may contribute to internal homeostasis in some cases, the maintenance of internal stability is not an overriding function. The stabilizing function of a behavioral system is to maintain relationships with the external environment that are optimal for survival, a function that frequently disturbs internal homeostasis.

Relationships between Behavior Patterns

Behavior patterns in a system affect each other in the following ways. The first is to serve as alternative courses of action. Thus, a mouse attacked by another mouse can either fight back, run away, assume a defensive posture, or freeze.

Second, behavior patters may be related to each other sequentially, each contributing to an overall function, as in the sexual behavior of a mammal, where courtship patterns are followed by patterns of copulation.

Third, in certain cases, behavior patterns may be exprcssed simultaneously, combining two different functions, as when allelomimetic behavior is combined with predatory attack in packs of wolves or African hunting dogs.

Unlike the situation in a physiological system, there is no direct interaction between behavior patterns. There cannot be, because behavior patterns do not exist continuously but are the expression of capacities inside the organism.

Relationships between Behavioral Systems and Physiological Systems

In every case, a behavioral system of a mammal is coordinated by the neuroendocrine system and expressed through the skeletomuscular system. In addition, certain behavioral systems are directly related to and facilitate physiological systems, as shown in Table 7.2.

Only half of the behavioral systems can be considered accessory to and outgrowths of physiological function. We must conclude that behavioral systems represent a higher order of organization that is primarily related to the function of the organism as a whole and therefore has unique qualities and functions.

At the same time, behavioral systems cannot be organized separately from physiological systems, and this is particularly true of the neuroendocrine and skeleto-muscular systems. A behavioral system, however, can be observed separately from its underlying physiological organization, and one of the principal areas of contemporary research, the neurosciences, is devoted to discovering the relationships between behavioral and physiological systems. Perhaps a better concept than that of the behavioral system *per se* is that of a physio-behavioral system.

Table 7.1 suggests that the evolution of behavior can be studied descriptively and comparatively on two levels: 1) the evolution of behavior patterns and 2) the evolution of function in higher order systems. A physio-behavioral system can function either on the level of the organism, or as part of social organization. Here I shall concentrate on the behavior of individual organisms, leaving a consideration of the evolution of function in physio-behavioral system for later chapters.

Table 7.2
RELATIONSHIPS BETWEEN BEHAVIORAL AND
PHYSIOLOGICAL SYSTEMS

Behavioral System	Physiological System
Shelter-Seeking	
Investigatory	
Defensive	
Ingestive, eating	Digestive
Ingestive, breathing	Respiratory
Sexual	Reproductive
Epimeletic (care-giving)	Reproductive, in part
Et-epimeletic (care-soliciting)	
Agonistic	
Allelomimetic	
Eliminative	Excretory, Digestive

MODES OF EVOLUTIONARY CHANGE IN
PHYSIO-BEHAVIORAL SYSTEMS

Evolutionary change in such systems has certain limitations. The first is that genetic changes cannot affect behavior directly, but must do so through changes in physiological processes: *There can be no evolutionary change in behavior without a change in physiology.*

Second, behavioral adaptation depends on variable responses to the environment. A behavioral phenotype is therefore much more variable than a physiological one. Differential survival depends on the behavioral variations of each individual as well as genetic variation among them, and the first may mask the second.

Third, since Differential Survival depends on function, the basic unit of behavioral selection must be the behavior pattern, which is the smallest segment of behavior that has a definite adaptive function.

Directions of Behavioral Evolution

Capacities for emitting favorable behavior have evolved in at least two ways which lead to quite different expressions in behavior patterns. The first of these evolutionary trends is that of evolving a special fixed pattern of behavior that is adaptive in a particular situation, and adding a new pattern for each differing situation. Such a trend is seen in certain protozoa, where a given species may have no more than five or six such fixed behavior patterns in its entire repertoire. Such evolution may take place even in higher animals. As I pointed out, in the agonistic system of behavior of mice, the behavior patterns consist of a biting attack, defensive posture, running away, and freezing behavior, each of which may be tried out in turn. It is obvious, however, that such organization requires an infinitely large number of behavior patterns if the animal is to adapt efficiently to a complex environment.

A second direction in behavioral evolution is that of evolving a small number of simple but readily modifiable patterns of behavior that can be easily related to a great variety of environmental situations. It is obvious that such an organization of behavior is much more adaptive to the complex situations met under natural conditions than is that of alternate behavior patterns; indeed, one wonders why the latter process survives at all. One possibility is that the latter may be more efficient in that the animal does not have to reorganize its behavior in each new situation. A modifiable pattern, however, combined with memory and other capacities of learning, can achieve that same efficiency as a fixed pattern. In fact, the process of learning produces fixed patterns.

As an example of variable patterns, we can point to the hunting behavior of a dog, which consists of a few simple patterns of behavior that can be combined and recombined in various ways. In one experiment (Scott & Fuller, 1965) we tested behavior on an artificial scent trail, assuming that the dogs would use the pattern of following the trail with nose to the ground. Beagles, however, usually solved the problem in a different way by running around over the nearby area until they caught the air scent of the goal object, then dropped their noses to the ground and investigated the whole area carefully with both eyes and nose. Following a natural trail in the field, a beagle may use a different combination, running along the trail and moving from side to side so that it is continually testing the direction of the scent trail by sampling different concentrations of the scent.

Another example is the hand-to-mouth pattern seen in human infants. The baby first simply puts its hand or digits next its mouth, then into it. Soon it begins to grasp objects and put them in its mouth and, by so doing, learns to discriminate between those objects which taste good and those which do not. Still later, the baby is taught to use a spoon and other eating tools, resulting in the elaboration of different patterns of eating behavior that we see in various cultures and individuals. The basic hand-to-mouth pattern is always there, but modified in dozens or even hundreds of ways.

But the most important example is the acquisition and elaboration of language. Beginning with no more than a behavior pattern of making babbling noises, and the capacity to make a great variety of such noise and sound combinations, a baby can acquire any language on earth, or more than one, and so learn thousands of the behavior patterns we call words, all elaborated from a few very simple but highly modifiable capacities.

It is obvious that a fixed and invariable pattern of behavior is adaptive only in a situation which does not change, which an animal encounters repeatedly in its own lifetime and which is similarly encountered by its descendents over many generations. Such, for example, are the three patterns of behavior (gnawing, splitting, and rotating) that a squirrel shows in opening a nut, which Eibl-Eibesfeldt (1956) has shown tend to be highly consistent and to be rapidly integrated into a functional unit through learning processes. This, in turn, is part of the symbiotic ecological relationship between squirrels and nut trees, whereby the squirrels bury the nuts at varying distances away and subsequently dig them up to eat them. The squirrel never finds all of the nuts that it buried, and consequently new trees are continually being planted. This aspect of the environment has presumably remained relatively constant over thousands of squirrel generations.

On the other hand, the squirrel patterns of climbing, running, and leaping are enormously variable. No two trees are alike, and as a squirrel passes through them it modifies these patterns from second to second. It is only when a squirrel has occasion to traverse the same branch day after day that its behavior becomes standardized and relatively invariant.

What we actually find in complexly organized animals is usually a combination of both evolutionary trends – a certain number of fixed behavior patterns, usually quite limited, plus a few modifiable kinds of patterns, When the fixed behavior patterns are examined, it turns out that a large number of these are patterns of social behavior and particularly patterns of social communication. This presumably arises from the fact that the social environment remains relatively constant and fixed over generations; indeed, for many animals this may be the only aspect of the environment that does not vary and fluctuate. Another factor arises from the special nature of the process of social communication. Signals are effective only if they can be understood, and they would be extremely confusing if they were constantly varying.

Again, the ability to communicate through fixed patterns determined by heredity is limited by the problem of numbers. The number of such signals used by nonhuman species is never more than a few dozen, even in the higher primates. It is interesting that human language has achieved the solution of the problem of clarity of symbols through a different route. Human language capacities are based on a very simple behavior pattern, that of producing variable noises on a voluntary basis, but these are almost infinitely modifiable, with the result that a language such as English may contain something like half a million words, each of these fixed, not by heredity, but by the processes of learning and habit formation. To be understandable, words must be pronounced similarly by different people.

It follows also that the evolutionary trend in a given species will vary considerably with its rapidity of development and the total length of life in which an individual has the opportunity to acquire modifications of variable behavior. Quickly developing and short lived animals should have a greater tendency to develop alternate stereotyped patterns than do slowly developing and long lived animals.

The Origin of Behavior

In order for behavior to evolve it must change in organization and produce new elements. It is almost impossible to imagine how a single gene change could result in anything as complex as a new pattern of behavior. While mutation will account for the variation that is the essential basis of evolution, it is always a combination of genes that produces a phenotypic effect; ultimately evolution rests on trying out new combinations. Some of the ways in which such new combinations could produce evolutionary changes in behavior are as follows:

In the first place, any living system tends to be stable and to resist change. It is therefore easier to modify a system by adding on a new element than by reorganizing the system as a whole. This device of addition rather than reorganization is well illustrated in the evolution of the vertebrate brain, where the older portions appear to be very similar in a wide variety of species, while newer portions, such as the neocortex of the mammalian cerebrum, vary widely.

In the case of the human language ability, this also appears to have been added to the non-verbal function of the brain rather than replacing it. We would expect a similar principle to operate with respect to the origin of new behavior patterns, but this still does not solve the question of how new patterns can originate.

Another limitation on system change is the fact that the nature of the system itself may determine the possible directions of change, as exemplified in organic evolution by orthogenesis. To use such a morphological illustration, it is difficult to imagine how the hooves of ungulates could ever evolve in the direction of hands and manipulative ability. In this group of animals, evolution has proceeded in the only possible direction, namely, toward larger, longer legged, and swifter running animals.

It is also possible that systems can evolve that are virtually unchangeable, i.e., that cannot be changed without destroying their functions. This is, of course, a restatement in systems terms of the old principle of overspecialization as stated by the comparative anatomists of the 19th century.

One possible way in which a rigidly organized system can change is to modify its functions without modifying its essential organization. There are may cases in social birds of behavior patterns that have altered their function or added a function with little change in form. For example, a movement useful in feeding may be given the added function of a courtship signal simply by making it out of context. This phenomenon has received the name of *ritualization* (Huxley, 1923).

Another way in which new behavior can originate arises from the basic capacities of variability and modifiability of behavior. As evolved in highly complex animals such as dogs, part of the general behavioral organization is a tendency to vary behavior when it is repeated. No matter how constant the environmental factors are kept, the young dog changes his behavior each time he is exposed to the situation, and it is only with many repetitions that his behavior becomes more or less standardized. This capacity for producing variation, which is the foundation of trial-and-error behavior, thus opposes the capacity to form a habit of that behavior which produces the most efficient and least effortful adaptation to the situation.

Once an animal has evolved these capacities of variability and modifiability, which appear to be common to most vertebrates, the problem of originating new forms of behavior largely disappears. These capacities intrinsically involve the ability to produce new forms of behavior. However, such new behavior in a non-social animal would have to be developed anew by each individual.

Baldwin (1896) suggested that if such a newly learned pattern of behavior has an important adaptive effect, there should be strong selection in favor of individuals that develop this behavior readily and easily, in effect, a return to the stereotyped behavior pattern with a specialized function. Such a "Baldwin effect" would account for the complex behavior of certain Galapagos finches (Lack, 1947) that use thorns or twigs to pry insect larvae out of their holes.

Still another way in which behavior could originate is through the principle of surplus capacities. Once an individual has evolved complex motor and sensory capacities, these can be used in ways that were not necessarily expressed under the conditions in which the behavior originally evolved. For example, the horse, having evolved the capacity to burst through restraining brush or grass, also has the capacity to pull loads. Similarly, under natural conditions the bluetit, a common bird in England, evolved the capacity to open snail shells. With the advent of paper-capped milk bottles, these birds readily adapted these capacities to opening such bottles left on a householder's doorstep (Hinde, 1969). These cases are a form of what the organic evolutionists called preadaptation (Chapter 6).

Finally, there should be in evolution a tendency to modify existing systems in ways involving the least amount of reorganization. For example, in the evolution of sexual behavior in mammals, the behavior of the two sexes has not been evolved separately, which would involve a different complex organization for each. Rather, each sex has the capacity for exhibiting the behavior of the opposite sex, but development is normally guided in only one direction, primarily by differences in hormones which channelize development in one direction or the other. Consequently, each sex has a certain amount of surplus capacities which make possible some overlap in behavior.

In the same behavioral system it would appear that the capacity for orgasm has evolved primarily around the function of ejaculation in the male. Because this orgasmic capacity is not limited to one sex, certain primate females including the human also can achieve orgasm under proper conditions of stimulation, although it is nonessential with respect to the process of fertilization. From one perspective, the female orgasm has been developed as a surplus capacity, but it also has obvious adaptive functions in a social setting.

The general tendency of systems to remain stable makes it possible to compare systems in widely separate groups and to draw conclusions regarding common ancestry. To use a morphological example, the tetrapod limb never has more than five digits. Even in those species in which the digits are reduced there are still traces of the original number, and their changes can be traced backward through time, but no species has ever evolved a greater number than five, although extra digits can arise by mutation. Similarly, it is possible to look at the organization of behavior in living species and come to conclusions regarding evolutionary relationships as Lorenz (1941) and others have done (Brown, 1975).

THE EFFECTS OF EXPERIENCE

Effects of Behavior on Physiological Organization

Any activity of the whole organism, however brief, must have an effect on physiological function. If the behavior is continued over a long period of time, it may result in the modification of physio-anatomical organization. In a vertebrate embryo, behavior begins early in development and is involved in the process of functional differentiation. This results in changes in the muscular and circulatory systems and also in the organization of the bones. As D'Arcy Thompson (1942) discovered, bony tissues are deposited along stress lines.

Because experience and behavioral activity vary from individual to individual, the result is increased inter-individual variation. That is, because of experience, some individuals will be physiologically better adapted for survival than others, differences that are not genetic in origin.

Effects of Experience on Behavioral Organization

The essence of behavioral adaptation is variation, differential responsiveness to varying external and internal conditions. Thus a sea anemone contracts its tentacles when touched by an organism that may be a source of food, but otherwise leaves them outstretched. Or if touched by a large object that may be a predator, the sea anemone withdraws all its tentacles and contracts into a ball.

More than this, if an organism is repeatedly subjected to the same situation to which a variety of behavioral responses may be given, it may begin to give only the response that has produced the most successful adaptation. This is the simplest form of learning, and it has been demonstrated in free-living flatworms as well as in organisms organized on higher levels (Corning & Ratner, 1967). That is, the capacity to organize behavior on the basis of experience is widespread in the animal kingdom. Whether or not it has a common origin, we shall never be able to say.

Without going into the specifics of and ramifications of learning processes, we can assess their effects on evolutionary change processes. With respect to Differential Survival, it increases variation among individuals that have varying experiences, and decreases variation within individuals, thus making Differential Survival a matter of experience as well as the result of genetic differences in adaptive capacity.

For example, we studied the development of learning in puppies repeatedly exposed to standard test situations. At the outset, there was a great deal of variability in response. As the puppies grew older, this behavior became less variable and more predictable. Furthermore, there was at first a great deal of overlap between breeds, and it was only after their behavior became more predictable that genetically determined differences began to appear (Scott, 1957).

If survival depends on differential responses of this sort, it is clear that differential survival depends on the interaction between learning processes and genetically determined differences and that this interaction cannot take place in development prior to the activation of the learning process.

As an example of a higher order interaction between functional behavioral organization and other genetically determined capacities, we set up a situation designed to test differential abilities for climbing and leaping. It was a set of boxes that could be stacked on top of each other, and a dog could either leap to the top or climb up a ramp that became steeper as the pile of boxes grew higher. On the top was a reward of food.

We had anticipated that basenjis, whom we had observed climbing over high fences, would do well on this test, while cocker spaniels, which are poor fence climbers, would do poorly. Actually, the basenjis were timid when confronted with the apparatus and approached it slowly and cautiously. The cocker spaniels, on the other hand, were not timid, appeared highly motivated by food and would rush up the ramp, and their momentum enabled them to scramble rapidly to its top. It was not until the task became extremely difficult that the basenjis made better scores.

That is, a complex organism like a dog can organize its basic physio-behavioral capacities in a variety of ways, so that the same adaptive end result is achieved (Scott & Fuller, 1965).

INTERACTION OF BEHAVIOR WITH EVOLUTIONARY CHANGE PROCESSES

All adaptive processes modify differential survival as well as being affected by it. In addition, behavior has an effect on two of the other evolutionary change processes, sexual reproduction and inbreeding. These processes are obviously modified by sexual behavior and the choice of mates. Finally, there is the possibility, at least in humans, of behaviorally modifying the mutation process by the use of mutagenic agents.

Sexual Behavior and Sexual Reproduction

Sexual reproduction can occur without sexual behavior, as it does in the dioecious plants. For example, in pine trees the pollen grains containing the male cells are windborn to the developing pine cones containing the female cells. But even plants are involved with behavior. The whole group of flowering plants, or angiosperms, has evolved in conjunction with insects that carry pollen from one flower to another, usually in the process of gathering food from the plants. The sexual behavior of the insects themselves is not involved, but from the viewpoint of the plant species such behavior has a sexual function. The whole evolutionary process must have involved mutual selection; on the one hand for plants that attracted and fed insects, and on the other, for insects that could utilize the plant food.

Many marine animals reproduce sexually by simple discharging sperms and eggs into the surrounding sea water. Such a process is extraordinarily wasteful, both of eggs that fail to be fertilized, and of the fertilized eggs themselves. Various devices to increase efficiency have evolved, such as seasonally coordinated reproduction. Then there is an almost universal tendency to evolve two types of germ cells, a larger, immobile egg containing a store of nutrients, and a smaller, motile sperm containing only a small store of energy.

When sexual behavior appears, its primary function is to facilitate fertilization and so reduce waste. This can be accomplished in ways as simple as aggregation, in which two or more individuals approach each other and release their germ cells into the surrounding water, or as complex as the courtship and copulation behaviors of Arthropods and Vertebrates.

The primary function of sexual behavior, therefore, is to facilitate sexual reproduction. Once a species has evolved sexual behavior, sexual reproduction becomes impossible without it.

Sexual Behavior and Inbreeding

As I pointed out earlier, inbreeding, defined as mating within a population, is a phenomenon which takes place on many levels. Ordinarily, the members of a species mate only with each other and not with members of other species; in fact, this is the best objective definition of a species. Cross-breeding between species is avoided in a variety of ways, but a major one is the evolution of sexual behavior patterns that are unique to each species. Put in other terms, behavior is a major isolating device.

Then there is inbreeding within subpopulations of a species. These may be very large, as in subspecies, or quite small, as in local demes. The major point is that sexual behavior can evolve in the direction of non-random mating. When it does, the result could be either outbreeding or inbreeding but in any case some form of at least temporary social organization. Since this is a higher level of organization, it will be considered in a later chapter.

The evolutionary consequences of non-random breeding thus take two directions. The effect of outbreeding is to maximize genetic variation in a population and in so doing to protect deleterious genes against selection. It should also have the effect of inhibiting the differential survival of gene combinations, as these would seldom be repeated. Outbreeding should therefore have the effect of slowing evolutionary change processes. Behavior that produces inbreeding, on the other hand, should facilitate this change process. The actual situation in any species depends on its social organization and the resulting mating system, if any.

Effects of Learning on Variation and Differential Survival

The effect of behavior itself is to increase variation both within and among individual phenotypes, which means that Differential Survival (Scott, 1981) is less dependent upon genetic variations and hence has less effect on behavior itself. Learned behavior, on the other hand, has the effect of decreasing variation within individuals and increasing it among them, again reducing the genetic consequences of Differential Survival. If anything is selected under these circumstances, it is the general capacity for learning, with much weaker selection of specific capacities.

Longevity

In an animal species in which the capacity to organize behavior through learning is important, it is obvious that an animal that has learned adaptive behavior survives more often than one which has not. Therefore, there should always be a selective advantage of older over younger individuals, and the mortality statistics of mammals and birds indeed show the highest death rates in very young animals. Such differential mortality has little to do with genetic differences, since an older experienced animal always has an advantage over a younger inexperienced one, no matter how great the potential capacities of the latter. An indirect consequence of this process should be selection for longevity, and one would predict a correlation between longevity and learning capacity among different species.

Behavior and Differential Survival

As indicated above, the effect of behavior is to slow down the process of Differential Survival in two ways. One is general; like all

adaptive processes, behavior promotes survival. The other is specifically related to the evolution of behavior. Behavior increases
non-genetic variation in a population. Our experiments with dogs
(Scott & Fuller, 1965) indicated that even with maximal genetic
variation and controlled environmental situations, the non-genetic
variation was at least 50% of the total. Therefore, any form of
selection of behavior, natural or artificial, is bound to proceed
more slowly than selection of characteristics having a greater
degree of genetically determined variance.

The problem of Differential Survival and social behavior is even
more complex, involving as it does, the behavior of two or more
individuals. This will be addressed in Chapter X.

CONCLUSIONS

The evolution of behavior is closely intertwined with organic evolution. Behavioral systems and physiological systems are never
completely independent. Behavior is organized in physio-
behavioral systems. Therefore, all of the phenomena associated
with organic evolution, such as adaptive radiation, orthogenesis
and specialization, should also be associated with behavioral evolution, and this appears to be the case.

On the other hand, behavioral evolution interacts with evolutionary change processes in ways that physiological evolution does
not. As with organic evolution, the general effect of behavioral evolution is to negate and buffer the organism against the effects of
Differential Survival, but to do this in new ways that greatly
extend this protective or buffering function. Primarily and primi-
tively, behavior releases the organism from factors dependent upon
location - in many cases, all an organism has to do in order to
survive is to move. In addition, behavior protects an organism in
a variety of other ways, including the facilitation of physiological
function. The learned organization of behavior greatly increases
non-genetic interorganismic variation, again protecting it from
Differential Survival.

Behavior affects other major evolutionary change processes in
ways that organic evolution does not. In particular, behavior may
alter the random nature of sexual reproduction and direct it
toward either outbreeding or inbreeding.

With respect to genetic variation of behavior, any aspect of behavior should be potentially subject to such variation. Other than movement in general, the smallest functional unit of behavior is the behavior pattern. When we examined the evolution of such behavior patterns in dogs and wolves we found that while a behavior pattern might be exaggerated, modified, or partially suppressed, nothing new had been created by thousands of years of selection (Scott, 1950b). While single genes can affect the expression of a behavior pattern, as I found with my studies on the tendency of fruit flies to crawl toward a light (Scott, 1943), such genes merely modified the expression of the pattern, making it faster or slower.

As one might expect from the systems organization of genes and their interaction, there are no "genes for" any particular pattern of behavior, whether it be aggression or altruism. The single-gene replacement hypothesis is justified only in a negative fashion; i.e., a single deleterious gene may make a pattern of behavior impossible. Eyeless fruit flies do not crawl toward the light.

In general, the genetic-systems theory of evolution indicates that the evolution of behavior presents new problems and new phenomena, particularly feedback and interaction with evolutionary change processes. Therefore, one cannot merely extend concepts derived from other evolutionary phenomena and reach satisfactory conclusions. Behavior provides a new evolutionary arena.

The dimensions of this new behavioral arena of evolution can be summarized as follows. Behavior has no effect on mutation, but does have extensive effects on all the other three evolutionary processes. Through sexual behavior, it may alter the random nature of sexual reproduction. Animal species may choose mates differentiatlly and, if this is consistent, it may result in a mating system. While the random natures of meiosis and fertilization are unaffected, random mating between individuals is reduced.

A system of mating behavior may either augment or reduce the degree of inbreeding within a species. Either result will have genetic and evolutionary consequences.

The major effect of behavior, however, is on the process of differential survival or natural selection. Any animal that can move can escape from injurious biotic or physical factors and seek out situations that are more favorable to its continued existence. The adaptive behavior of individuals thus enormously increases the proportion of non-genetic variance in the total variance of a population. It follows that it is much more difficult to select for genetically-determined aspects of behavior than it is to select for similar variation in anatomical or physiological characteristics.

This conclusion applies to any form of selection, whether natural or artificial. It should also be easier to select for a relatively invariant pattern of behavior than for one that includes much variability. On the other hand, variation itself may be the principal adaptive feature of a behavior pattern. It should be possible to select for the capacity to emit variable behavior, and the fact that such variability is so prominent a feature of mammalian behavior indicates that this has taken place in the past.

As with any form of adaptation, adaptive behavior reduces the effects of the factors that bring about differential survival. While natural selection is a major change process in evolution, it must work against itself; i.e., to reduce the degree of differential survival and so minimize the process.

With behavior, an animal can not only escape from various factors that bring about selection, but its behavior can actually change the physical and biotic environments. Shelter building, of whatever nature, results in the modification of the physical environment. Biotically, the behavior of an animal may modify other species in various ways, not only with respect to its own evolution, but by bringing about evolutionary changes in other species, or co-evolution. This topic will be taken up in a later chapter in more detail.

Chapter VIII

On Current Theories of the Evolution of Social Behavior and Social Systems: Evolution in Terms of Genetic-Systems Theory

We now come to the crucial topic of this book: biological evolution and its relationship to social organization. Evolution is an historical subject and consequently poses all the problems and difficulties that face historians, with the additional one that there are no written records of biological history. The closest approximations are fossil remains, what the older naturalists called the record of the rocks. Even that is largely missing with respect to social behavior and organization, which have left very few traces in the sediments of geological strata.

Consequently, the value of an evolutionary theory is usually estimated through argument. A scientific argument can be an exciting and productive exercise provided it does not degenerate into passionate remarks that question the motives and good sense of the participants. There is a fine line between mental excitement that leads to new ideas and destructive passions involving pain and anger that inhibit rational thought.

In criticizing the work of other thinkers I have followed two general rules: 1) that no theory can be said to be useless. The example of Mendel's theorem which lay fallow for more than three decades before its value was appreciated is a classical example of the dangers of negativism. Positive criticism, whenever possible, leads to constructive thinking. 2) I myself may be in error in some respects, and so will respect contrary arguments. It is in the spirit of inspiring fruitful scientific dialog that the following comments are offered.

In addition, I suggest certain criteria that are especially useful in evaluating theories of biological evolution:

1. *Where did the theory come from?* Ideally, the best scientific theories should come out of observed phenomena, and this has certainly been true of the origin of the major theories of biological evolution. Darwin's theory came from several sources: the observed variation of plants and animals in nature, the changes in domestic plants and animals that agriculturists had produced, and Malthus' theory of population growth, presumably based on observation of humans. To this Wright added the concepts of inbreeding and random drift from his experience with inbred lines of guinea pigs and analysis of livestock pedigrees, and later derived his overall shifting balance theory. In this tradition I have added still another concept, the selection of mated pairs producing desirable gene combinations, again derived from animal breeding practice. In contrast, theories derived from other theories, or by metaphorical extensions from unrelated phenomena should be weaker, but still may be useful.

2. *How generally applicable is the theory?* Theories can be either limited in their application to certain classes of phenomena, or be more broadly generalizable. Here the danger is overgeneralization, a weakness that is inherent in human symbolic language. As I have suggested in previous pages, of the major theories of evolution that have been developed each has validity for some sorts of biological phenomena, but there is no completely general theory of evolution except possibly that living organisms must change in order to survive. From this reasoning, it follows that theories of evolution of social organization should be limited to that class of phenomena.

3. *Is the theory useful?* A theory may be useful in many ways. For research scientists, this question usually means, is it testable? Evolutionary theories rarely can be tested experimentally, but a theory can inspire research designed to discover whether the phenomena that the theory predicts are found in animal societies. Much of the recent field research in such groups has come from fruitful theories of this sort. Or a theory can pose an intellectual challenge that leads to the production of more elaborate theories. Such exercises are useful and valuable in that they provide pleasurable and esthetic creative intellectual enterprise, but unless they lead back to biological function in some more direct way, their usefulness is limited.

4. *Is it theoretically sound?* Any theory should be logically consistent within itself but in this book I have added two additional criteria derived from two basic theories, as follows: Since all biological evolutionary theory postulates changes that are biologically inherited, any such theory should be consistent with the modern genetic theory of evolution. And since all living organisms function as systems and parts of systems, biological evolution becomes the evolution of systems. Therefore, any workable theory of biological evolution must be consistent with both systems theory and the genetic theory of evolution.

The classical genetic theories of evolution (Fisher, 1930; Wright, 1932, 1977; Haldane, 1932; Dobzhansky, 1937) were developed by biologists who were primarily geneticists and who knew little about behavior. Only Dobzhansky eventually became interested in behavior, did research on it in fruit flies, and published some wise comments on the relationship of genetics to human behavior (1962). The others, if they considered it at all, assumed that behavioral evolution would proceed by the same processes that govern the evolution of morphological and physiological characters.

INFLUENTIAL THEORIES OF SOCIAL EVOLUTION

In the 1960's and later, a group of biologists who were primarily interested in social behavior began to theorize about its evolution. The first of these works was Wynne-Edwards' book, *Animal Dispersion in Relation to Social Behavior* (1962). An ambitious attempt to relate the ecological problems of population and dispersion to social behavior, it only incidentally dealt with behavioral evolution, but the author introduced two important ideas. One was the extension of Darwin's concept of sexual selection to include all cases of selection within a social group, irrespective of whether they were brought about by selection of one sex by the other. He called this *social selection*, a term that I had previously found useful to describe all cases of selection of individuals by a social system (Scott, 1958). He said, furthermore, that in addition to selection on the two levels of individual organisms and species, there must be a third level related to social groups, which he called *group selection*. To Wynne-Edwards this latter phenomenon was self-evident "as with other social phenomena, the evolution in locusts of this migratory or gregarious phase has been brought about by group selection – it could not have been otherwise..."

Not so to other evolutionary theorists, especially those wedded to the concept of simple Darwinian selection between individuals. To them, group selection was heresy, but their main argument was that it was probably unimportant (Lack, 1966), and they devoted a great deal of time to demonstrating that individual selection could account for almost everything. Maynard Smith (1964) soon added a new concept, that of kin selection, namely that an inherited behavioral characteristic favorable to the survival of descendents should result in selection of the descendents of the individual transmitting such a characteristic. This is, of course, a form of group selection but taking place within a larger group or deme (Hamilton, 1975; Wright, 1980).

As stated in this book, there is no logical reason why selective processes cannot act at every level of organization. Since the organization of living systems is inclusive, such processes should be going on simultaneously, so that an individual organism may be affected at all levels. If they act in opposite directions, the result should be some sort of balance or equilibrium (Scott, 1968).

As long ago as 1975, Brown recognized that selection can take place on at least four levels: individual organism, kinship group, deme and species. Biological evolution is the result of genetic change, and all four of these result in genetic change within a species. The net change of an entire species affects the ecosystem and so brings about change on that level. In many cases, a socially organized group may be the equivalent of either a kinship group or a deme, or a deme including several kinship groups. From the genetic viewpoint, selection can take place on any level on which genetic variation exists. This is true of all the levels listed above. In addition, genetic variation can occur with respect to any level of organizational development within the organism, beginning with the fertilized egg and ending with death itself.

The difficulty that some theorists have with the concept of selection at levels other than that of the individual organism is based on their assumption that the only possible evolutionary process is mass selection based on competition between individuals, often further simplified by the assumption that the genes on which individual differences depend are themselves individually selected. Genetic population research over the last half century has demonstrated that both these assumptions are wrong: that genes are parts of interacting systems, and that there are four major genetic evolutionary change processes which themselves interact. Further, in an organism in which sexual reproduction takes place and gene combinations are the basis of variation, such selection must involve both the individual and the other individuals with which it mates.

One hopes that the group selection controversy will be quietly and respectfully buried as having served its purpose of clarifying certain evolutionary issues. But I have the feeling that its uneasy ghost may rise again (Trivers, 1985), simply because few scientists have the patience to become experts in both animal behavior and genetics.

With respect to those four major criteria that I laid down at the outset of this chapter, Wynne-Edwards' theories obviously fulfill that of sound biological origins, being derived from observations of populations as they exist in nature. This has led to a great deal of observational and theoretical work on the relationship of behavior to ecological phenomena. Further, he did not overgeneralize, applying his theories only to the field from which they were derived, and his theories are testable insofar as evolutionary theories are testable, chiefly by argument as above. Finally, their theoretical bases do not conflict with the postulates of genetic-systems theory; the severest criticism is that Wynne-Edwards did not attempt to develop such deeper theoretical bases. Nevertheless, his ideas proved highly stimulating to the thinking of others. Dozens of papers appeared in the following years, of which I shall cover only those that have had major impact.

Hamilton's Genetical Theory of Social Behavior (1964)

Of all the papers that followed Wynne-Edwards' book, this one is most important, as it developed all of the basic concepts employed by other authors in the next two decades.

From the viewpoint of genetic-systems theory, the paper has one major flaw. It is based on a single gene model and its extension to all other genes. Thus it makes no use of the concept of genetic systems, although this had been strongly presented in the earlier work of Darlington (1939) and Huxley (1942). It therefore presents a limited mathematical model that conflicts not only with the concept of systems, but with the well-established genetic phenomenon of gene interaction: one gene never acts by itself.

The general problem addressed by Hamilton was "... the only parts of the theory of natural selection which have been supported by mathematical models admit no possibility of the evolution of any characters which are on the average disadvantageous to the individual's possessing them. If natural selection followed the classical models exclusively, species would not show any behavior more positively social than the coming together of the sexes and parental care" (p. 1). Hamilton thus assumed that most social behavior is disadvantageous to the individual and concentrated his attention on so-called "altruistic" behavior.

Hamilton pointed out that, from the viewpoint of natural selection, the survival of an individual has little importance. What is important is its survival to adulthood and taking part in the reproduction of the next generation; otherwise, the heredity of the individual could not be passed along. He called the capacity to produce similarly reproducing members of the next generation *inclusive fitness*, essentially the genetic contribution of an individual to the next generation. One can point out that this concept also involves the survival of the next generation after that, and so on indefinitely, making it a difficult quantity to measure or calculate. Hamilton got around this difficulty by developing a mathematical definition based on Wright's coefficient of genetic relationship which is .5 for children, .25 for grandchildren, and so on.

Similar thinking had been employed by Haldane (1955), who calculated that if one wished to preserve one's genes, one child is worth two nieces or nephews. Of course, one must always remember that the coefficient of genetic relationship is based on probability; one never can pass along more than one-half of one's genes to a single individual, and which half is purely a matter of chance. Consequently, although a parent must pass along one-half of his or her genes to each offspring and the true genetic correlation is exactly .5, no such restriction applies to collateral relatives. The *mean* correlation between siblings is .5, but the actual correlation for any particular gene pair is *either* 1.0 or 0.0, and the mean correlation between a particular pair of siblings for all gene pairs varies between these two extremes. Though highly improbable in close relatives, it is theoretically possible for either collateral relatives or grandparents and grandchildren to share none of the same variable genes, and the chances of this happening rapidly improve as the coefficient of genetic relationship declines.

A further complication ensues when we consider the effect of gene combinations. The probability that a single gene at a particular locus will be identical in siblings is .5, but the probability of receiving identical genotypes is less. If we assume that both parents are heterozygous for genes at the locus, (Aa x Aa), then the genes will segregate and recombine to form 3 genotypes in the ratio of 1/4, 1/2, and 1/4. The probability that any 2 siblings will receive the same genotype is the sum of each of the probabilities squared, or 3/8. This is less than .5.

If we now assume that the parents are heterozygous for other genes in a combination, the probability of identical genotypes becomes 9/64 for a 2-gene combination and 27/512 for a 3-gene combination. In decimals, the series becomes .375, .141, and .053.

This means that with respect to genotypes, or gene combinations, siblings are much less closely related than the simple gene index of relationship would indicate. The figures are somewhat different for parent-offspring correlations of combinations. The figure is .5 for a single factor, the same as the genic correlation, but for a 2-factor combination the figure is .25, and so on.

Dominance changes the picture somewhat. If we assume dominance in the above example, the ratios produced for each gene pair independently are 3/4 and 1/4. The probability of identical *pheno types* in siblings then becomes 9/16 + 1/16; or 5/8, a figure greater than .5. Extended to other gene pairs in a combination, the series becomes .625, .391, .244 and so on.

The above result is a consequence of the effect of sexual reproduction in magnifying variation. It means that a relatively small amount of genic variation can greatly reduce the genotypic and phenotypic correlations both between parents and offspring and between collateral relatives. Mathematical models need to take this possibility into account, and we need to rethink our method of analysis of the correlation between relatives.

From the viewpoint of survival of a single gene, the concept of inclusive fitness is a useful one that lends itself to direct measurement through counting numbers of surviving offspring. From the viewpoint of genetic systems, the measure is still useful but based on a more complex phenomenon. The survival of offspring will depend not on single genes, but on combinations of genes, and there is no way that an individual can pass along his or her combination through the process of meiosis; the combinations present in the offspring will depend on the other parent or parents as well. This has given rise to a well-known technique among animal breeders, usually called nicking. If a complex trait such as conformation in a show dog is desired, the best technique is to mate two individuals and rear their offspring. If desirable puppies result, the mating can be repeated; if the puppies are undesirable, mating in other parental combinations can be tried. A successful mating will produce at least some individuals equal to or superior to the parents.

Effect of a Given Behavior

	Neighbors Gain	Neighbors Lose
Individual Gains	Positively Selected	Selfish Behavior
Individual Loses	Altruistic Behavior	Counter-selected

Figure 8.1. Hamilton's model for selfish and altruistic behavior. This is a slightly modified version of that which appeared in Hamilton's (1964) paper. As suggested in the text, it is a perfect example of conceptualization in terms of bipolar opposites.

From the viewpoint of selection, the technique is dependent a) upon progeny testing (similar to Hamilton's inclusive fitness), and b) on the selection of a combination of two parents. The unit of selection here is not the individual, but a pair and its offspring. The breeder has selected a group from a population of such groups.

Practical selection procedures may involve either selection of individuals, a technique that is very successful where a single major gene is involved, or pair+offspring selection. Given the fact that major genes do not appear to be important in evolution, it is apparent that pair+offspring selection is probably the more important process in natural selection. Hamilton did not provide a mathematical model for it.

Moreover, a mathematical model dealing with the evolution of complex genetic systems had already been developed by Wright (1932, 1977). This shifting balance theory, described in detail in Chapter III, applies to the evolution of any adaptive characteristic, social or otherwise. The challenge of the future will be to produce an equally sophisticated mathematical model that will extend Wright's theory to the special conditions of the evolution of social behavior and organization.

Hamilton also introduced the idea that selfish and altruistic behavior may be balanced against each other, and he assumed four possible combinations as shown in Figure 8.1, depending on the effects of behavior upon an individual and its neighbors. If a behavior is harmful to both an individual and its neighbors, it will be selected against. If it benefits both, it will be positively selected. The consequences of the other two combinations are less predictable. If a behavior benefits an individual but harms its neighbors (selfish behavior), it should be selected positively, but only if the neighbors are unrelated; if they are related, such behavior should be selected against. If a behavior harms an individual but benefits its neighbors (altruistic behavior) it should be selected against, unless the neighbors are related, in which case it could be selected positively. In the case of a parent-offspring relationship, care of the offspring (altruistic in terms of parental survival) obviously promotes offspring survival and inclusive fitness and should therefore be positively selected.

Such considerations led Hamilton to conclude "the social behavior of a species evolves in such a way that in each distinct behavior-evoking situation the individual will seem to value his neighbor's fitness against his own according to the coefficients of relationship appropriate to that situation" (p. 19). Testing this hypothesis led to much subsequent research on the adaptive value of behavior in animal societies under natural conditions. Whether true or not (and many results support it), it has been valuable in stimulating research.

Returning to Hamilton's binary conceptual framework (Figure 8.1), it has certain weaknesses. The first is that it makes use of a dichotomy involving bipolar opposites. While such a formulation fits our cultural heritage, and hence is inherently attractive to scientists in our culture, it does not correspond to the facts. Behavior falls along a continuous scale of adaptivity from 0 to 100 percent, and most of it is somewhere in between the extremes. Also, the same behavior may be adaptive in some circumstances and maladaptive in others. Behaviors as well as genes belong to systems and thus modify each other. In short, the actualities are far more complex than Hamilton's scheme postulates.

Second, the analysis suffers from the use of the common terms "selfish" and "altruistic", both of which are loaded with surplus meanings. This has led to sloppy thinking, especially where this has been translated into genetics. Thus even Hamilton speaks of "the gene's point of view", as if it were an independent and even conscious entity.

Genes do not "stand for" a particular trait. If they did, it would be consistent with the theory of preformation, a primitive biological theory that died as soon as biologists obtained the necessary optical equipment to look at embryos. A gene always acts in cooperation with other genes, as part of a system. All a single gene can do is to modify variation in a trait, in ways depending on its interaction with other genes. While Hamilton doubtless meant "selfish gene" as a bit of shorthand for "gene modifying behavior in a selfish direction," the results have been unfortunate.

Hamilton's formulation (Figure 8.1) is similar to that which I have used in a different context, to examine the effects of selection on different levels of organization (Scott, 1968). In either case, it leads to a concept of balance or equilibrium, which I consider to be a useful one in analyzing selection.

The final section of Hamilton's paper is devoted to the applications of his hypothesis to the social insects, particularly the

Hymenoptera, whose genetic system is peculiar in that the males are haploid. In a colony of honey bees, all of which may be produced by a single mating, the male has a zero genetic relationship with males in the next generation but a 1.0 coefficient with his daughters (that is, he contributes all his haploid chromosomes to every daughter). Consequently, his daughters are more closely related genetically than are sisters ordinarily (.75 instead of .5). Hamilton predicts that since every female (including the sterile workers) is more closely related to its sisters than is the mother, sisters should be more solicitous than usual of each other's welfare. And since the workers are sterile, they can lose their lives to defend the colony without endangering the reproduction of the next generation. Such self sacrifice is what Hamilton would call "altruism," and is surely appropriate in the human sense of the word. But genetic relationships do not explain the behavior of a new queen in the colony, who kills all her sister potential queens. That is, genetic relationship is not a universal determining factor.

Finally, Hamilton's paper suffers from the assumption that most social behavior is inherently disadvantageous to the individual, leading to concentration on a narrow range of problems related to this assumption. But social behavior is always expressed within social systems exhibiting two-way causation and feedback. Thus, behavior that seemingly benefits only others may in fact benefit the whole society and through it all its members, including the individual that exhibits the behavior.

In summary, Hamilton's paper is important because it presents a mathematical model related to a topic of basic general importance, the evolution of social behavior, and because it has had a strong effect on the thinking of other evolutionary theorists. Its logic is impeccable and his conclusions have stimulated research. A mathematical model, however, is only as good as the assumptions that go into it. The basic assumption in this case is flawed – that of a single gene, rather than that of a genetic system. This means that the model will only directly apply to major gene effects. It is possible that a mathematical model based on an assumption of genetic systems and combinations of genes might lead to the same conclusions, but this remains unproven.

I shall now introduce an alternative model that avoids some of the difficulties inherent in Hamilton's formulation, based on two fundamental biological concepts: function and systems theory. It is derived from a comparative study of social behavior and organization as it exists in the animal kingdom, and it is consistent with the genetic-systems theory of biological evolution.

Rather than using popular phraseology such as selfish and altruistic, I employ the term *epimeletic behavior* (Scott, 1956), defined as giving care or attention to other members of the same species. It has no connotation of good or evil, and there is no implication of bipolar opposite traits; it exists in measurable amounts on a continuous scale. It can be considered as a physio-behavioral system based on the *function of caregiving* (Chapter 7), and its evolution analyzed from that viewpoint.

The Evolution of Function in the Epimeletic Physio-Behavioral System

The most widespread examples of caregiving are those of care of offspring, and these in turn are related to the care of fertilized eggs. An obvious theory is that caregiving behavior has its origin in the general function of reproduction which involves the sexual system as well.

I have surveyed major animal phyla for examples of caregiving. Among the lower invertebrates, caregiving first appears in the polychaete worms, an example being the tube worm, *Neanthes caudata* (Reish, 1957). The male guards his tube against intruding males, but allows a mature female to enter, mate and lay her eggs. He then ejects her but stays with the eggs, pumping water over them until they hatch. It is noteworthy that it is the male who performs the caregiving function.

Epimeletic behavior is rare among molluscs, the best example being that of *Octopus vulgaris*, the common octopus (Wells, 1978). After mating and insemination, the female retires to a nest in some convenient cavity, lays her eggs and guards them continuously until they are hatched, usually dying thereafter. In general, epimeletic behavior among the lower invertebrates is poorly developed, amounting to a few cases of protection of eggs until hatching. Both the cases studied here have arisen in connection with shelter-building behavior.

It is only in the two more highly organized phyla that there is any elaborate social organization based on epimeletic behavior.

Among the Arthropods, protection of the eggs is relatively wide-spread. For example, female decapod crustaceans, such as the crayfish, commonly attach their fertilized eggs to their swimmerets, carrying them until hatching. Actual care and feeding of offspring has arisen in several other groups, of which I shall give a few examples.

Among Arachnida, spiders of the species *Stegodyphus sarasinorum* from Afghanistan cooperatively build huge connected nests, live together in these without agonistic behavior, cooperatively kill insects and share them (Kullman, et al. 1971-1972). Each mated female will build a cocoon, often side by side with others, lay her eggs and, when the young are hatched, feed them with regurgitated food. Later she catches insects and brings them to the nest, where they are eaten by the young. Still later the young catch their own food. In the final phase of reproduction, the female dies and is eaten ("sucked out") by her offspring, the ultimate example of "altruism" in Hamilton's sense. (Death following reproduction is fairly common, though not universal in animals. Death itself has an evolutionary function: If there were no death, evolution would be impossible, as it depends upon the replacement of previous generations.)

It is, however, among various orders of Insecta that epimeletic behavior reaches its highest development among Arthropods. The elaborate examples of female care of offspring in the bees, wasps and ants of the order Hymenoptera are well known (Michener, 1974; Wilson, 1971). These involve nest building protection against predators, cleaning, and feeding. The peculiar Hymenopteran pattern of sex determination has diverted attention away from the fact that epimeletic behavior has evolved in several other major orders of insects. Among these, termites (Order Isoptera) have evolved elaborate social organizations on a different genetic basis. In the termite colony such as the relatively primitive *Incisitermes minor* of the western United States, (Harvey, 1934) a new colony is founded by a single reproductive pair that builds a burrow in dry wood and begins to reproduce. The resulting nymphs are capable of metamorphosing into adults but do not do so in the presence of the reproductive pair. They stay in the colony, enlarging the burrows and feeding the younger nymphs. Feeding is essential in termites, as they cannot digest wood but harbor protozoan parasites that perform this function. These are transferred during the feeding process. The nymphs not only feed the younger ones but extend this behavior to all members of the colony.

Thus as with the Hymenopteran societies, social organization among termites is founded on epimeletic behavior. In both these groups reciprocal feeding is a prominent feature of social organization. In this case, care is extended to other adults including the reproductives. Wheeler (1923) called this trophallaxis and theorized that it was the basis of social organization in insects. Similar to the bee and ant colonies the members of the termite society are all related to each other through a founding pair. Epimeletic behavior is not extended to unrelated animals.

As Wilson (1975) pointed out, social organization among insects is based on caste recognition, or reacting to classes of individuals, whereas vertebrate organization is founded on recognition of individuals. There is some degree of caste organization among vertebrate societies, such as differential responses to males and females and to adults and young, but, in addition vertebrates also distinguish between individuals within these classes.

Some form of caregiving behavior is found in all five major classes of vertebrates. Among freshwater Teleost fishes, the pattern of a male building a nest and guarding it until the eggs are hatched is fairly common and was elaborately described and analyzed by Tinbergen (1953) for sticklebacks. It even occurs in *Amia*, the river dogfish, one of the most primitive of modern fishes. Here the male guards the newly hatched young for a time. The only case of parental feeding of fishes of which I am aware was described by Ward and Barlow (1967). Parents in the orange chromid (*Etroplus maculatus*) secrete mucus over their scales which is eaten by the newly hatched fry for approximately three weeks.

Cases of parental care of eggs are relatively common among salamanders, frogs and toads in the class Amphibia. One remarkable case is that of the gastric brooding frog that swallows its own eggs and lets them hatch out in its stomach, feed on food swallowed by the parent, undergo metamorphosis, and finally emerge from its mouth as tiny frogs (Tyler & Carter, 1981). In this case the care of offspring is primarily physiological, but in three species of the tropical frog genus *Dendrobates*, a female carries individual tadpoles to tiny pools formed in the leaf axils of certain plants. Each tadpole is then fed for several weeks with unfertilized eggs laid by the mother (Duellman & Treub, 1986).

Epimeletic behavior other than providing nests is relatively rare among Reptilia, but Pooley (1974) has described more elaborate maternal care in the Nile crocodile. She builds a nest on land and guards it until the eggs are hatched, 84-90 days later. She then collects the hatchlings in her mouth, stores them in a pouch below her jaws and carries them into the water where they are released. No further care was observed.

It is among the two classes of warm blooded animals that vertebrate epimeletic behavior reaches its most complex development. Birds have primarily exploited the aerial environment, and mammals the terrestrial one. Associated with this are a number of anatomical and physiological divergences, but those most directly associated with epimeletic behavior concern reproduction. Birds lay eggs and, being warm blooded, must incubate them. Except for two aberrant species, the duck-billed platypus and the echidna, mammals bear their young alive, a task that devolves upon the female. Further, all female mammals lactate and feed their newborn young in this fashion. Ring-doves and related birds produce "crop milk" which serves a similar function, in this case produced by both males and females who share the care of the young equally (Lehrman, 1965). But most species either feed their young by bringing them food (altricial birds) or do no more than lead them where food may be found (precocial birds).

These differences in epimeletic behavior are associated with divergences in the mating systems of birds and mammals. The vast majority of bird species mate in monogamous pairs, contrasted with the polygynous systems found in many mammals. Kleiman (1977) estimated that only 3% of mammalian species are monogamous. Associated with this, paternal care of offspring is much more common in birds, ranging from relatively slight participation in some of the perching birds through equally shared care as in the ring-dove, to complete male responsibility for incubation, as in the mallee fowl (Frith, 1962).

Care may be extended to the mate. Feeding ("tidbitting") is part of the male courtship pattern in domestic fowl, and the male African hornbill provides the female with all her nourishment during incubation.

Hamilton's theory that altruistic behavior should be extended to species mates in proportion to the degree of genetic relationship has lead to a search for species in which this occurs. Emlen (1984) provides an extensive list of species such as the acorn woodpecker where young birds may stay with the parents a year or more and help with the care of the next brood. To date, I have seen no recorded cases of epimeletic behavior extended to non-relatives except to mates responsible for producing related offspring. A possible further exception is the cedar waxwing, a berry-eating bird that not only feeds its young but sometimes passes berries from bill to bill among the flocks in which it lives. The relationships of birds in these flocks are not known (Tyler, 1950).

In general, the class Aves is the most successful vertebrate group adapted to the aerial habitat and includes a large number of widely divergent species. One is impressed by the great variety of epimeletic strategies (to use Maynard Smith's term) seen in this group.

Mammals likewise show a great deal of divergence, not only between the major orders such as the Rodentia, the two orders of hoofed mammals, the Carnivora and the Primata, but also within these groups. Among rodents, beavers have evolved one of the more complex forms of social organization (Bradt, 1938; Willson, 1971). They live on bark and twigs, and build the most elaborate structures of any non-human mammal. They either construct burrows in the banks of large streams, or dam small streams and build protective lodges out of small logs in the resulting ponds. Living in cold climates, they cut and store their winter supply of food in the bottom of the pond and need not emerge from the lodges when ice forms, hence are protected against predators.

A beaver colony is formed by a mated pair. Young are born within the lodge, where they are suckled by the female but later provided with wood by both parents, soon being able to retrieve this on their own. The young remain through the following year as helpers in the work of maintaining the dam and lodge and providing food for the next litter. Eventually, they move away to form new colonies, again as mated pairs.

In contrast to the small societies of the beavers, some species of ungulates live in herds of hundreds or even thousands of animals, especially during migrations. In the mountain sheep, for example (Geist, 1971), females perform all the care of the young, the two sexes being together only during the mating season. The mating system is polygynous but polygamy also occurs. The attachment process in the females only operates for a couple of hours after birth, ensuring that the female will become attached only to her own lamb, or in some cases, twin lambs. There is no extension of this behavior to any other individuals, related or not.

Terrestrial carnivore young are often born in litters in an immature state and require relatively long periods of nursing, feeding, and cleaning, usually within a den. In addition to the well described case of wolves (Murie, 1944) where there is usually one litter born in a pack to the most dominant female and where other adult members, both male and female feed the young and guard the den, there are several other cases in the family Canidae and other Carnivores. Black-backed jackals (Moehlman, 1979) mate as monogamous pairs, with biparental care except for nursing, but in 11/15 of observed cases, one or more young from a previous litter stayed on for a year, and helped rear the next litter before moving away.

The banded mongooses of East Africa live in packs in a communal den, where several females produce young together which are indiscriminately nursed (Emlen, 1984). Males guard the den when females are abroad. In the dwarf mongoose (Rood, 1978, 1980) some nonreproductive females apparently develop teats and nurse the young communally. This may be a case of false pregnancy, and needs further physiological study.

Caregiving behavior among primates has special interest because its members are man's closest genetic relatives. The order Primata is anatomically and behaviorally highly specialized with respect to manipulative digits, predominately those of the forelimb. These long and unprotected fingers limit the distribution of their owners to tropical and mild temperate climates except for humans with protective clothing. Within these limits, they have penetrated two biotic habitats, forests and plains, and have produced both diurnal and nocturnal forms, with accompanying behavioral and anatomical differentiation. Most species are omnivorous, but some, such as the gorilla, are almost entirely herbivorous and a few of the prosimians feed almost entirely on insects and thus are carnivores.

They have evolved a variety of mating systems, ranging from monogamy among the single pair troops of lemurs, through polygyny in the single male troops of many monkey species such as langurs, to partial polygamy in multi-male groups such as baboons and rhesus monkeys.

Primate young are born in varying degrees of maturity, but all are carried by the mothers, either ventrally or riding on the mother's back as in the baboons that habitually walk on all fours. A prominent feature of primate behavior is grooming with the hands and teeth. This is extended from self to infants and also to other adults, particularly between males and females. Males will sometimes hold younger animals and groom them. Males also have the function of guarding a troop and repelling predators in many species.

Grooming has some relationship to the removal of parasites such as ticks, but Saunders (1988) concluded that its function in baboons was primarily social integration. While grooming is strongly related to maternal relationships, it may be extended to non-relatives (Silk, 1986), both in the laboratory and in the wild. As an example of how this can occur, the social organization of rhesus monkeys leads to contact between males and unrelated others. In the usual troop of 40-50 animals all are genetically and socially related, except that young males frequently leave their natal troops, penetrate other groups (often where they have older brothers) and attempt to work their way up the dominance hierarchy to the point where they achieve mating (Meikle & Vessey, 1981). At this point it would be possible for mutual grooming to occur between unrelated male-female pairs and also between males and unrelated young.

An obvious evolutionary theory that will explain the observed phenomena listed above is that of extension of function, from self-care to care of fertilized eggs, from this to the care of the resulting offspring, from this to the care of related adults, and also to adult mates that are not genetically related but become related to offspring that are produced.

This progression does not take place in a straight line, and it can take very divergent forms. The advantage of the theory from the genetic-systems viewpoint is that it does not require gross disturbance and reorganization of previous physio-behavioral systems, but rather elaboration of existing organization.

The ultimate extension of this function is to non-related young and adults. Extension to non-related young leads to the phenomenon of adoption, which can be easily produced experimentally both within species and in some cases across species. All that needs to be done in birds is to substitute the eggs of one individual for another as used to be done frequently for setting hens in farmyard practice. It was just as easy to substitute duck eggs for chicken eggs.

Cross species adoption occurs regularly in nature among semi-parasitic birds such as the cowbird that lays eggs in warblers nests, and the European cuckoo with similar habits. Such parasitic cross species adoption is also a regular phenomenon in the so-called slave making ants.

Cross fostering is a common experimental technique used in rodent experiments, and we found that domestic dog mothers would as readily accept a strange puppy of a different breed provided the mother was absent at the time of introduction and the new pup had contact with others and so lost its distinctive odor.

Adoption of infants whose mothers have disappeared occurs in several primate species, including chimpanzees (Silk, 1986). Because the members of a primate troop are usually genetically related, this is not a clear case of extension to unrelated individuals.

It is thus clear that the *capacity* to extend care to non-related individuals is widely distributed. This is another example of the principle of surplus capacities (Chapter 7), cases where behavior primarily evolved for adaptive function in one situation is also useful in another. I would therefore predict that we shall eventually find numerous cases of extension of the caregiving function to non-related adults in mammals. For example, porpoises are reported to support other porpoises that are ill or disabled and have difficulty in swimming. What their relationships might be cannot be determined in most cases. But there are also reported cases where porpoises have helped a drowning human swimmer (Kellogg, 1961).

The wide extension of care to non-related individuals among humans is well documented. Human social organization at the tribal level is based on the institution of the family; i.e., every individual is related to every other one in the tribe in some way. Burhoe (1976) suggested that religions have played a strong part in extension of social organization to non-related individuals and along with this caregiving. An example is the Mosaic injunction that "you shall not oppress a stranger for you were strangers in the land of Egypt."

Whatever the function of religion, it is clear that the extension of caregiving behavior to non-relatives among humans is associated with language and culture transmitted by language. Nevertheless it has its biological roots. There are many subjective reports that

individuals enjoy and obtain emotional satisfaction from caregiving, and there is recent evidence that human caregivers also live
longer than those who do not give care.

The extension of caregiving behavior to non-relatives becomes
a difficult evolutionary problem only if one assumes that all evolutionary change was brought about by competition. Here we may
reflect that competition does not occur within physiological systems. (If it does, there is something radically wrong, as in the case
of cancerous growth that competes with normal cells). And so
many philosophically minded biologists have wondered why
humans cannot behave like their constituent cells, in cooperation,
peace, and harmony (Dunn, 1961).

The answer is that competition *is* possible *between* systems.
Something new appeared with the evolution of behavior and social
organization based on behavior. Organisms must cooperate in
order to achieve social organization, but they are still capable of
competition between organismic systems. This is the evolutionary
paradox stated in the most general way, and I shall return to this
in the next chapter.

Caregiving behavior is so widely related to social organization that
many scientists of the past were led to the statement that "the family
is the basis of society." This is a case of overgeneralization, as there
are at least four behavioral roots of social organization: shelter seeking behavior leading to shelter construction and shared shelter,
defense against predators evolving into agonistic behavior, sexual
behavior leading to caregiving behavior, and epimeletic behavior
itself. Use of these may arise independently in different species but
their functions may be combined in complex societies.

To return to Hamilton's model, the extension of the function of
caregiving (which he dismissed as an unimportant kind of social
behavior), will easily account for the evolution of "altruism."

Williams' Adaptation and Natural Selection (1966)

Another important work of the 1960's was that of Williams. The
author presented it as a critique of evolutionary theories then current rather than as a new contribution. Because his arguments are
well organized and readable, his conclusions have had major
effects on the thinking of other writers, especially for those who
have not gone to his primary sources.

The principal limitation of the book was that it made no use of the systems concept. On the genetic level, Williams briefly considered gene interaction, but did not appreciate its implications for genetic systems. Thus "the genetic environment can be considered to be all other genes in the population, at the same and other loci. In practice, it is possible to consider only a few of the more important loci and treat the remainder as noise" (p. 58). Thus he repudiated the systems concept in favor of the old heredity vs. environment dichotomy long since discarded by geneticists. The only aspect of genetic systems organization considered by Williams was that of meiosis and the process of sexual reproduction, and this only as a result of evolution rather than an intrinsic process. Thus the whole book was founded on a false assumption, that of individual gene action. Why then has it had such an effect on the thinking of others?

Essentially, the book was a tightly reasoned theoretical argument to the effect that group selection is an unimportant factor in evolution compared to selection between individuals, which he reduces to selection between individual genes. By group he meant "something other than a family and to be composed of individuals that need not be closely related" (p. 93).

Thus Williams accepted Hamilton's formulation without criticism although, as I and others have pointed out, it involves selection of groups in the strict sense of the word. Wright (1977) distinguished between *group selection* based on genetic correlations (as in Hamilton's and most of Wynne-Edwards' cases) and *intergroup selection* (Wright, 1931), which he also called *interdeme selection*, referring to small local populations. He considered "group selection" to be a special case of the more general phenomenon of interdeme selection. Wright did not, however, appreciate the degree to which social organization, whether or not the individuals are related, will create the small, somewhat isolated populations that he considered essential for rapid evolution.

Williams' argument, therefore, boiled down to one directed against the importance of interdemic selection. He dismissed Wright's theories on the basis of a criticism by Simpson (a paleontologist), who argued (1944) that the conditions specified by Wright could occur only rarely. Williams apparently did not consult Wright's (1931) original paper on the subject but referred only to a review of one of Simpson's books (Wright, 1945). Nor did

Williams see Simpson's (1953) volume in which he came around to Wright's viewpoint.

Wright, who was a physiological geneticist as well as a population geneticist, based his theory on two major phenomena that were well-known even in the 1930's: non-additive interaction effects between genes, and pleiotropy (a gene usually affects several different characters). For example, Dobzhansky (1927) had examined the effect of 12 mutant genes in Drosophila on the effect of spermatheca shape, an internal characteristic which was not one of the main effects ascribed to any of the mutations. He found that 10 out of 12 of these genes had an effect on the shape of this organ.

Wright (1932) then developed a mathematical model based on two recessive genes each on a different locus and each of which by itself had unfavorable effects on survival, but in combination produced a favorable effect. In order for the combination to survive and spread through the population, there must be a fairly high incidence of each of the two genes, which Wright arbitrarily set at 5%. Also, the favorable effect of the combination must outweigh the unfavorable effects of the two genes separately. If it does, selection of the population will drive it up an adaptive peak. As the increased survival occurs, numbers of individuals will increase in the local population and migration will take place into adjacent populations, enabling them to move up to a similar adaptive peak. This implies that genes with strongly unfavorable effects (and this includes the majority of genes studied in the laboratory) are not likely to be important in evolution. Rather, it is those with relatively mild effects.

Wright later extended the model to multiple loci and stated that the success of the process depends upon the existence of thousands of heteroallelic loci (1980). Also, there may be hundreds or thousands of local populations in the species, increasing the chance that a favorably interactive pair of recessive genes may occur. Wright called his theory that of "shifting balance" and concluded (1977) that "... the interaction system should be more adaptive than mere gene substitution" (p. 472). Wright also stated that the model applied equally well to selection of family groups. Wright's theory therefore is not an exclusive but an inclusive one.

We thus have two genetic theories of natural selection, the shifting balance theory and the genic substitution theory, each with its strengths and its limitations.

The strength of the shifting balance theory is that it deals with the fact that genes are not independent entities but must operate as interdependent entities comprising a system. The limitation of the theory is that it applies only to populations employing biparental reproduction. Obviously, new combinations of genes cannot be tried out in species that are reproducing asexually or by self-fertilization. But since the great majority of plants and animals do reproduce sexually, this is not a serious limitation. From the systems viewpoint, a logical criticism is that the actual system is more complex than assumed in the mathematical model.

On the other hand, the strength of the gene substitution theory lies in its simplicity; it is easier to understand and demonstrate in artificial selection models. Its weakness is that it does not correspond to the fact that the effect of a gene is always interactional. Williams' assumption that interactional effects are "noise" is patently unfounded. Nevertheless, selection against a single gene can obviously produce effects. The recessive gene for albinism, which occurs relatively commonly in mammalian species, has pleiotropic effects on coat color and eye color, not only rendering individuals more conspicuous to predators, but also producing defective eyesight. Except in protected laboratory populations, natural selection should keep the frequency of this gene at a low level where selection becomes rather ineffective and reaches a balance with mutation rates. A single major gene with positive effects should also be selected, but such genes rarely if ever occur.

Predicting the relative importance of each of these processes of natural selection then becomes a matter of defining the situation under which the evolution takes place. The variables should include, for each particular species, complexity of the genetic system, generation time, physiological organization, social organization, population organization, and finally the nature of the adaptive character (involving physiology, behavior, or social organization).

Summarized, Williams' arguments against the importance of the shifting balance theory chiefly depends on Occam's razor, that the single gene substitution theory is simpler, as indeed it is. Unfortunately, simplicity is not necessarily equivalent to reality, and it should be remembered that William of Occam (ca. 1280-1349) lived before the dawn of the scientific method and devised his razor to curb the proliferation of philosophical theories. Genes exist only as parts of complex, interacting systems and cannot act independently. A similar criticism has been voiced by Wilson (1975) who names it "the Fallacy of Simplifying the Cause" (p. 30).

Competition

Williams' thinking is permeated, as is that of other authors with similar views, with the concept of competition. While competition does occur, it is by no means universal. As I have pointed out above, natural selection is based on differential survival and reproduction. Competition may play a part, as it does in the mating of mountain sheep, but differential survival may also occur in the absence of competition, as when a female sheep provides better care and more milk for her lamb than does her neighbor, without taking anything from her. And if one actually looks for behavioral competition under natural conditions, it is often hard to find. This is partly because competitive situations are rare in the everyday lives of animals, and partly because an animal that can move can usually walk away from unprofitable competition. In fact, the situation that best fits the strict doctrine of competition is that of two trees growing closely together. I therefore conclude that competition, on whatever level, is only a special case of the more general phenomenon of differential survival.

Also, in employing the systems concept, I wish to avoid two sorts of dichotomous thinking involving bipolar opposites: selfishness vs. altruism, and competition vs. cooperation. Both of these are, after all, concepts that arose directly out of our culture, and when applied to other species impose limits both on observation and conceptualization. Dichotomous distributions do exist in pairs of genes on a pair of chromosomes, but they produce corresponding dichotomous phenotypes only if there is a single allele at the locus, dominance is present, and there is a major gene effect, usually deleterious.

Consider the case of allelomimetic behavior, in which each animal does what the animals next to it do, with some degree of mutual imitation. The result is a mobile and coordinated group that has many possible adaptive functions. Such groups are widely found in certain species of fishes, birds and mammals. Instead of a pair of eyes, the school or flock has hundreds or thousands of

eyes that may be used for the location of food, a dangerous predator, or, in the case of social carnivores such as wolves, for locating
prey and coordinating group attacks.

One can test out the function of such groups under natural conditions by simple experiments. For example, if one drops a peb-
ble near a school of small fish in a shallow fresh water lake they
will all swim to the bottom and stir up mud with their tails, obviously blocking the view of a potential predator such as the
experimenter.

The evolution of such behavior was a puzzle to Williams (1964),
because it is noncompetitive. He attempted to make a feeble case
for fishes trying to get into the center of the school and so be safe,
but such behavior would obviously be self-defeating as it would
destroy the school and provide a solid mass of fish that would be
easier for a predator to attack. Hamilton (1971) pointed out that
it is only necessary for a fish to approach another to reduce the
chance of predation and that marginal predation is a common phenomenon in predator-prey relationships.

Allelomimetic behavior is mutually beneficial and possible only
for the members of a group. The vast majority of social behaviors
are of this sort; that is, they are mutually beneficial and noncompetitive. If we look at the basic physiobehavioral systems of social
behavior (Table 7.1), each has an adaptive function and only one,
the agonistic system, is directly competitive. As I have pointed out,
animals do not spend their lives in agonistic behavior.

Furthermore, the adaptive function of allelomimetic behavior,
or its survival value, does not depend on the other individuals
being close relatives, although this may be the case in many social
groups. There is no need to invoke competition to explain its origin. Even one fish following the movements of another independently moving fish should obtain some benefit from it and should
show differential survival, enabling the behavior to spread
throughout the population. Once this has occurred there should be
a strong differential survival compared to a lone fish, thus maintaining the behavior.

Such behavior is not universally adaptive in every situation. It
obviously benefits human predators such as fishermen as well as
other predators such as porpoises, who are able to locate their prey
more easily and, in the case of man, to capture it enmasse. The
behavior, therefore, must have evolved under conditions where

positive and negative survival functions came into some kind of equilibrium in which the advantages heavily outweighed the disadvantages.

Corning's The Synergism Hypothesis (1983)

Like Darwin's *Origin of Species*, this book was an attempt to develop a general theory of evolution, but based on a broader set of premises and a much broader foundation of factual information now available in the biological and social sciences. Also like Darwin, Corning reviewed a vast array of scientific literature relevant to the evolution of living systems.

From his study, which extended over many years, Corning developed what he calls a theory of progressive evolution. While it emphasizes and includes Natural Selection, it is different in several important respects. The first and most important of these is the concept of *synergism*, which Corning defines as a group of combinatory processes that may produce additive, multiplicative, or non-linear effects, but in any case can result in discontinuities that produce novel effects and so bring about change. This extends the phenomenon of creative or emergent interaction that is inherent in systems theory, to the phenomenon of evolutionary change. Combinatory processes thus comprise a major change process in evolution.

Further, synergistic processes occur at all levels of organization, and each is related to function. In this sense synergisms are goal directed or purposive, and Corning therefore states a second principle, that of *teleonomy*. Some combinations (which is another way of looking at interactions between systems entities) are dysfunctional or dysergic. Natural selection should eliminate those that are dysfunctional, and Corning therefore derives a secondary principle of *teleonomic selection*.

A third principle that Corning emphasizes is that of *cybernetic interaction*. This is equivalent to the concept of two-way causation and feedback that I have used in connection with systems theory but emphasizes the element of unequal causation (an inherent and highly probable outcome of two-way interaction), and thus leads to the concepts of governance and steering that are associated with cybernetic theories.

On these bases, Corning introduced the hypothesis that evolution has been guided by synergism acting in combination with natural selection: i.e., a major change process in evolution has been the trying out of the effects of new combinations on every level from the genetic to the human political, which is where he stops, not proceeding to ecosystems. This leads to change in the direction of greater and greater degrees of combinatory processes, or progressive evolution. In this view, combinatory processes are both major sources of change and a major guiding process in evolution.

This approach avoids the old dichotomy of cooperation versus competition, substituting the proposition that even in competitive situations a combination will almost invariably triumph over individual effort. To one well versed in human political organization (as is Corning), this is a self-evident truth. It also has the ring of truth when applied to phenomena on lower levels of organization and in noncompetitive situations. Applied to evolution, the species that has the ability to form combinations should be the one to survive, and if it also has the ability to form new combinations, it should evolve more rapidly.

Applying the synergism hypothesis to the four basic genetic processes of evolution, Corning pays little attention to mutation, emphasizing instead combinatory processes (gene combinations) as the basic change process. He thus finds his theory consistent with Wright's shifting balance theory. Sexual reproduction, including meiosis and fertilization, has in this context a major function, that of trying out new gene combinations. Corning pays little attention to inbreeding (whose change processes are largely random), but includes natural selection as a discriminator between synergic and dysergic combinations.

Corning's approach to the genetic basis of evolution therefore de-emphasizes its random change processes (except for sexual reproduction), neglecting the fact that there is a strong random element in evolution, and that it is not completely directive.

Further, Corning did not fully appreciate the general tendency of genetic systems, in common with living systems at all other levels, to develop and maintain stability. Therefore, in a highly organized system most changes are likely to be either dysfunctional or to lack function altogether. To be viable, a change cannot destroy the system of which it is a part. But Corning states that new combinations may produce entirely new effects that are functional, and so he finds no difficulty in accounting for discontinuous change such as is postulated in the theories of saltation and punctuation that have been applied to paleontological data with respect to organic evolution (Gould & Eldridge, 1977).

There are difficulties also with the principle of teleonomy. Goals and purposiveness are obviously important determinants of human behavior and are associated with consciousness; a human can state why he or she wants to follow a certain course of action. But it is difficult to assign purposiveness to nonhuman animals other than that they act as if they had two goals: to stay alive, and to reproduce. These activities are functional, but they need not be consciously purposive. Corning would say that there is continuity between functional adaptation on this level and conscious purposiveness among humans. Undoubtedly, purposiveness is more important on the human social level; human behavior is directed by a great variety of goals, many of which have little or no relevance to the basic goals of maintaining the existence of the organism and the species.

Putting these criticisms aside, Corning's hypothesis is a major contribution to evolutionary theory, for several reasons. First, his book is the only recent work that deals in a comprehensive fashion with the problem of cooperation, and it does this from a fresh viewpoint. Second, it does not attempt to replace other evolutionary theories with a single simple formulation, but to include them in a comprehensive framework. Third, because the author has trained himself in both the social and biological sciences, he speaks with a great deal more authority concerning the evolution of human social organization than do more narrowly trained scientists. This is particularly important with respect to cultural evolution, which I shall treat in a later chapter.

MOVEMENTS AND MODELS

Following World War II there was a world-wide flowering of interest in animal behavior and the social behavior of vertebrate animals, and this soon became organized into scientific conferences and societies. In Europe, the Ethological Conference began as a seven-man committee whose most prominent members were

Lorenz, Tinbergen and Von Frisch on the continent and Thorpe in Great Britain. Research reported at these early meetings and indeed for the next 20 years was dominated by the concept of instinct. It stimulated a great deal of descriptive research on "fixed action patterns," and inadvertently on the social organization in which these were expressed.

Eventually it became apparent to younger researchers that the concept of instinct led to a dead end. Logically, it should have led to study of the physiological basis of organized behavior, and its development under the influence of genetic factors. Instead, biologically trained workers chose to study behavior as it was exhibited in the field, largely influenced by the new evolutionary theories of social behavior that arose in the 1960's. An offshoot of the Ethology Conference was a group of scientists working under the aegis of Behavioral Ecology (Krebs & Davies, 1984), and a new scientific society by that name was formed.

Likewise in America, the movement was first organized by a committee, the "Committee for Research on Animal Societies under Natural Conditions," a group that arose out of a meeting in 1946 at Bar Harbor, Maine on "Genetics and Social Behavior." Its most active early members were C. R. Carpenter, T. C. Schneirla, F. A. Beach, J. T. Emlen, and J. P. Scott. The Committee soon organized regular scientific meetings on "Animal Behavior and Sociobiology," in conjunction with the American Society of Zoologists and the Ecological Society of America. Eventually, the group was formally organized, as the "Animal Behavior Society."

Unlike its European counterpart, the American movement was much more eclectic, and dominated by no particular theory. Its members early recognized that there was a need to describe existing animal societies. Largely influenced by Carpenter, who pressed for field work on primates, primate behavior described by biologists, comparative psychologists, and especially physical anthropologists, became a flourishing world-wide enterprise that still continues (DeVore, 1965; Smuts, et al., 1986).

Also unlike the European movement, the American one was strongly interdisciplinary from the start, having its roots in comparative psychology as exemplified by Calvin Stone, T. C. Schneirla, and C. R. Carpenter, and students of the ecologist W. C. Allee (such as N. E. Collias, A. M. Guhl, E. M. Banks, and E. A. Beeman). Other ecologists such as D. E. Davis and F. H.

Bronson were also influential. The movement has been dominated by no particular theory but rather by the intrinsically fascinating nature of animal behavior and the new discoveries of fact that await the observer. But comparative studies inevitably led to evolutionary explanations, and much recent work has been guided by attempts to verify evolutionary models.

The study of the genetic basis of behavior was undertaken by a different group who formed the Behavior Genetics Society. Its members have concentrated on the proximal effects of heredity rather than its remote historical influences, and hence have had little influence on evolutionary thinking.

In the years since the publication of Hamilton's stimulating paper (1964) there has been a proliferation of evolutionary models, of which I shall describe those that have major effects on descriptive and experimental studies of social organization.

Kin Selection

This concept arose directly out of Hamilton's (1964) theory that individuals should favor other individuals in the species in accordance with the coefficient of genetic relationship. This led to a large amount of research on the behavioral interactions of related vertebrate animals, especially birds and mammals (Emlen, 1984). Not surprisingly, these studies confirmed that parent animals do indeed take care of their own offspring. More interestingly, such studies revealed many new cases of care by nonparental siblings. I have discussed the evolutionary implications of such behavior in an earlier section.

Hamilton's formulation would seem to rule out cases of alarm calls which could help out unrelated neighbors. In the prairie dog, a highly social ground squirrel, close neighbors tend to be related, but more remote individuals also benefit (Hoagland, 1983). Another obvious case of extension of social behavior to include unrelated individuals is the "mobbing reaction" of groups of grackles directed against crows that are potential nest predators.

The importance of this research is that it has led investigators to analyze animal societies in terms of genetic and social relationships, as well as with respect to behavior patterns and individual recognition.

Kin Recognition

A corollary of kin selection is kin recognition. If animals selectively favor their offspring or near relatives, how do they know which is which? Neither birds nor mammals emerge from the egg and womb with a fore-knowledge of relatedness. This is produced by the process of attachment, usually a mutual affair, although it was first studied as a process in the newly hatched bird and named imprinting by Lorenz (1935) and later studied extensively by Hess (1973) and others. A similar process takes place in mammals (Scott, 1978) and I have suggested that it has a common evolutionary origin in the more general process of site attachment. I have also suggested that social attachment is one of the roots of social organization; indeed that no long-lasting or permanent society can be maintained without it.

Recent research has centered around the problems of whether animals do indeed recognize individuals, and the sensory modalities through which recognition is achieved. For example, Porter (1987) found that Egyptian spiny mice reared together preferred each other's company, whether they were related siblings or fostered siblings, indicating that in this species also an attachment process takes place early in life. Recognition is achieved through olfactory cues in this species, as seems to be the case in many mammals. Even human infants can be recognized by their mother through odors, although humans obviously use other cues, including visual and auditory ones. Kin recognition, as evidenced by preferential association, has been reported in a variety of vertebrate species ranging from frog and toad tadpoles to man. Kin recognition is a special form of individual recognition, the whole forming the basis of vertebrate social organization.

What the function of kin recognition may be in such species as frog and toad tadpoles is a puzzle. It is possible that there is some advantage in maintaining contact in early life, but there is as yet no clear evidence on how tadpoles might benefit their siblings under natural conditions (Blaustein, 1983).

The mechanisms for kin recognition in these species are also unclear. Eggs produced by a single female may have some common biochemical properties that becomes familiar to the larval frogs in the clutch. Alternatively, there could be a genetic mechanism that facilitated recognition, but it is difficult to see how this would work. In order for all members of a clutch to share one gene, one of the parents would have to be homozygous, but if this were true, how could differences between parents be maintained?

Since the concepts of kin selection and kin recognition were directly derived from Hamilton's (1964) theory, this research provides abundant evidence that the theory is testable, both in the field and the laboratory, and the results are positive. Animals do indeed favor their close genetic relatives, although genetic relationships and social relationships produced by attachment do not necessarily coincide. As shown earlier in this chapter, the facts show that care-giving behavior may be extended to non-genetically related individuals. Finally, researchers in this field are still using the single-gene replacement model and have not yet come to grips with the complexities attendant on gene combination theory (e.g., Charlesworth & Charnov, 1981).

The Investment Model

One influential line of evolutionary thinking was inspired by the human science of economics. One would have supposed that this would have proceeded from the science of ecology, whose name was derived from the same root word, but, on the contrary, the theory was directly derived from the human science.

The chief difficulty with this model is its origin. The science of human economics, out of which the term investment is derived, is based largely on the assumption of rational symbolic thought, an assumption that is frequently not justified even in the human species. However, if one equates it with its ecological equivalent, the expenditure of energy, it becomes a viable concept.

The model is consistent with systems theory, but one must remember that all living systems are open ones, that living energy is not limited in total quantity but only by the capacity of the organism to obtain or utilize it and by the extent of available resources.

A major concept in this model is that of "investment," a term straight out of economics and capitalist economics at that. (One wonders what the model would have looked like it if had been derived from Marxist economics.) Investments, of course, are made in the hope of obtaining return or profits, so that the investor gets back more than he gave.

In the evolutionary context, investment means the expenditure of energy, and in most cases the animal receives a return in the form of food, shelter, and continued existence. But the evolutionary economic theorists are interested in a form of return that the investor usually never sees, the survival of offspring carrying similar heredity. In short, this is an attempt to relate energy expenditure to reproduction, particularly the behavioral aspects of reproduction such as mating and parental care.

The concept of parental investment was first strongly stated by Trivers (1972a, b; 1985), who suggested that a parent should spend energy in the process of reproduction in ways that would maximize the numbers of surviving offspring and near relatives. Whatever the soundness or weakness of the theory, it does have the advantage that it makes a definite prediction of a phenomenon that can be objectively measured as amount of activity although, as Trivers pointed out, the ultimate investment is the life of the individual. This theory has been tested numerous times in such studies as that of Hoagland (1983) on the alarm calls of prairie dogs in response to a model of a predator. The prairie dogs called more frequently when their descendants were near, but their calls also reached nearby collateral relatives. But prairie dogs that had no close relatives also called, showing that the response is extended beyond genetic relationships. In another study, Pugesek (1983) found that aging gulls, whose reproductive life was approaching its close, expended more effort in rearing their chicks than did younger pairs.

Trivers' reasoning, and that of others such as Maynard Smith (1977) who have followed this line of thought, makes no use of the systems concept. Thus the model omits feedback except in the sense that differential survival affects the gene pool of the species and through this the behavior of future generations. This, however, neglects feedback from the social system itself.

The human analog of investment implies that the investor has choices (which are in fact limited by the economic system within which he operates). But for a male animal born into a polygamous mating system, there is often no choice. A sagecock has no option but to compete for females on the mating ground or lek, and the nature of this competition is rigorously regulated by the dominance organization developed in this species. He does not have the option of mating with a single female and investing his energy in parental care. Similarly, a male pigeon or dove, belonging to species in which the system of biparental care is equalized to the point where both sexes produce crop milk for the young, there is no way that a male can go off gayly and mate with female after female and still produce living offspring.

Other social systems are more flexible with respect to the male role in reproduction, and it is perhaps here that the theory of investment has most predictive value. In some duck species reproduction starts out with biparental care. A male must mate every day with the female in order to assure fertilization of the eggs, which are produced one per day. But, unlike geese, a drake may leave before the brood is completely reared, and so have a chance to mate with a second female. This can be seen as the male maximizing the numbers of his offspring; or on a higher level, of insuring that all females, especially those that have lost mates, have a chance to be mated.

Much of this sort of thinking is obviously influenced by the idealized, carefree human male who loves 'em and leaves 'em, leaving a trail of offspring in his wake with relatively low effort. It is true that our culture provides some limited options of this sort to a sexual psychopath, but human culture like that of other primate societies, is based on some degree of biparental care, a common pattern being that of females caring for infants and males caring for and training older children, especially males. Or the social system may require that a male support both females and offspring. To take an extreme example of polygyny. Abdul Aziz, the founder of the kingdom of Saudi Arabia, had 43 sons and an unrecorded number of daughters from his numerous wives. But this was not cost free; the social system required him to support all of these women and their offspring. He obviously invested more than any one woman and, from a strictly monetary standpoint, invested more than all of them put together (Lacey, 1981).

Finally, from the viewpoint of genetic systems, it is obvious that the genetic contribution of either parent is essentially equal (except for such cases as the X and Y chromosomes, where the female contributes more than the male), and the adaptive outcome is not the preservation of individual genes but the creation of new viable genetic systems. Mating with a variety of females, a male parent has a better chance of producing viable systems, but their survival is also dependent upon adequate parental care.

Considered generally, the investment model is a metaphoric translation of Hamilton's principal of inclusive fitness, that the adaptability of behavior is dependent upon the survival of a group of related individuals, as well as upon the survival of the individual itself. This metaphor has the advantage that it suggests that the adaptability of behavior can be measured and so directly test the theory. It also escapes the defect of Hamilton's mathematical model, in that it makes no assumption regarding the single or multiple gene modes of evolution. The investment model attempts to predict how an animal should act in a given social system and makes no assumptions as to how it got there. It thus leaves unanswered the question of how particular social systems originated.

The Strategic Model

In a culture addicted to war as a science and, associated with this, competitive games, it was perhaps inevitable that scientists would begin to think of the evolution of behavior in these terms. Maynard Smith (1977) wrote an influential paper in which he employed the concept of "strategy" – straight out of military science – and went on to develop a concept that he called "evolutionarily stable strategies".

As Maynard Smith has used the concept, it includes not only patterns of behavior but also patterns of reproduction and by implication other patterns of physiological organization. Later (1982) he defined it as a phenotype, behavioral or otherwise, "such that, if all members of a population adopt it, then no mutant strategy could influence the population under the influence of natural selection" (p. 10).

This poses a basic problem of evolution in the context of systems theory: What produces the general tendency to develop stability in living systems on any level? and how do evolutionary processes overcome this tendency? In evolutionary terms, stability is adaptive in that it permits a system to function more efficiently. Therefore, stability should evolve. As I suggested in Chapter I, the apparent paradox of evolutionary change in the direction of stability can be resolved by the theory that greater complexity of organization produces greater internal stability within a system and that this leads to progressive evolution toward higher levels of organization.

The four evolutionary change processes in combination should therefore lead to greater complexity in the organization of systems which in turn produces greater internal stability. Paradoxically, one source of stability lies in the process of selection itself. As Wright (1977) pointed out, change brought about by selection depends upon the degree of selection. Weak selection produces correspondingly little change, and very strong selection of a favorable gene combination will eventually eliminate all other combinations and so produce stability. But in order for this to be maintained, the strong selection must be continued. There are several sorts of conditions where such strong selection is maintained. First, the physical environment may be stable, as it usually is for marine organisms. Second, organisms living in such an environment should be stabilized, leading to a stable biotic environment. Third, the social environment of the species may be stable, as it often is in highly organized animal societies, even if the physical and biotic environments are not.

It is interesting that most of the stable behavioral patterns studied by the ethologists as fixed action patterns and renamed Modal Action Patterns by Barlow (1977) are patterns of social behavior. In turn, it is possible, since communication is only understood if the constituent signals or symbols are clear, that variation in patterns of communication must be greatly restricted (J. P. Scott, Jr., personal communication). Thus, one explanation of an evolutionarily stable strategy is intense selection maintained over long periods of time.

In a variable environment, stability is not necessarily adaptive. Although the constituent behavior patterns may be stable, the organization derived from them may not be. For example, the same species of tree squirrels is territorial in one ecological setting (Smith, 1968) and not in another (Layne, 1954). Obviously, variable social organization, or the employment of several alternative strategies, will increase the survival value of a species. If one disregards the surplus meaning derived from its origin in human culture, the concept of strategy is a useful one for analyzing social organization and its evolution. As noted above, birds and mammals have different reproductive strategies, egg-laying and viviparity, and these are associated with different strategies with respect to mating systems and parental care. The use of the concept has led to much fruitful research (Parker, 1984). In the broad sense, a strategy is a way of performing some function within or between systems. The degree of stability is a researchable question: a useful strategy may be variable as it is in the example of the squirrels cited above.

Finally, since the concept makes no assumption as to the nature of the underlying stable genotype, it need not be inconsistent with the genetic theory of evolution.

As Maynard Smith first applied the concept, he was thinking of various mating systems seen in animal species, particularly birds, and developed some simple mathematical models. But as one examines the sexual and epimeletic behavior of animals, one is impressed first by the great variety of reproductive behavior seen in different species, and second by the many different ways in which they achieve reproductive success, in contrast to the one behavioral and two physiological parameters employed in Maynard Smith's early model (parental care, seasonal breeding, and egg laying).

To give some examples of the widely different ways in which birds achieve reproductive success, there are the colonial nesting sea birds such as gulls, which usually produce no more than two eggs per year, but nest in colonies that are largely inaccessible to terrestrial predators and that are cooperatively defended. Within the colonies, parents compete for nest sites and attack the young of other pairs. With no more knowledge than this, one would predict a species struggling for existence. Actually, such birds live for many years and are subject to low mortality rates once they become adults. Sea birds can be extraordinarily successful as measured by size of populations, as shown by the fulmars in the British Isles.

In a very different example, song birds usually live not more than one or two years, rear one or two clutches of eggs per year, with perhaps one or two birds surviving beyond those required to replace the parents. With respect to numbers, red winged blackbirds exist in enormous populations but a species that has the same basic breeding strategy, Kirtland's warbler, is well on the way to becoming extinct. The critical factor here is not the "mating strategy" but ecology: blackbirds exploit an almost unlimited food

supply in marshes and cultivated fields, while the warblers are confined to a restricted niche in a burned over forest area in Michigan. In short, what enables survival is the interaction of complex
systems on many levels, behavioral, physiological, and ecological,
with an almost infinite variety of evolutionary solutions to the
problem of existence.

If one looks only at the metabolic cost of producing germ cells,
a male animal should mate with as many females as possible. This
makes puzzling the behavior of nest building fishes, where the
male guards the nest and the female moves from nest to nest
depositing her eggs and paying nothing for having them guarded.
The male does mate with more than one female, but it is the
behavior of the female, who also has many mates, that determines
this. It is the male fish who is tied down to home and the female
that acts like the "carefree" human male.

Anyone who has watched the mating behavior of salmon is
impressed by the tremendous waste of energy involved. Here is a
river full of hundreds of magnificent fish weighing many pounds
each, the males constantly competing with one another for a few
square feet of stream bed where they may mate with the females
who pass through their ranks and deposit eggs as they go. The
longer the fish stay, the more their bodies deteriorate, and finally
all of the adults will die. In terms of energy, it is a costly and inefficient enterprise, but it works, and in the absence of human predators, salmon flourish in many different species. It is, as Maynard
Smith would say, an evolutionarily stable strategy.

One can only conclude that, unlike the strategies of war, evolutionary reproductive strategies are almost unlimited in their variety, depending on variation in behavior, physiology, social systems,
and ecosystems. It is fascinating to discover and describe the
reproductive strategy of a new species, but no one could predict
these outcomes from a knowledge of the basic strategy of bisexual
reproduction.

Game Theory

The concept of strategy comes straight out of human culture, and
its ultimate extension is the application of game theory to evolutionary problems (Maynard Smith, 1982). And as cross-cultural

surveys show, games involving strategy are associated with cultures showing more highly developed technology, class stratification, and organized warfare (Sutton-Smith, 1971). That is, competitive games are found in human societies that emphasize competition and conflict. Is it then justifiable to extend such a narrowly based concept to all animal societies?

Now, some animals play, and some even appear to play games, but the examples are almost entirely based on the behavior of mammals, and among them are confined to young individuals. For example, young lambs will mount each other, a playful form of sexual behavior, they may run and leap together, a playful form of allelomimetic behavior; or they may butt each other gently, a playful form of fighting. They may even show what looks like a competitive game of "king of the castle", when one lamb stands on a rock or stump and threatens others that come near (Scott, 1945).

As the above description implies, not all playful interactions are competitive, and this is equally true of adult sheep behavior. When contests do appear, they are far from playful. In mating contests between mountain sheep, a pair of males may rush together headlong and meet with a thunderous crash. One or both is likely to get hurt; it is no longer a game.

Nevertheless, these mating conflicts have some of the characteristics of a game in that there are limitations, almost as if the sheep were obeying rules. In these headlong charges there are always two contestants; two males never gang up on a third. Butting is done in a stereotyped fashion; the males attack each other on their least vulnerable spots: the head and horns. The usual outcome is that the male with the largest horns and in prime physical condition wins. If the loser is a younger male, all he has to do is wait a few years until his horns become larger, and it will then be his turn to mate most freely.

In actual situations behavior is much more variable and complex. As a female comes into estrus she attracts the rams in a herd, but at first runs from them. Sometimes as many as nine rams may race after her at top speed, but if she draws ahead she usually waits till they catch up. Eventually she stops and mating takes place, sometimes repeatedly with one male and sometimes with several males; there are no exclusive mating rights in the herd and receptivity continues for two or three days (Mills, 1937). In the herds that he observed Geist (1971) found that the male with the largest horns did 50% of the mating, the males with the next largest horns did 25%, those with the smallest horns did 20%, and even the yearlings did 5%. Serious fights of the type described above occurred occasionally, but usually between males of different herds. The loser is not driven off but permitted to remain if he allows the winner to treat him like a female. In short, the loser accepts subordinate status but by so doing still has a chance to mate.

One of the common adaptations to conflict within Vertebrate societies, and to a much more limited extent in others, is the development of dominance-subordination relationships, in which fighting is reduced to a largely symbolic level not harmful to either individual. It may take a great variety of forms beside that described in sheep. In goats, for example, the relationship may be one in which a subordinate individual never initiates butting but always retaliates. In another relationship the subordinate never retaliates, and in still another may retreat as soon as the dominant looks at it (Scott, 1948).

In contrast, Maynard Smith (1982) postulated only three possible strategies in a competitive situation: display, escalation, and retreat. But the dominance-subordination relationship opens up all sorts of other possibilities, including a different theoretical approach. Vehrencamp (1979) has analyzed the evolutionary effect of dominance in terms of fitness – defined as lifetime reproductive success, thus avoiding the problem of single gene replacement vs. shifting gene combinations – and concludes that there must be a balance between reproductive success of dominant and subordinate animals such that the mean reproductive success of the group to which both belong will not be adversely affected. Like any other mathematical model, this one can be criticized on the ground that it over simplifies the actual situation. Nevertheless, this approach seems more likely to be useful than that of game theory, being based on an actual rather than a hypothetical phenomenon.

As used by Maynard Smith, the game theory of evolution makes two assumptions. One is that the outcome of a contest can be measured on a unidimensional scale of "Darwinian fitness". As I have pointed out, survival (and survival of offspring) is the result of many different factors; consequently, fitness has little analytic usefulness unless it is defined in concrete terms – "fit with respect to what?"

The concept of strategy and its derivative, game theory, has the advantage that it assumes the existence of social systems, albeit much simpler systems than usually exist. It does not deal with the polysystemic organization of life, being confined to only one limited aspect of social organization, that of competition. While competition may have highly significant physiological and social consequences, the amounts of time spent in competitive activity turn out to be very small in well organized animal societies (Jay, 1965; Southwick, 1972; Winslow & Miczek, 1985).

Thus, while the theory of games is an interesting mathematical puzzle, its application to evolutionary problems is limited. Nor has anyone attempted to relate it to the gene combination theory of inheritance and the four-process theory of evolution. Game theory as now used applies only to the process of Differential Survival, and there only to phenomena that are competitive.

Game Theory and the Evolution of Cooperation

If one adheres to the two-process theory of biological evolution (mutation and natural selection) and further assumes that all evolutionary changes are produced by mass selection of individuals within a species, it follows that all evolutionary change must come about through competition. How then, could cooperation be evolved?

Axelrod and Hamilton (1981) suggested a solution to this problem using a simple competitive game known as "The Prisoners' Dilemma." The rules are as follows. Each player has two choices: to defect or to cooperate, but does not know the other player's choice. If one player defects and the other cooperates, the defector wins and the cooperator loses. If both defect, both lose, but if both cooperate, both win more than they would by defecting. If the game is played over and over again, what is the best way to signal the other player to cooperate? The overall best strategy is to play Tit for Tat; i.e., to cooperate on the first round and thereafter do what the opponent did in the previous round, thus punishing him for defecting and rewarding him for cooperating.

On this basis the authors make a persuasive case for the evolution of cooperation based on reciprocity, or mutual aid, using Maynard Smith's concept of an evolutionarily stable strategy. Several assumptions are made in the model: that alternative heritable strategies are available to individuals in a population, that the competing individuals meet repeatedly, that the individuals can choose between them, and that the choices are made simultaneously.

As I have pointed out above, cooperation is essential to social organization; otherwise individuals will not stay together. Therefore, the model assumes the pre-existence of cooperation. But the basic criticisms of this model are 1) its origin in human culture and the rational thought processes by which the game is played and 2) over-generalization. The theory does not consider other models of the origin of cooperation, such as that of Allee (1951) or the one since proposed by Corning (1983). The importance of the model is that it theoretically demonstrates that cooperation could evolve even under the assumption of the strict competitive model. With respect to genetic systems theory, the 4-process theory allows a great deal more flexibility than that postulated by the authors, and they made no attempt to deal with the problem of gene combinations.

In summary, the greatest weakness of the strategic model is its origin in human culture, and in a particular culture that emphasizes competition and competitive games. Such games are based on verbal rules (by their nature fixed and rigid), rational thought, and conscious decisions based on learning. It is inherently unlikely that actual situations in the biological world of non-verbal animals would fit the game-playing format.

Further, the games that have been used as models are overly simple. If one wishes to explore game theory, why not use the game of bridge? The two partners receive hands dealt at random (the suites could represent chromosomes and the cards, genes) which are combined in play (the offspring) and in the ensuing competition, the partners having the best combination of cards are likely to win. The game combines cooperation and competition in a way that is much closer (though still overly-simple) to the realities of biological inheritance than is the Prisoners' Dilemma game. I suggest that those interested in game theory should try out some alternative game models.

With respect to generality, game theory obviously applies to human behavior in specified competitive games. Whether or not it can be usefully extended to other species is a matter of argument. Biological systems are so complex that it is unlikely that any one simple theory will explain all aspects of the organizations that have evolved. Axelrod and Hamilton's (1981) theory presents a theory of how cooperative behavior *might* have evolved but it does not eliminate or replace other theories. It is most satisfying to those persons who adhere to the idea that all evolution is the result of competition, ignoring the modern genetic theor/y of evolution. Selection is a modifying and directing process, but not a sole cause. Change is produced by the interaction of selection with the other three major categories of change processes.

Strategy, on the other hand, is a useful tool for describing and analyzing the ways in which a species adapts to its environment – physical, biological and social – ways that combine physiological and behavioral adjustment. These strategics interact with each other, and one could develop a theory of social organization based on strategic interaction. But without a knowledge of what strategies are actually available to a species, it is impossible to predict what will occur. To date, the strategic model has spawned more theories than data collection.

Finally, there is no obvious conflict between the strategic model and systems theory. Human strategies are born out of human verbal systems. But the evolutionary strategy modelers could improve their products by consideration of the biological systems in which they are expressed and in part produce. An important aspect is that of genetic systems. Again, the modelers could bring their product into agreement with gene combination theory.

The Moralistic Model

The use of the term "altruism", originally used to describe a culturally desirable sort of behavior, inevitably introduced other concepts derived from human morality codes into theoretical explanations of the evolution of behavior. Perhaps the ultimate extension of this line of thought was Dawkins' *The Selfish Gene* (1976). In the introduction to his book, he stated that it should be read as if it were science fiction, and indeed it should, for in it he has genes acting like little persons with alleles "competing to the death".

If there is anything that genetics has established, it is that genes do not exist as individuals, but only as parts of interdependent systems. Dawkins recognized this, but thought – metaphorically speaking – of genes as analogous to a group of rowers, each of whom adds something to a common purpose of driving the shell ahead. But a second principle of genetics is that interaction between gene loci is usually non-additive and that most if not all genes produce multiple effects. In short, the attribution of the human moral quality of selfishness to genes is an amusing metaphor, but only that.

Similar problems have bothered other evolutionary theorists; their basis is the assumption that all evolution is based on competition. This being the case, animals (and by extension humans) should do anything to win the game of inclusive fitness. And so it has been fashionable to look for nonhuman animal equivalents of murder, rape, incest, stealing, cheating, and even infanticide (Hrdy, 1977). When these are found, no matter how rarely or whether accompanied by social disorganization, they are used as verification of the original assumption.

Actually, the range of behavior in nonhuman animal societies is so great that one can find almost anything that one looks for. A few generations ago, Ernest Thompson Seton (1938) looked for evidence – and found it – that animals behave in accordance with the Ten Commandments of Moses. Today certain scientists as earnestly look for the equivalent of cultural deviations, and find them (Barash, 1982).

Apart from this, competition, in the sense of differential survival of offspring of one mating at the expense of offspring of another mating, seldom takes place in direct fashion in animal behavior. All that is necessary for differential survival is that one sort of animal, be it an individual, a pair, or a larger group, outreproduces another. The fact that one female may have a dozen offspring as opposed to one or two, does not necessarily inflict harm on the second.

Second, the evolution of social behavior takes place cooperatively as well as competitively. It is unnecessary to assume that cooperation must arise through inter-individual competition within a species, although it could arise through inter-species competition as numerous examples of cooperative behavior attest. As an example, the members of a gull colony will all rise in the air and attack an intruder, no matter whose nest is threatened. I have already described the cooperative behavior inherent in allelomimetic behavior. The evolution of cooperation and mutually beneficial behavior, a problem first set forth by Prince Kropotkin (1902) and broadly researched by Allee and his students (1951) has been too long neglected and is only now being brought back into focus (Corning, 1983).

The simplistic emphasis on competition as a sole evolutionary process leads to the conclusion that all individuals should act selfishly, either directly or indirectly involving their offspring, in direct contradiction to the highest principles of Judeo-Christian morality. This has been especially bothersome to Alexander (1971, 1979) and others who feel that all things should be consistent.

As I have pointed out above, this conclusion is based on an unsound, or at least incomplete theory of evolution, that of the single gene substitution hypothesis, combined with faulty observation which selectively singles out competitive behavior and neglects mutually beneficial and cooperative behavior.

Further, as Emerson (1942) and numerous others have pointed out, when humans evolved communication through verbal language, they largely escaped from biological controls. Language has a biological basis, the capacity to speak, and is subject to genetic variation in that capacity. Otherwise, any human can learn to speak any language in the world. Languages evolve and change and cultures evolve and change, but on entirely different bases from genetics. And so the world has seen a wide variety of cultures that justify and explain behaviors that are sometimes completely contradictory. There are human cultures that glorify war, others that glorify peace and some, like our own, that glorify both. Cultures can justify completely maladaptive (from a biological viewpoint) behavior, as did that of the Shakers who did not believe in sexual intercourse. Needless to say, this particular culture is on the verge of extinction.

Without explaining the process of cultural evolution, Campbell (1975) has suggested that cultural change should be subject to natural selection, in that cultures including systems of morality should survive if they promote the welfare of their members, and become extinct if they do not. This does not mean that the individuals within the culture must die; in most parts of the world large human populations survive indefinitely, but they may change from one religion to another and even from one language to another.

Therefore, it should surprise no one that evolutionary theories and ethical principles should conflict. Biological evolution and cultural evolution are almost completely independent phenomena. But I do suggest that the conflicts that have been most bothersome are based on faulty evolutionary science, namely, the tendency to overly extend and simplistically unify in a science whose basis is diversity.

Mathematical Models

The utility of mathematical models in the biological and social sciences lies in the fact that such a model can be considered as a symbolic experiment. Given certain hypothetical assumptions, their logical outcome can be predicted, often in a quantitative way that can be verified or denied in actual experiments. Any such model must, of course, be tested in a real experimental situation.

Mathematical models are particularly useful in explaining evolutionary change, precisely because they are the *only* form of experimentation that is available in most cases. To be employed most productively, two or more mathematical models should be compared, simulating a symbolic controlled experiment with two or more variables.

Mathematical Models for Systems Theories

The general technique for the analysis of function in a system is first to define the boundaries of the system, next to identify the entities within the system, and finally to study the interaction between the entities. The final step can be taken in at least two ways. One is to measure the interaction of each entity with every other entity in the system, and the other is to remove or inactivate each entity in the system one at a time and observe the effect on the functions of the system as a whole.

Applying mathematical models to these procedures calls for modification of the conventional statistical techniques which are usually based on probability theory. Simple probability theory is founded on two assumptions: 1) independence of the units in question, and 2) random or chance variation of these units. These assumptions obviously have great validity and importance in genetics, as in Mendel's principle of independent assortment. This was based on the behavior of chromosomes in mitosis and meiosis, where they do indeed exhibit random assortment with respect to other chromosomes.

But as soon as one considers genes on the same chromosome, or effects of a combination of interacting genes, the assumption of independence breaks down. In fact, one assumption that one must make in models of living systems are that the entities are never independent, but exhibit reciprocal causation. We need to develop new mathematical models where assumptions are consistent with various sorts of system organization. I shall make some attempt to do this in the next chapter.

In the meantime, any mathematical model that is based on the assumption of single genes, or single genes with additive effects, is bound to be limited in its applications, to major genes that have the same effects in any gene combination and are almost always injurious. Random probability theory still has usefulness as the null hypothesis, namely that the entities in a system are not organized with respect to each other, and any coincidence in function is purely random.

But I doubt that any single mathematical model will ever encompass the enormous complexity of living systems interaction on all its various levels. For this reason, I feel that verbal, non-quantitative models of evolution may be more useful in the long run. Words will describe the unmeasurable in ways that mathematics cannot, and the nature of verbal symbols permits greater complexity. For that matter, living systems are so complex that any symbolic system, verbal or mathematical or diagrammatic, can never be more than a close approximation of reality. I hope that the mathematicians will keep on trying, particularly in the area of developing mathematical models that explain basic systems phenomena such as two-way causation and feedback, even though they may never completely succeed.

SOCIOBIOLOGY AND EVOLUTIONARY THEORY

A major work of the 1970's was E. O. Wilson's (1975) *Sociobiology*. This is a remarkable and clearly written book and is a mine of information about social behavior in animals. From the subtitle,

"The New Synthesis", it is obvious that Wilson hoped that evolution would integrate the diverse facts of this field in the same way that Darwinian evolution integrated the diverse facts of comparative anatomy.

Wilson is not a geneticist, but he recognized the genetic basis of evolution and summarized its general processes, with one important omission, that of genetic systems and gene interaction. Thus he recognized, but did not use Wright's shifting balance theory. Like the *Origin of Species*, the word system does not even appear in the index of the book.

The second limitation was that, instead of looking at the phenomena of social behavior and social organization in various species of animals and postulating that their evolution might take different forms from that of organic evolution, Wilson attempted to use a relatively simplistic model of evolution and to fit all of the facts of social behavior and social organization into it. In short, his thinking was deductive rather than inductive.

A final limitation was that Wilson's thinking was mechanistic and reductionistic. This leads to the untenable conclusion that all social behavior and organization can be explained by genetics; this was the basis of most of the criticism that was directed against Wilson in the years following the publication of his book. This line of reasoning is often extended as follows: all behavior has been evolved under the influence of natural selection; therefore, all behavior must be adaptive. This provides, in human affairs, an excuse for morally inexcusable behavior. Similar thinking in the 19th century led to Social Darwinism: the idea that it was right to exploit and starve the poor and needy because this led to the survival of the fittest. Wilson himself disclaimed Social Darwinism – he is an enlightened man – but his line of reasoning almost inevitably leads to the conclusion that everything that exists is good; hence, there is no need for social change. Needless to say, I and many other persons do not agree.

Nor do I agree with Wilson's circumscription of sociobiology as an evolutionary science; i.e, a historical one. As I saw sociobiology in the late 1930's when I first became interested in the subject, sociobiology should be an integrated merging of biology with the social sciences, each making its own contribution, integration being achieved by overlapping concepts and principles derived from each. Evolution is not the only biological principle; I have emphasized in this volume the equally important concept of systems organization. And there are many other concepts besides. Furthermore, the social sciences can be experimental as well as historical and so introduce a higher level of scientific thought than is possible on a purely historical basis. Wilson's "new synthesis" was thus not a new synthesis but an old one.

Despite these criticisms, evolutionary sociobiology has had desirable results. It has awakened social scientists to perceiving that their sciences might be enriched by the contributions of biology, and it has encouraged animal behaviorists to look at animal societies in new ways and, motivated by evolutionary theory, to gather information that otherwise would not have been assembled.

At the same time, it has also generated a certain amount of confusion. The fact that humans *may* consciously do what is biologically adaptive does not prove that one is derived from the other. The essence of behavioral function is adaptation, but behavioral adaptation may take place in seconds as opposed to evolutionary adaptation that may take millennia. The animal that can behave adaptively (which means varying its behavior according to the situation in which it finds itself) has to that degree negated the effects of natural selection. In fact, the whole story of evolution is one of escape from natural selection.

CONCLUSIONS

Each of the evolutionary theories discussed above has its merits as well as its weaknesses. Many are flawed by a lack of appreciation of systems organization, the fact that genes are organized and function as parts of systems and that all biological phenomena that result from their activities are organized into interdependent and interactive systems on higher levels.

With the exception of Wilson, most authors have followed the early and over-simplistic lead of R. A. Fisher and based their ideas on the two-process theory of evolution. They do not even use the three-process theory, but consider sexual reproduction only as an outcome rather than an integral part of the overall evolutionary process. Finally, in common with almost all evolutionary theorists who have not consciously used the systems concept, they oversimplify the selection process in two ways, neglecting on the one hand gene combinations as the unit of selection, and the enormous complexity of the ecological variables that determine selection on the other. The concept of fitness does not represent a fixed quantity; if it has useful meaning at all it is as a mean for an entire population for a given unit of time.

While the two-process theory has a major application among the simplest organisms such as viruses, it has quite limited applications among species that develop complex behavior and social organization. Even the three-process theory, (mutation-sexual reproduction-differential survival) applies chiefly to the less complex marine organisms with simple behaviors and low levels of social organization. And it is precisely to the terrestrial species with complex behaviors and high degrees of social organization, among which all four evolutionary processes operate almost universally, that the above authors have attempted to apply the less elaborate theories.

A final criticism is that of over-generalization. Rather than striving for a theory that will fit all possible cases, evolutionary research of the future should recognize the fact that each species is evolving under a different set of conditions. This is particularly true of Differential Survival, but each of the other major evolutionary processes may also vary. Inbreeding may be very strong or completely absent; bisexual reproduction, though almost universal among the more complex organisms, may be absent. Even mutation rates vary among species, as might be expected with differential exposure to radiation and also as an outcome of mobile genetic elements.

The theorists of the future should recognize that each time a new mode of adaptation comes into being, the evolutionary process changes. Evolution in multicellular organisms has different outcomes from that in unicellular species. Similarly, the transition from physiological adaptation to behavioral adaptation and the resulting social organization creates new levels of systems organization and modifies evolutionary processes accordingly. Among other things, new feedback loops are created. Thus, the processes of evolution may themselves evolve.

Chapter IX

The Evolution of Cooperation and Competition

In terms of systems theory, the appearance of behavioral adaptation brought about a gross change in the nature of living systems and their evolution, producing what I have called the great behavioral divide (Figure 1.3). On one side, the nature of systems is primarily determined by anatomical structure and the resulting spatial relationships between entities making up physiological systems that interact within organismic systems.

On the other, behavior, defined as the activities of a whole organism, has introduced a new form of organization. Spatial relationships still have an effect, as when organisms become attached to a common site, and they regulate their distances from each other as part of social organization (McBride, 1964), but there are no longer any fixed directions or distances between the entities composing the system. Organization is there, but based on movement rather than structure.

In anatomical structural organization, competition is strictly limited because of the interdependence of the entities in the system; there is no way that entities can compete without mutual harm. But the emergence of behavior makes it possible to evolve social organization whose entities (the organisms) must cooperate; otherwise there would be no social organization, but their behavioral interaction makes it possible to compete also. And, as species have evolved more elaborate forms of social organization, they have also evolved a physiobehavioral system with the specialized function of competing and regulating competition, i.e., agonistic behavior. This is the heart of the evolutionary paradox discussed in Chapter 8. In order to resolve it we must consider the evolution of both cooperation and competition, starting with open minds and no prior assumptions. First, these are not bipolar opposites with fixed boundaries between them. Both cooperation and competition may occur in many different ways and on many different levels. They may overlap, and even serve a combined function, as when members of a hyena pack cooperate in order to compete with another pack. Second, there is no need to assume that one is derived from the other; that is only one of many possibilities that are not mutually exclusive.

THE EVOLUTION OF COOPERATION

The first workable theory of the evolution of cooperation was developed by the ecologist W. C. Allee (1951; Allee, Emerson, Park, O., Park, T. & Schmidt, 1949). He proposed that the study of animal societies should begin with a description of animal aggregations and the analysis of their functions. He and his students discovered and demonstrated many instances of animals that survived better in groups than singly; i.e., the environment provided by bodies of species mates was superior to the surrounding one. He called this the Theory of Unconscious Cooperation, and demonstrated its occurrence in dozens of cases from Protozoa to Mammals.

From this he predicted that in animal populations there should be a level at which survival would be poor, a higher level that is favorable to survival, and a still higher one which would be unfavorable to the individuals involved. It follows that one of the functions of social organization should be the regulation of numbers, or population control. This should be a fruitful field of research for those interested in optimalization. The discovery of how social organization affects numbers may provide an answer to the problem presented by Malthus (Wynne-Edwards, 1968).

Allee's theory is directly related to the physiobehavioral system of shelter-seeking. Given that animals seek out sheltering environments, they should come together to produce aggregations. These are not organized groups, however, and the associations so produced last only as long as the general environment remains unfavorable. But the association does provide an opportunity for the evolution of organization, and this may be one of the roots of social organization. Its function is obviously related to shelter-building. Animals frequently aggregate in sheltered spots for protection. Once a shelter is improved by digging or construction, it should attract others.

Another possibility is that coming together for mutual protection against biotic selection processes might lead to a more permanent association through allelomimetic behavior, in those animals that have the sensory and motor equipment to follow each other's movements. A further result is to produce a mobile group.

The unique feature of the Allee theory is that it is based not on the concept of an individual transforming itself into a social individual, but suggests the origin of sociality through behavior in populations. Thus it might be called a *population theory* of social evolution.

A second sort of aggregation observed by Allee was sexual aggregation. Many marine animals simply broadcast their germ cells into the water, as occurs in some of the marine annelids, their activities being coordinated through the moon and tides. But this is a very wasteful process, and would be completely impractical on land. Internal fertilization involving sexual behavior occurs in many marine animals and in such lowly organized forms as the flatworms. It is universal among highly organized phyla.

Even semi-solitary animals must come together for mating behavior, and the result is an association that may last for a few minutes or, in some animals, for life. In any case it provides an opportunity for the evolution of social organization. In particular, it could lead to the extension of epimeletic behavior to the care of eggs, offspring, relatives and eventually to non-relatives. (See Chapter VIII.) Therefore, one of the major roots of social organization is sexual reproduction.

Still another root is site attachment, a phenomenon that is universally found in the multicellular animals except for pelagic forms in the ocean. Some animals are literally attached, such as mussels on a wharf piling, and so cannot interact behaviorally, but if behavior is maintained, animals attached to neighboring sites must become neighbors and must interact, whether cooperating or competing, again providing the opportunity for the evolution of social organization.

None of the physiobehavioral systems will in themselves produce more than temporary associations. Long lasting social organization is therefore dependent upon social attachment, a process that has been extensively studied in birds as imprinting and in mammals as primary socialization, and is now being further studied as kin recognition (Chapter 8). Because of the great similarities of the process in such distantly related species such as chickens and dogs, I have suggested that social attachment has evolved out of a basic process of site attachment common to all vertebrates.

The above theories of the evolution of cooperative behavior have in common that they postulate the evolution of cooperative behavior from physiological function. In one case, that of sexual behavior, it is directly related to a physiological system; in others such as shelter-seeking, it is related to the physiology of the whole organism.

Stated broadly, the functional theory says that cooperative social organization facilitates physiological function and that it is successful to the degree to which this is produced. This in turn promotes survival and implies differential survival, or selection, on all levels: individual, group, social organization, and species.

This set of theories is compatible with the systems theory of evolution and indeed has its origin in part from the concept of systems. It is compatible with the four-process genetical theory of evolution and the theory of gene combinations, and is also compatible with the two-process and three-process theories. Finally, it is compatible with a major new theory of evolution of cooperation, Corning's (1983) Synergism Hypothesis. He postulates that combinatory processes on every level are a major source of change and direction in evolution.

Still another root of social organization is defensive behavior, primarily an adaptation to predation, where it is often cooperative, but extendable to conspecifics, thus providing the most likely hypothesis for the origin of agonistic behavior.

THE EVOLUTION OF COMPETITION

Of the eleven categories of behavior patterns listed in Table 7.1 only agonistic behavior is intrinsically competitive, but most of the others can become competitive indirectly. For example, ingestive behavior can become competitive when a group of animals devour a limited supply of food. Shelter-seeking can be competitive if animals attempt to crowd into a small and limited space, such as one produced by shelter-building. Sexual behavior leads to competition for mates. Even epimeletic behavior may produce competitive behavior between a parent and offspring under special conditions. Therefore, competition must have existed prior to the evolution of agonistic behavior but in a sporadic and unorganized fashion, as it does today in species that lack agonistic behavior.

Because competition may produce physical injury to the participants, one of the physiobehavioral systems is an obvious candidate for the origin of agonistic behavior. This is defensive behavior against predators, which is extensible to the prevention of injury by species mates.

Predation itself is not included in Table 7.1 as a social physiobehavioral system because it usually applies to interaction between species, but, because it always involves injury to the prey animal, it also is a possible precursor of agonistic behavior. It is less likely for two reasons (Lorenz, 1966). One is that agonistic behavior occurs in prey species such as mountain sheep that never hunt or eat other species. Another is that in predator species, the patterns of behavior and underlying physiological-motivational bases are distinctly different. Predators do not appear to be angry at their prey, destructive as they may be. Further, predation is a complex activity involving investigative behavior, pursuit, attack, killing, and finally ingestive behavior. While the evolution of agonistic behavior from predation may have occurred in some species, it is unlikely that this should have been a general event (Figure 9.1).

Table 9.1
DEFENSE AGAINST PREDATION (RELATIVE IMPORTANCE OF EACH PHENOMENON INDICATED BY NUMBER OF X'S)

Phylum	Anatomical Defenses (Armor)	Avoidance	Defensive Behavior Shelter-Building	Injury
Protozoa	X	XXX	–	–
Coelenterata	XX	XXX	–	XXX
Platyhelminthes	–	XXX	–	–
Nemathelminthes	XX	XXX	–	–
Annelida	–	XXX	X	X
Echinodermata	XXX	XXX	–	–
Mollusca	XXX	XXX	X	X
Arthropoda				
Crustacea	XX	XXX	XX	XX
Arachnida	X	XXX	XX	XX
Insecta	X	XXX	XXX	XX
Vertebrata				
Pisces	X	XXX	–	X
Amphibia	–	XXX	–	–
Reptilia	XX	XXX	–	XX
Aves	–	XXX	X	XX
Mammalia	X	XXX	X	XX

THE EVOLUTION OF DEFENSIVE BEHAVIOR

Physiological-Anatomical Defenses

Many species of animals have evolved protective coverings or armor. As shown in Table 9.1, all but two of the major phyla (excluding sponges, which have no behavior) include at least some armored species. Even among the Protozoa, the Heliozoa have protective siliceous shells, and among Coelenterata (Cnidaria), the class Anthozoa includes the corals that secrete massive limestone skeletons.

Among the worms, neither the flatworms or annelid worms have external protective skeletons, but the roundworms are covered with a heavy but flexible body covering that is highly resistent to injury whether by force or chemical contact.

As their name implies, most of the Echinoderms have spiny external skeletons, although a few like the sea cucumber have lost these. But it is in the Mollusca that we see the most extensive development of external armor. All the Molluscs have shells, at least in rudimentary form, and those of the Bivalves such as clams can be extraordinarily massive.

All Arthropods have external skeletons. The most massive ones are found among Crustacea such as the lobsters and crabs. In any of these organisms the external skeleton carries the disadvantage that, in order to grow, the animal must molt and so discard its armor temporarily, leaving it vulnerable and unprotected for at least a short time.

Among Arachnids and Insects, the other two major classes of Arthropods, almost all species are either terrestrial or aerial. Correlated with this, the external skeletons are relatively light and thin. Among Insects, only those in the order Coleoptera, or beetles, have heavy external shells, and these insects are among the poorest flyers. Exceptions among the Arachnids are the scorpions which have moderately heavy protective skeletons.

Finally, among vertebrates, whose skeletons are internal, external armor is relatively rare. In some fishes such as the Ganoids, the scales are developed into bony plates, but the modern forms of armored fishes are quite rare.

Present day Amphibia have no armor, nor do birds, whose adaptations for flight would prohibit it. Certain aquatic reptiles, particularly the Chelonia, or turtles, possess heavy bony shells, and some of them have ventured out onto land (the tortoises). Alligators and crocodiles have leathery armor, but again, live largely in water. Most of the land living reptiles, such as the snakes and lizards, are either unarmored or lightly so.

Among mammals, external armor is quite rare, but there are a few exceptions. Armadillos have external shells, porcupines have quills, and elephants and rhinoceroses have evolved an extremely heavy skin which serves as flexible armor for these large and relatively slow moving animals. Thus in our own class, armor has been sacrificed for mobility, which means that behavior must take the place of armor in the function of defense.

External Armor, Ecology and Behavior

The lighter the armor the more mobility is facilitated. This is particularly true of animals that fly. In flying insects, flying birds and flying mammals armor is reduced or absent. Skeletons, whether internal or external are as light as possible, particularly in insects, the major group of flying invertebrates. Since their external skeletons increase in size and weight in proportion to the surface of their bodies, insects have been successful competitors only in the smaller size ranges. An insect that is eight cm long is a giant among these animals.

Terrestrial animals can afford to carry more weight, and we do find exceptional species with heavy armor, but it is among aquatic animals, particularly those that live in the ocean, that we see the greatest development of shells, whose weight is largely borne by the water. Even here, there is an inverse correlation between heaviness of armor and activity. One would also expect an inverse correlation between armor and agressivity, since an animal that is well defended by armor has little need for defensive behavior, nor does its heavy weight allow much behavior. Thus we would expect to find decreased aggressivity among heavily armored animals, and this is indeed the case. There is nothing more peaceful than a mollusc with a heavy shell. In contrast, many groups of animals have specialized in the evolution of behavioral adaptation.

Avoidance or Retreat

This is one of the two most primitive universal kinds of behavior. Any animal capable of movement has the capacity to move out of an area which is noxious, dangerous, poisonous, or unpleasant, and to find, through investigative or exploratory behavior, a place that is more favorable to continued existence. Avoidance behavior certainly exists in every animal phylum (except sponges, which are like plants in that they do not move) and likewise in every species that is capable of movement. As indicated in Table 9.1, its importance is universal.

Avoidance behavior thus has a far older evolutionary history than does attack behavior and is by implication more fundamental and basic.

Shelter-Building and Digging

Closely related to avoidance behavior is that of building or digging a shelter into which an animal can retreat when threatened with injury. Such behavior requires considerable manipulative ability, and we first find examples among the annelid worms, many of which dig holes, as does the familiar earthworm, and some of which like certain marine worms, strengthen the walls of their burrows with body secretions. Among Molluscs, the octopus finds a cleft in the rocks and makes it into a more effective shelter by piling small stones around the entrance. And, of course, the common clams dig into the sand and mud for concealment and protection.

But it is among Arthropods that this behavior reaches its height. The Decapod Crustaceans include the fiddler crabs that regularly construct burrows, as do crayfish. Among Arachnids, the spiders use their capacity for spinning filaments not only to construct webs for catching insect prey, but also for building elaborate nests, of which those of the purse-web spiders are most elaborate. *Atypus abboti* digs a deep burrow in the damp ground of a swamp, lines it with silk, and extends it up to 25 cm on the side of a tree, with an entrance that can be opened and closed like a purse.

Among insects, the construction of burrows and nests is extremely common. The tropical termites build enormous mounds out of earth glued together with a cement-like secretion. The papernest wasps similarly build large nests of plant fibers glued together in elaborate designs. The fine manipulative skills of these animals greatly exceeds anything that is possible for vertebrates, with the possible exception of some birds like the oriole, that weave fibers into nests. Some birds even dig holes, as do the bank swallows. But for the most part, bird constructions are used for protection and rearing of young rather than places into which the builders can retreat.

Among mammals, the dams, lodges and burrows of beavers are impressive in size, but crude in form compared to the constructions of insects. Many other rodents, small herbivorous animals for the most part, are diggers of burrows, and some of their constructions are quite elaborate, consisting of tunnels many meters long and connecting with lined living chambers. But the larger forms of mammals chiefly rely on escape behavior rather than digging or building shelters, and among primates it is only man who is a builder and digger.

Injury

Finally, there is the defensive behavior of injury or threat of injury. In Table 9.1, I have estimated the relative importance of this and other behaviors by rating each group with Xs from 0 to 3. Surprisingly, it is not highly organized animals that excel in this behavior, but the Coelenterates. The stinging cells on the tentacles of these creatures are one of the most effective repellent devices ever evolved, and Coelenterates are still one of the most successful of all animal groups, although far from highly organized in their anatomy and physiology.

Some Annelid worms have biting mouth parts, and the Cephalopod molluscs can resist a predator with tentacles and beak. Among Arthropods, some crustaceans such as lobsters can resist attack with their biting claws. Spiders have fangs, and some secrete poisonous substances, and scorpions have a poisonous sting. Among insects, it is chiefly the Hymenopteran social insects who resist attack with an injury. Many species of ants have workers who bite and pinch with their mouth parts, and some bees and wasps have the female genitalia of the workers modified into poisonous stings.

Among Vertebrates, most fish species depend on escape rather than threat, although some can deliver severe bites, and others have evolved sharp and even poisonous spines that can be raised defensively and produce serious injuries. The behavior of the puffer fish is a remarkable example. When threatened, this fish inflates itself with air and becomes a floating ball with spines pointing in every direction.

Modern Amphibia, without teeth, claws, or armor, can threaten little injury to attackers, although some toads secrete poisonous substances. Reptiles, on the other hand, resist attack with a variety of injurious behaviors: the threshing tail and bites of alligators, and the poisonous fangs of some snakes and lizards.

Among terrestrial mammals, defensive threat behavior is common, ranging from the bite of the cornered rat to the lowered head and horns of musk oxen, and the kicking of horses and zebras.

In order to injure a potential attacker, an animal must have the ability to actively inflict injury. Such capacities have evolved in many directions. Some simply employ the means by which an animal makes its living: stinging cells on the tentacles of the Coelenterates, which are also used to kill prey, and teeth and claws of the carnivorous mammals. Some species have evolved injurious behaviors useful only in defense, and along with these the capacity for chemical as well as physical injury, as in the stings of bees. But defensive behavior, especially that of avoidance, is found even more widely in the animal kingdom. What then is the relationship of these general defensive behaviors to social defense and attack?

THE EVOLUTION OF FUNCTION IN AGONISTIC BEHAVIOR

Occurrence

Table 9.2 lists the occurrence of agonistic behavior in the major groups of present-day animals. New instances are constantly coming to light as the behavior of more and more species is studied, and the known distribution should become wider. Until Francis (1973 a, b) reported the occurrence of agonistic behavior between members of certain species of sea anemones, it was unknown in Coelenterates. Sea anemones reproduce by fission, as well as sexually, and the result of repeated fission is a clone of genetically identical individuals. Members of a clone never attack each other, but if two clones come into contact, combat may ensue. These particular species have special organs (acrorhagi) loaded heavily with nematocysts, or stinging cells. When brought into contact with another anemone of a different clone, these organs break off and adhere to the body of the other animal, discharging nematocysts. If the attack is to heavy, the attacked animal may disintegrate and die, or if only slightly injured, it may move away. Since both clones are equally well-equipped with these injurious organs and since sea anemones have no defense against such injury except avoidance, the result of this behavior is to keep clones separated. Similar behavior has been described in another species by Kaplan (1982), who reports that in *Metridium senile*, males do not attack females of different clones, and vice-versa. Such behavior would facilitate out-breeding.

Another instance of the occurrence of agonistic behavior among relatively primitive groups is that of the behavior of the Polychaete annelid worm, *Neanthes caudatum* (Reish, 1957). A male *Neanthes* will build a U-shaped tube in the sea floor. If another male attempts to enter, it is driven off, but a female is allowed to come in, mate, and deposit her eggs. Afterwards, she is ejected and the resident male guards against all future comers.

Among molluscs, which are generally peaceful animals, it is only among octopuses that social fighting has been described, chiefly that of females defending a nest containing developing young, although a male in captivity will attack and sometimes kill another smaller male of the same species (Wells, 1978).

Table 9.2

AGONISTIC BEHAVIOR IN THE ANIMAL KINGDOM
(RELATIVE IMPORTANCE INDICATED BY NUMBER OF X'S)

Phylum	Occurrence	Examples
Protozoa	–	–
Coelenterata (Cnidaria)	X	sea anemone
Platyhelminthes	–	–
Nemathelminthes	–	–
Annelida	X	*Neanthes*
Echinodermata	–	–
Mollusca	X	*Octopus*
Arthropoda		
Crustacea	XX	crabs, crayfish
Arachnida	X	spiders
Insecta	X	dragonflies, bees
Vertebrata		
Pisces	XXX	many (not all) species
Amphibia	X	bullfrog
Reptilia	XX	lizards
Aves	XXX	most avian species
Mammalia	XXX	most if not all species

Among crustaceans, instances of agonistic behavior are found in scattered species. Of particular interest is the behavior of the fiddler crab (Crane, 1975). The males of these species dig burrows and defend them against other males, but will try to entice females into them where mating can take place in seclusion, presumably protected against the attacks of predators. Also, if a male is threatened by a predator, he may rush down the nearest hole. The owner eventually attacks and ejects him, but this usually happens after the predator has departed. Fighting is relatively harmless to both parties and has the function of regulating space and protecting mating.

Agonistic behavior occurs relatively rarely among spiders. Most spider species are solitary hunters, and if agonistic behavior occurs, it has the function of keeping them apart. In some cases, such spiders seem to react as if the strange animal is a prey species. But among the most highly social of all spiders, *Stegodyphus sarasinorum* of Afghanistan whose members build enormous communal webs and make group attacks on prey, agonistic behavior does not occur, even between strangers (Kullman, Nawabi, & Zimmermann, 1971-72).

Again, in insects, agonistic behavior only occurs sporadically. In certain species of dragon flies (Campanella & Wolf, 1974), the males patrol temporary territories in which mating takes place. The result is to keep the males spread out so that any female is likely to come in contact with one. Among the highly social honey bees, workers still attack any non-colony bee that attempts to enter the hive. Within the hive itself the only agonistic behavior is that between rival young reproductive females who attack and kill each other, with the result that there is only one queen or reproductive female in the hive.

But it is among vertebrates that social fighting reaches its zenith. Many but not all species of fish show agonistic behavior. In nest building species such as the sticklebacks and sunfishes, a male will guard a nest against another male, but admit females who mate and deposit their eggs. Subsequently, the male guards the eggs until hatching and sometimes guards the young for a short time thereafter.

Amphibians are relatively peaceful animals, but fighting among the males has been described in several species of frogs, particularly the bullfrog (Howard, 1978) and green frog. A male will attempt to drive other males away from the area that he occupies. He then attracts females by his vocalization, the pair mates, and the female deposits her eggs in the area.

Like amphibians, reptiles are remnants of a once dominant life form. The most highly social and also those that show the most agonistic behavior are the lizards. The fights that occur are largely a matter of signals and threats and seldom result in serious injuries.

It was among birds that the first scientific studies of agonistic behavior were made. The pioneer studies of Schjelderup-Ebbe (1922) on the peck order in chickens were contemporary with the work of Elliot Howard (1920) on song and territoriality. Almost all bird species show some form of agonistic behavior and in most of them it is related to territoriality. Being primarily adapted to locomotion by flying, birds tend to develop visual and auditory senses and signals to the exclusion of those signals that are detected by olfaction. And so most of the signalling that goes on among fighting birds is visually oriented or vocal. Little of it is fatal, or even produces serious injuries. It is only when birds are especially bred for fighting and equipped with man-made, lethal weapons, as in the sport of cock fighting, that they inflict fatal injuries.

In many bird species, agonistic behavior is seasonal, occurring only during the process of reproduction when territories are maintained. Fighting is most severe among the ground living chicken-like birds, or Galliformes, which employ flight chiefly for escape. Male birds compete for small territories on a lek, or breeding ground. Among grouse species, the seriousness of fighting is inversely related to the complexity of organization on the lek (J. W. Scott, 1950).

The chief function of agonistic behavior in birds is thus the regulation of use of space through the establishment of territories. This in turn regulates the use of space to rear the young and indirectly the population level (Wynne-Edwards, 1968). In lek systems, it also regulates access to females, but there is no competition for particular females as may occur in ducks.

Agonistic behavior in mammals has been thoroughly studied in only a few species, but has been widely observed. It probably exists in all mammalian species, but in those that have been studied extensively it occurs in a great variety of contexts and functions.

In the great majority of reported cases, there is a differentiation of function between males and females, males being larger and tending to be more aggressive. There are two interesting exceptions. One is the golden hamster, a semi-solitary rodent that hoards food under natural conditions. Females are larger than males and occasionally kill them if caged together (Kislak & Beach, 1955).

Even more exceptional is the spotted hyena (Kruuk, 1972). These animals live in large packs and cooperatively hunt large animals such as zebras, as well as being scavengers. All adult females are larger than males and are dominant over all males in the pack. There is relatively little agonistic behavior within a pack, involving mild contests over food, females with young chasing males away from a den, and groups of males combining to "bait" or tease a single female. The principal function of agonistic behavior is territorial defense. Hyenas mark boundaries and, if members of one clan cross such a boundary, they may be severely attacked and sometimes killed.

I shall now describe two widely different mammals whose agonistic behavior has been intensely studied in both captive and semi-wild conditions. The first is the house mouse, available as a laboratory animal in a variety of inbred strains and genetic stocks and also living in wild or semi-wild conditions in many parts of the world as a facultative parasite on man. Ecologically, it is a prey animal, but itself is omnivorous and may prey on insects when available. It is nocturnal in habit, and digs holes and builds nests for shelter. Physiologically and anatomically, it is a small mammal, short lived (two years is old for a mouse), a rapid developer (about 80 days from egg to sexual maturity), and a rapid reproducer, with large litters sometimes born as little as 21 days apart. The two sexes are very similar in size and appearance. All these features contribute to a strategic analysis.

Its agonistic behavior has been more thoroughly studied than that of any other mammal over a period of some 60 years, beginning with Uhrich's (1938) paper, and continuing with hundreds of subsequent reports. Currently, it has been proposed as a model for the study of social evolution (Brain & Parmigiani, 1988).

In the usual procedure for studying agonistic behavior in male mice, a single male is placed in a cage for at least 24 hours and allowed to thoroughly explore it. If another strange male is then introduced, the resident will attack in the majority of cases, and a fight ensues. Females so treated and exposed to strange females fight much less frequently, not fighting at all in many laboratory strains. In wild strains, males fight almost 100% of the time, and about 25% of females will fight in the same pattern (Ebert, 1983). Mice therefore follow the usual mammalian pattern of increased aggressiveness in males, and this is related to the presence or absence of the male hormone.

The sex difference is of course a genetic one. In addition, strain differences in the amount of fighting have been repeatedly demonstrated (Maxson, 1981) some of which are related to the Y-chromosome (Maxson, Ginsburg, & Trattner, 1979).

Characteristic patterns of agonistic behavior appear in the above sort of fighting. Tail rattling and hair fluffing may appear prior to an attack. A male may also approach and show rough grooming, biting and pulling the hair. In the attack, a male runs toward the other and bites, usually on the back or rump. In response, the attacked male may (1) fight back, biting the attacker in the same way; these two animals then roll over and over in a ball, biting and scratching; (2) if badly hurt, one of the participants may run away with the other mouse in pursuit; (3) if unable to escape, it may assume a defensive posture, standing on its hind legs with fore legs outstretched, and squeaking when approached; and (4) if caught in a corner it may crouch passively. Wild females, if they fight, will employ the same patterns of behavior. The adaptive strategy in an inexperienced animal (to use Maynard Smith's term) is to try out these patterns in rotation. Experience has a strong effect. A mouse that has previously won several encounters will attack immediately, with no preliminary behavior, and a mouse that has lost will not attack, but employ whatever pattern of behavior has been effective in the past.

Analyzing similar behavior in male rats, Blanchard and Blanchard (1977) found that bites are always directed away from parts of the body where crippling or fatal wounds could be inflicted, and directed toward the back or rump where most wounds are painful but not fatal. This supports Lorenz' (1966) theory that agonistic behavior should evolve in ways that are effective but not destructive. Females defending a nest, on the other hand, show a different pattern, with bites directed at the nose and face. Similar analyses of mouse fighting lead to the same conclusion.

However, if one leaves two fighting mice together in the same small cage, within 24 hours one may be dead and sometimes cannibalized. How then to explain the occurrence of destructive behavior? An obvious answer is that in a free situation, a beaten mouse would escape and survive. Looked at more generally, the experimenter, by bringing two strange mice together, has removed them from whatever socially organized group of which they have been a part, and produced a disorganized group. I have suggested that social disorganization is a major cause of destructive agonistic behavior (Scott, 1975).

What do mice fight about? The obvious effect, given freedom of movement, is to increase the space between two individuals. Given sufficient space, male mice may mark and defend small territories within which one or more mated females may live. The fighting between strange females should also serve to maintain possession of an area.

But mice do not fight over females per se, although this may result indirectly. Nor do they fight over food; their food is seldom in a form that permits exclusive possession. In my efforts to discover a method of inducing fighting in 100% of males, I found one thing that always worked; an attack by another mouse, involving biting and hence painful stimulation. The function is defense against injury.

With respect to the reciprocal effects of agonistic behavior and social organization, mice are unable to develop dominance-subordination relationships which reduce fighting to symbolic forms. If unable to move apart, a group of male mice soon develops one winner, the rest being losers, always bearing fresh scars.

Nor are mice capable of developing fixed territorial organization as do many birds. In a well populated area they may develop small discrete territories, but not in areas where wide ranging is necessary to find food. As Bronson (1979) puts it, house mice are an ecologically (and I would add, socially) opportunistic species.

A second species whose agonistic behavior has been thoroughly studied is the domestic dog (Scott & Fuller, 1965) together with its wild ancestor, the wolf *Canis lupus* (For a sample of general publications, see Banks, Pimlott & Ginsburg 1967; Klinghammer, 1979; Mech, 1966; Murie, 1944). Ecologically, wolves are primarily pack hunting predators of the large herd animals in arctic and temperate regions of Eurasia and North America, but will also hunt mammals as small as mice, and birds on the ground. They will also scavenge on dead carcasses and occasionally eat some vegetable food such as berries. Hunting is cooperative, its precise form depending on the prey species. In general, the pack attempts to corner or surround an animal such as a moose so that it cannot escape, then attacks simultaneously from the rear and front, attempting to avoid the striking front hoofs that are the chief defense of the moose.

Agonistic behavior takes very different forms from the above. Its basic elements appear in contests over bones in young puppies. Each animal attempts to seize the other by the hair and skin over the shoulders and force it to the ground. Note that, like the mice, the vulnerable feet and belly are not attacked but rather an area of thick skin covered with long hair. Adult wolves show a more elaborate version of the behavior, with the winning wolf taking the snout of the other in its jaws, but not biting.

On the basis of such contests, dominance-subordination relationships are developed in which fighting is reduced to an elaborate system of signals. The dominant animal may growl and snap. If standing, its tail is always erect, while that of the subordinate one is down, usually with head and ears also down, always alert and ready to retreat if threatened. Many variations on these basic patterns are possible, but all result in a reduction of agonistic behavior to non-harmful forms.

What do dogs and wolves fight about? Primarily for the possession of food. Giving two puppies one bone small enough to be carried will almost inevitably provoke agonistic behavior. I have observed puppies as young as two weeks of age, with eyes barely open, growling when presented with a fresh bone. In a wild wolf pack, similar behavior gives prior access to certain parts of a carcass.

Both dogs and wolves mark with urine and feces, and attempt to defend the areas so marked. But since a wild wolf pack may have a hunting range of 85 km, constant defense is impractical except for a small area around the den. Packs usually respect marked boundaries, but if shortage of food forces invasion of a neighboring territory, serious fighting and even death may result (Mech, 1977).

Males are larger than females in both dogs and wolves. Males are usually dominant, but not always. Females dominate their own pups, for example. In Ginsburg's (personal communication) captive wolf pack, a female was dominant for several years. Females and males have separate dominance orders in a wolf pack. One would expect that the most dominant male would do all the mating, but this is not always the case, at least in captive groups. Mating is primarily regulated by the females. The most dominant female prevents the more subordinate ones from mating by driving them away from the male. The result is that there is seldom more than one litter born in a pack in a given year. All members of the pack, both males and females, act as helpers in bringing food to the den and vomiting food for the pups. In this case it is the offspring of the dominant female whose survival is favored. She is inevitably replaced by a younger female as the composition of the pack changes, but the replacement is more likely to be one of her own offspring rather than that of others. This results in both control of numbers and increased survival rates. Wolves can multiply rapidly, however, if the food supply is increased and the territory sizes are reduced (Fritts & Mech, 1981).

Wolves are also capable of forming alliances, usually on the basis of litter relationships. These can serve either as a protection for subordinate animals, or as a basis for a revolt against a dominant one.

In contrast to mice, wolves are relatively long-lived animals and live in long-lasting, close, social groups. They are capable of reducing agonistic behavior to symbolic and relatively harmless forms in highly elaborate dominance-subordination relationships; otherwise living in groups would be impossible.

Agonistic behavior takes still other forms in herbivorous mammals. In the mountain sheep, one of the species on which wolves prey, agonistic behavior chiefly regulates sexual behavior, and is rarely seen outside the mating season. A male with larger horns has a better chance to mate, but this is only a greater probability (Geist, 1971; Mills, 1937). The result in this species is to favor individuals with large horns, hence older ones, and hence to favor longevity. The horns themselves involve a large energy cost, both to produce the bone and to carry it around for several years. They are little help against predators; the chief defense of this species is flight, especially to rocky cliffs where wolves cannot follow.

Outside the mating season, males live in separate flocks with no fighting. But there is some evidence of dominance organization, as when a large horned male may occupy a higher spot when bedding down.

Sheep do not fight over food. Sheep migrate, usually between familiar areas, and so show site attachment, but they do not defend territories. Domestic goats, when grazing or browsing, defend a small area on either side of themselves that can be called a "mobile territory," although it is actually a space and has nothing to do with land. Hungry goats can also be induced to contest for food placed on a small board, and so demonstrate the existence of dominance orders (Scott & Stewart, 1947).

Finally, agonistic behavior among primate species has been more completely surveyed than in any other mammalian order, chiefly under natural conditions, but more intensively in a few captive species (Walters & Seyfarth, 1986). The unique feature of primate evolution is the specialization of the limbs for manipulation, particularly the fore-limbs, and this has an effect on agonistic behavior. Actual fighting in most species is very similar, consisting of hitting, grappling, holding down, and biting. The potential severity of biting varies widely in different species, some having evolved massive jaws as in the dog-like baboons, or in chimpanzees. In others such as squirrel monkeys or humans the jaws are relatively weak, but they all can be used to bite species mates.

Like birds, primates have well-developed visual and auditory senses, and like them they have evolved a variety of visual and auditory signals in connection with agonistic behavior. This means that they can interact over some distance as well as in close contacts. For example, the howler monkeys of Central America maintain distance between troops through calling.

Except for the nocturnal lorises, tarsiers and bush babies that are usually solitary foragers, primates live in long-lasting groups ranging in size from a mated pair plus offspring among gibbons to troops of 40-50 animals in the ground living baboons and rhesus monkeys. Mating systems vary from monogamy in the mated pairs through polygyny in single male troops such as langur monkeys, to polygamy in the multimale groups of rhesus monkeys.

Primates show wide variation in sexual dimorphism, ranging from near equality in gibbons to males that are 2-3 times as large as females in some baboons. This specialization seems to be associated more with the function of defense against predators, to which the ground living primates are particularly vulnerable, than with social function. Smuts (1986) critically reviewed the evidence for male-female differences in agonistic behavior, and found that

while males wound each other more often than females, there are
no overall differences in the amount of aggressive behavior exhibited, nor do there appear to be sex differences in the form of agonistic behavior, such as occurs in mice and dogs. Males and
females fight in different contexts and for apparently different
goals, however.

Apart from sex differences, intraspecies genetic variation in agonistic behavior has been little studied in non-human primates
because of the obvious difficulties of accumulating large populations and conducting breeding experiments with long-lived animals. Interspecies differences, on the other hand, have been widely
studied and show much variation and presumably have a genetic
basis. The new molecular-genetics techniques have so far been
applied chiefly to evolutionary relationships between species, but
may eventually be used to analyze intraspecies variation in
behavior.

As might be expected in long-lived animals living in groups, primates are capable of developing dominance-subordination relationships and exhibit an unusual variety and complexity of them.
Alliances are common, and both males and females exhibit such
relationships. In the multimale groups of macaques, the offspring
of females having high dominance ranks tend to assume similar
ranks in their respective hierarchies as adults. In some species,
males clearly dominate females, but through alliances females can
overcome any single male.

What do primates fight about? The primary effect of agonistic
behavior is to increase spatial distance between contestants. This
is not always obvious within troops whose members remain in
close contact, but is clear in the maintenance of distance between
troops. Site and social attachment are universal. In wide-ranging
species the areas occupied often overlap without the precise
boundaries that are found in birds, but species with small ranges
may guard territorial boundaries.

Male contests for breeding females are widespread among primates. For example, each hamadryas baboon male in a troop
attempts to round up and guard a small group of females, attacking other males, but also punishing females that stray. In other species with multimale groups, females often choose a mate, but do
not contest for one. Contests for the possession of food depend on
its type and distribution. Frugivorous and arboreal species rarely

fight over food, but this does occur in ground-feeding forms such as rhesus macaques, whose members may fight over food or not, depending on its distribution. If concentrated, fights occur, but if widely scattered, fighting over food is rare. Agonistic behavior among primates may have some effect on population growth in areas where food supplies are abundant and population levels are high, but such control is produced by breakdown of social organization rather than by organization itself. Limits to population growth appear to be mainly ecological (Dunbar, 1986).

Primate societies as described in a recent landmark volume (Smuts, Cheney, Seyfarth, Wrangham, & Struhsaker, 1986) are impressive both because of their diversity and complexity. At the same time, because most non-human primates are adapted to specialized ecosystems and are marginally successful with respect to numbers, there has been relatively little study of within-species diversity.

As many species have now been studied throughout the lifetimes of both the animals and their investigators, the great potential complexity and flexibility of primate social organization has been revealed. Many authorities find the evolutionary concept of strategies useful, but not that of stable strategies. That is, non-human primates have evolved capabilities for labile behavior modified by experience, and so are able to use strategies in ways that are similar to those employed by humans.

TRANSFORMATION OF FUNCTION

The principal theory that arises out of these comparative studies is that of transformation of function. It has the advantage that, because it requires no drastic reorganization of behavior, it is consistent with systems theory which states that one of the determinants of the direction of biological evolution is the organization of the pre-existing systems.

The theory predicts that closely similar patterns of behavior having different functions should be found in the same species. For example, in the house mouse, one of the defensive patterns against predators is flight, and a beaten mouse likewise flees from a conspecific attacker. Another anti-predation pattern is the response to pain. Even an infant mouse will turn and attempt to bite your finger if you pinch its tail, and it is easy to see how this could be transformed in function to an agonistic attack. The pattern of biting directed at the back and rump could have evolved from the fact that these are exposed parts of a fleeing mouse, plus selection against survival of strains of mice that attack the more vital parts. (Agonistic behavior always involves at least two individuals.) Evolution of the defense posture is not so obvious, but even it is a combination of motor patterns that are common in the mouse: standing on the hind legs, holding out the fore paws, and squeaking with pain.

Similar examples could be culled from any of the above described species. This does not exclude the possibility that agonistic behavior could have been derived from predation. The arguments against it are that predation against one's own species would definitely be harmful to the survival of the species, that the physiological and motivational bases of predation and agonistic behavior show no overlap in existing species, and that strictly herbivorous mammals such as the bighorn sheep have nevertheless evolved elaborate patterns of agonistic behavior. Both flight and butting in sheep could have evolved from defensive behavior. The case of the sea anemone is less clearcut. The acrorhagi are obviously tentacles, but tentacles are used both for defense and catching the small organisms on which the animals live.

Figure 9.1 illustrates the various evolutionary pathways through which the function of agonistic behavior has probably been transformed. These are not the only pathways, and not all of them will occur within a single species, with the possible exception of humans.

The concept of transformation of function is obviously related to that of ritualization, a transformation of a behavior pattern into a signal or symbol that may be unrelated to the original function. (See Chapter 7.) Both dominance-subordination and territorial defense involve ritualization, with the difference that the ritualization is not an evolutionary process per se but a developmental one that must be repeated in each generation. What is evolved is the *capacity* to develop these forms of organization. As shown above, dominance organization evolves in animal societies that live in close and stable social groups; without it group living is incompatible with agonistic behavior.

An outcome of transformation of function is that agonistic

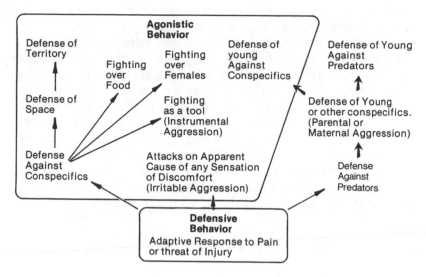

Figure 9.1. Transformation of Functions of Agonistic Behavior. This illustrates the chief pathways through which the functions of agonistic behavior could have been evolved into the various sorts of agonistic behavior described by Moyer (1971) and others: (1) Defense of self against predators should be transformed or extended to defense of offspring, and this extended to defense against conspecifics. (2) Defensive behavior can be transformed into attacks on the conspecifics whose presence is associated with feelings of discomfort, whether or not they are the actual causes of these sensations (irritable aggression), a condition that often occurs among humans. (3) Defensive behavior is extendable to conspecifics that injure or threaten injury, and this can be transformed into defense of space and defense of territories. (4) Conspecific defense can be transformed into fighting over food, contests for the possession of females and, ultimately, fighting as a tool to obtain a variety of results (instrumental aggression). (From Scott, 1975)

behavior can evolve different functions in different species. Even the above brief survey brings out the wide variety of functions that species in the same taxonomic category can show. Once a species has split off from another and genes are no longer exchanged, evolution goes on completely independently, except for the nature of the ancestral genetic system.

Nevertheless, there are some agonistic functions that commonly occur. The most basic is the regulation of the use of space and of the distance between organisms; the simplest function of an agonistic attack is to drive another organism away. This function actually occurs by itself in some semi-solitary mammals such as the woodchuck, which are always spaced out from each other except briefly during mating and rearing of young by a female.

From this other agonistic functions can arise, as in Figure 9.1. In many cases, as Wynne-Edwards (1968) pointed out, agonistic behavior will have an effect of controlling population size and density. If there are only so many breeding territories of a uniform size, the number of young birds produced in these will be limited. A fundamental question in the study of an animal society is how population levels are controlled. Many prey species, such as deer have no limit except factors in the ecosystem such as food availability or predation. On the other hand, most predators, such as wolves, and including birds that feed on insects during their reproductive season, have some form of population regulation.

AGONISTIC BEHAVIOR AND SOCIAL ORGANIZATION

Social Relationships

The basic unit of social organization is the social relationship, defined as regular and predictable behavior between two or more individuals belonging to the same species. The simplest relationship is a dyadic one, which may be regarded as a miniature social system having all the fundamental characteristics of such systems. Actually, such dyadic relationships are usually parts of larger systems or may be subsystems within them.

With respect to agonistic behavior, an unorganized dyadic contact that evoked agonistic behavior – it could not be called a relationship – would occur if an animal attacked every similar animal that it met, and such behavior would result in the widest possible distribution of individuals as they attacked and retreated from each other. Also, such generalized agonistic behavior would render sexual behavior impossible. Such cases of unorganized agonistic behavior are quite rare, if they occur at all.

Caste Organization

In such cases, agonistic behavior is directed against one whole class of individuals and is not directed against another class or classes. Examples are the honey bees and other Hymenopteran social insects, whose workers will not attack colony members, but do attack bees from other colonies. Discrimination is based on colony odor, which is different in each colony.

Dominance-Subordination

In most cases, if not all of the vertebrate species that exhibit it, agonistic behavior is organized on the basis of inter-individual recognition, although there may be some caste organization as well, as when no agonistic behavior is directed by males toward females, or by adults toward the young.

In contrast to caste organization, agonistic relationships between individuals are based on interaction and subsequent organization through learning. The result is a dominance-subordination relationship, in which one animal, the dominant one, expresses attack or threat, and the other expresses avoidance or defensive behavior. It is characteristic of such relationships that the amount and severity of agonistic behavior becomes greatly reduced as the relationship is developed. The dominant animal may only have to look at a subordinate in order to cause it to retreat.

It is also characteristic of such relationships that they occur in species that live in groups or have continuous contact. Solitary and semi-solitary animals such as raccoons lack the capacity to develop dominance, as is also the case in house mice.

Functions of Dominance-Subordination Relationships

Dominance gives the dominant animal priority. Among non-human animals, that have no language to explain what they want, such priorities are limited. The most fundamental priority is that relating to space, and McBride (1964) has analyzed such organization in societies of feral fowl and other species.

Dominance can regulate either the distance separating animals, as it does in flocks of goats, or, if site attachment is involved, can result in the exclusive use of a particular area, or territory. Dominance may result in priority of access to females by males, as in many herd animals and primate troops, or in access to a male by females as occurs in wolf packs. It also may regulate priority of access to scarce food items, as it does in packs of dogs or wolves.

Territoriality

A territory is defined as an area where boundaries are defended against conspecifics. In the well-known examples among song birds, a male maintains exclusive use of an area in which he is mated to a female or females and in which a nest or nests are built. He defends the area by attacks on any male bird that enters the territory, and in some species the females will attack entering females. In most cases, the males from adjacent territories recognize each other, and each is dominant within his own territory and subordinate to his neighbors in theirs. Another type of territorial organization is found in the sage grouse, where males and females separate during the rearing of the young. During the mating season the males gather on a mating ground and by fighting establish small territories into which females may enter and be mated. In this case, the most dominant animal is usually in the center, and the majority of females will mate in the central area with this particular bird (J. W. Scott, 1942, Wiley, 1973).

Among mammals, there is a great variety of expression of territoriality. No territory can be maintained in the open ocean by marine mammals, but male elephant seals fight for territories on the shore during the breeding season. Within his territory a male enjoys exclusive mating with a group of females (LeBoeuf, 1974). On the other hand, ungulates, the hoofed animals that live in herds, usually do not maintain territories although certain species of African antelopes such as the kob develop a lek system similar to that of birds during the mating season. These are small, temporary territories, each guarded by a single male (Buechner, 1974).

Inter-Group Relationships and Coordinated Attacks

In the vast majority of vertebrate species agonistic behavior is an affair between two individuals, with no coordinated group attacks. It is only among wolves and primates such as the rhesus monkey that such relationships may develop. A single rhesus male is usually stronger than a single female and in an individual encounter is dominant, but females occasionally gang up on a male and defeat him. By such alliances, the offspring of a dominant female in the group maintain her relative rank, i.e., immediately below her but above the monkeys which she dominates.

Also, one troop may be dominant over another, as reported by Southwick (1972) in India and also by observers in Puerto Rico (Vessey, 1971). That is, if two troops meet at a feeding station one gives way to the other, usually following a certain amount of threatening behavior.

Studies on the social organization of agonistic behavior in vertebrates lead to the following general conclusions. Except for the preliminary stages in the development of a relationship, as when two strange animals meet for the first time, *agonistic behavior among vertebrates is always expressed within a social relationship, and the nature of the relationship is the major determinant of the amount, form, and intensity of that expression* (Scott, 1983). Therefore, a major objective of research on agonistic behavior in any vertebrate species is to discover the capacities of the species to develop such relationships. It does not follow that relationships based on agonistic behavior and the resulting dominance and territorial organization are the only forms of social organization, important as they may be. Social relationships can be developed on the basis of any sort of social behavior. For example, in most bird species, agonistic organization is functional only during the breeding season. During the rest of the year, organization is based on allelomimetic relationships involved in flocking behavior and, in the case of such species as the Canada goose, is based on attachments between family members and leadership by older birds.

INFANTICIDE

Infanticide, defined as the killing of an infant by an adult of the same species, is an apparent exception to the theory that agonistic behavior should evolve toward the least harmful form that is consistent with its function within a social system. Inspired by sociobiological theory, Hrdy (1977), who studied infanticide by males in the Indian langur monkey, hypothesized that in this species, infanticide by an unrelated male increased the probability that his offspring would be present in the next generation, i.e., there should be selection in favor of males showing this trait.

In the langurs, a troop is composed of a single male and several adult females and their offspring. In areas where the population density is low, agonistic behavior is seldom observed, but where it is high, clashes between troops are more frequent. Cases of infanticide are observed when either a single male or a group of males attempts to take over a troop from the resident male. In the course of the melee, the intruder attacks not only the resident male but also the females carrying young, and it is at this point that infanticide may take place.

Several alternative hypotheses are possible, none of which are exclusive; i.e., infanticide might have more than one function:

(a) Infanticide is an aberrant maladaptive behavior induced by social disorganization resulting from high population levels.

(b) It has evolved as a means of controlling population levels, as it has been employed in several past human cultures.

(c) It may be adaptive for individual survival of adults through cannibalism (this is not the case with langurs).

(d) It provides more immediate access to estrus females, as it does in langurs, because females go into estrus sooner if not lactating. This would lead to the same result as the theory of reproductive advantage.

(e) Infants are more helpless than adults and less able to defend themselves.

A basic research question is, how important is infanticide? The answer may help to discriminate between some of the above hypotheses, and also provide a way of estimating the strength of the hypothesized selection process, or selection pressure as it is often called. As we know from experiments with selection, such processes must be strong and continuous in order to maintain a genetically variable condition at a high level.

The best available data come from Struhsaker and Leland's (1986) paper, which tabulates reported instances of male infanticide among non-human primates. There were 24 cases where this was actually observed, eight of which occurred in two species of langurs. All but two of the rest occurred in the Old-world monkey and apes. This is consistent with Itani's (1982) survey of intraspecific killing among primates. He reported that almost all cases of adult killing occurred in the Old-world monkeys and chimpanzees, with very few among the New-world monkeys. The great majority of deaths occurred in infants. These comparative figures would be more meaningful if they were in terms of rate per population size and rate per hour of observation. Many times these figures have been inferred or estimated, but such figures are even less meaningful. Nevertheless, they suggest two additional hypotheses. One is that killing in primates is associated with ground living. The South American monkeys are predominately arboreal and frugivorous, whereas many of the Old-world primates live on the ground and only occasionally climb trees. Among the Old-world Hominoidea, killing has not yet been reported in the arboreal gibbons and orangs. This is consistent with observations in birds that the most injurious fighting occurs among ground-living birds such as the gallinaceous ones rather than among perching birds.

Second, on the basis of data so far available, the phenomenon of male infanticide occurs in primates on a level that could result in only weak selection. If it is an adaptive phenomenon it occurs only in restricted cases, such as that of over-population.

From the viewpoint of genetic theory, the male killer may win an advantage, but the mother whose infant he has killed loses correspondingly. Therefore, there should be selection in favor of females who effectively protect their infants, leading to some sort of equilibrium.

Sommer (1987) observed five langur troop takeovers in a 14 month period, of which 3 were infanticidal and 2 were not. This reality of the infanticidal phenomenon was demonstrated, but also that its occurrence was variable, suggesting some sort of balance between the various genetic evolutionary processes that may be involved.

One of the species in which male infanticide has been reported is the yellow baboon. Yet in the same species an adult male will pick up an infant apparently to ward off or ameliorate an attack (Stein, 1984), suggesting that this behavior inhibits or buffers agonistic behavior.

Male infanticide has been reported in two non-primate species, house mice (Svare & Mann, 1981; vom Saal & Howard, 1982) and lions (Schaller, 1972). Among mice it has been experimentally studied in the laboratory by Svare, Parmigiani, and vom Saal who each report that it is consistent with the reproductive advantage hypothesis (in Brain & Parmigiani, 1988). Agonistic behavior in this species as described above should function to distribute populations rather than limit them, but mice that are reared together do not fight, with the result that enormous numbers can accumulate where a concentrated food supply is available. Reproduction in mice is also affected by strange males in a peaceful fashion. Contact with a strange male will cause a pregnant female to abort if this occurs at four days or sooner (the Bruce effect). The effects and importance of male infanticide in wild mouse populations are still to be determined.

Lions are unusual in many ways. They are the only highly social species of the cat family, and the males tend to be parasitic on the females, who are the active hunters. A male that takes over a pride from a resident may kill the cubs in it. Lions have a high reproductive capacity, but, as successful carnivores at the top of the food chain, their populations must be small lest they outrun their food supply, which suggests that in this species population control may be as important as reproductive advantage.

Infanticide by a dominant female has been reported in some other pack-hunting carnivores such as wolves and the Cape hunting dogs. Here the reproductive advantage obviously goes to the female, but the cubs so killed are likely to be related to her.

Male infanticide does not occur in all species of mammals nor in all species of primates but is associated with social disorganization following intrusion by a strange male or males. It has not been reported in rhesus monkeys where a strange young male intruder is always dominated both by the resident males and alliances of resident females. Infanticide in each case needs to be analyzed in the context of the systems organization of the species: ecological, social, behavioral and physiological.

CONCLUSIONS

The evolutionary theories discussed in this chapter have in common that they are based on the functions of living organisms, whether these are internal physiological functions, physiobehavioral functions, or interactive social-organizational functions. Stated most broadly, social organization has evolved out of internal and external functions, in contrast to most selection theories that have been previously used, which assume that evolutionary change proceeds solely from a group of external processes called selection that act on a passive organism. Many if not all selection theories have therefore been mechanistic rather than systems theory based. This does not imply that selection has no role in evolution but rather that it has an interactive role.

Some of these functional theories are classical, such as Allee's theory of social organization through aggregation, and Wynne-Edwards' theory that social organization functions to control population levels. The more novel ideas that I have presented are:

1. Specialized social functions have evolved in physiobehavioral systems. The more complex groups of animals have independently evolved one such system that has the express function of regulating competitive behavior, i.e., agonistic behavior, usually having the function of limiting competition to useful or non-harmful forms. The nature of agonistic behavior in a species will in turn regulate the nature of evolutionary processes that are dependent on competition, and, by implication, affect the operation of any evolutionary theory dependent on competition.

2. A major evolutionary theory is that of *Transformation of Function*. This is consistent with systems theory and states that new functions of social behavior evolve out of pre-existing functions. This avoids the difficulties inherent in theories that assume that new functions arise out of opposing functions, such as that cooperation is evolved through competition.

To apply the criteria for evaluating evolutionary theories stated in Chapter 8, the theory of transformation of function, and indeed all the functional theories described above are, first of all, impeccable in their origins, being derived from studies of animal societies and populations as they exist in natural conditions.

Second, these theories are broadly general, their application not being limited to any particular species or set of conditions. Nevertheless, none of them will explain all evolutionary phenomena. Living systems are so complex that no one single theory will explain all aspects of their operation and organization.

Third, these theories are eminently testable by observation and experiment. A basic question derived from systems theory is, how does the system, or set of systems work? Function theory leads to detailed observation and description of social behavior and social systems and from this to experimental analyses, either in wild or captive populations. Such experiments can be as simple as removing a territorial male from a songbird population, and measuring how the system reacts, or recording and playing vocal signals such as bird song and wolf howling, and recording the effects. Or a group of strange individuals can be experimentally assembled, and the development of social organization (or lack of it) observed.

Fourth, these theories are all compatible with systems theory and the systems concept. One of them, the combinatory theory of Corning, was directly derived from one aspect of systems theory, namely the creativity effect of higher levels of organization. But while none of the functional theories is inconsistent with genetic systems theory, their authors have made little effort to relate the two, and that will be the task of the next chapter.

Chapter X

On the Evolution of Social Organization

Any sort of social organization involves at least two individuals of the same species. If this behavioral interaction becomes regular and predictable, we have a dyadic social relationship, the simplest form of social organization. The number of dyadic relationships in a group is given by the formula $n(n-1)/2$, where n is the total number of individuals in the group. That is, each time a new individual is added to a group, the number of dyadic relationships is increased by a figure equal to the number of individuals previously in the group.

In many cases, behavior involves more than two individuals, which renders relationship organization progressively more complex. As we have seen previously in analyzing interaction between the four evolutionary processes, in a social group of four there is one possible relationship involving all four individuals, three involving three at a time, and six involving two each.

This phenomenon provides one of the basic and still only partially solved problems of behavior genetics: One cannot observe and measure the expression of one genotype on social behavior without involving the expression of at least one other genotype (Scott, 1977). How complicated this becomes even in a single dyadic relationship is shown by Figure 10.1 (Scott & Fuller, 1965), and the complexity becomes almost unimaginable if several individuals are considered. A similar problem is presented by the evolution of social organization, since biological evolution rests on genetic change.

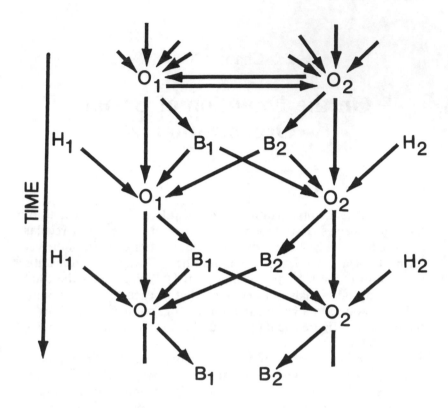

Figure 10.1. The expression of social behavior by an individual organism is modified by the heredity of all individuals with whom it interacts, as shown in this diagram of dyadic interaction. Beginning at the top of the diagram, both organisms (01 and 02) have been modified by previous experiences and interactions. They stimulate each other, resulting in behavior (B1 and B2), which feeds back on both organisms. Since the behavior of both is affected by hereditary variation (H1 and H2), the social behavior expressed by each of the two organisms reflects the heredity of both. If continued, such behavior will eventually become organized as a stable social relationship. (After Scott & Fuller, 1965, reproduced by permission of the University of Chicago Press.)

If there were a 1:1 relationship between genetic change in an individual and social organization, the problem of analysis would be simple: social organization would reflect the sum of the constituent genotypes. It is possible that this assumption is justified in certain limited cases, but to arrive at a more general analysis we must make different assumptions: 1) behavior between individuals is usually interactive in a non-additive fashion, and 2) the interaction between each pair or more of genotypes belonging to such individuals is unique. The only limitation is that interactions should tend (but not necessarily so) to be adaptive; i.e., to promote and facilitate life processes.

The inevitable conclusion is that while genetic variation and hence evolutionary change rests on individual genotypes, any such change that produces a change in social organization must involve more than one genotype. Indeed, the logic of the analysis of social organization argues that such a change reflects the interaction of a given variable genotype with every other genotype included in the social group. With this in mind, we can now consider the effect of the major evolutionary processes on social organization.

EFFECTS OF EVOLUTIONARY PROCESSES ON SOCIAL ORGANIZATION

Kinds of Social Organization

Social organization is composed of social relationships, and these in turn depend on the nature of the social behavior involved. A dyadic relationship may be simple, based on one sort of social behavior (Scott, 1953) or it may be complex, involving more than one kind of behavior. If more than one, the relationship may be expressed either serially or simultaneously in combination. Table 10.1 summarizes the resulting relationships. It should be added that any form of lasting relationship is dependent on the process of attachment, either to other individuals or to localities.

Considered from a descriptive rather than an analytic viewpoint, temporary aggregations commonly occur in a wide variety of animals, but chiefly in the lower invertebrates. In the case of more permanent groups held together by processes of attachment, parent-offspring groups are fairly common and exist in a variety of forms such as the female-parent+offspring group in honey bees and other Hymenopteran insects and some semi-solitary mammals, the biparental-offspring group of termites, many bird species and some mammals, and the male-parent+offspring group as in many fish species. Groups may include more than one parent of one or both sexes: In sheep and many herd mammals numerous females and their offspring comprise a group; a single male and several females form a group in polygynous species of birds and mammals; or a group may include numerous males and females as it does in rhesus monkeys and certain other primate troops.

Allelomimetic groups are common only in Vertebrates: schools of fishes, flocks of birds, and herds of mammals. Such groups may contain only young individuals (as in some fish schools), adults of one sex, or adults of both sexes. Many parent-offspring groups also are allelomimetic, as they are in primate troops. The social relationships involved may be undifferentiated allelomimetic, with each individual responding to every other individual in the same manner, or they may be differentiated into leader-follower relationships based on individual recognition and different degrees of attachment.

Only agonistic behavior has a dispersive effect. Consequently, it can be organized into dominance-subordination relationships only if the group is held together in some way, usually by some form of attachment, either social or to a place.

Table 10.1
SIMPLE SOCIAL RELATIONSHIPS

Social Behavior	Relationship	Group
Investigative	1-way or mutual investigation	Temporary Aggregation
Shelter-Seeking	Contiguity	Temporary Aggregation
Shelter-Building	Contiguity	Lasting Aggregation, usually with complex relationships
Sexual	Sexual relationship	Temporary Aggregations: mating pairs or mating swarms. With attachment: mated pair, polygynous or polygamous groups
Ingestive	Feeder-fed	Usually Parent Offspring
Epimeletic (care giving)	Care-dependency	Usually Parent Offspring
Et-epimeletic (care soliciting)	Care-dependency	Usually Parent Offspring
Agonistic	With attachment Dominance-subordination	
	Without attachment	Tends to disperse group
Allelomimetic	Leader-follower or Mutual following	Schools, flocks, herds, troops

The relationships described in Table 10.1 are not equally distributed among all combinations of individuals. In most animal societies, individuals vary with respect to their capacities for social behavior. The simplest variation is that associated with sex: two kinds of sexual behavior appropriate to the sort of fertilization found in a particular species. And since most animals go through a period of development prior to sexual maturity, there may be differentiation based on age.

Most vertebrate societies are composed of adult males and females, and young of both sexes. Within each of these three basic groups there may be further differentiation based on individual recognition. Assuming that immature individuals already behave differentially and that there are actually two kinds of young, there are six possible dyadic combinations involving physiologically unlike individuals, making a total of 10 such combinations. In addition, innumerable specific combinations of individuals within and between these groups are possible. Among invertebrates, and especially among the highly social insects, there may be more than the above four classes of individuals. For example, honeybees have only one kind of male, the drone, but two kinds of females: the reproductive females or queens, and the sterile workers that build nests and care for the young. In an ant species there may be more than one kind of sterile female: the so-called soldiers that have the function of defending the colony, in addition to the workers. In some termite groups there may be as many as seven kinds of animals: three sorts of reproductive individuals, workers, soldiers, larvae, and nymphs. In some species there are two kinds of soldiers. Such classes of individuals have been called "castes" in analogy with social organization in certain human societies in India.

However, individual recognition, though it sometimes exists, has relatively little importance in invertebrate social organization. The result is to greatly simplify the possibilities of social organization. If there are only four castes in an invertebrate society, there can be only ten possible sorts of relationships, whatever the size of the social group. But in a vertebrate group of only ten individuals organized on the basis of individual recognition, there are potentially 45 different dyadic relationships. The result is that social organization among vertebrates is potentially far more complex than that seen in insect societies.

Evolutionary change in social organization can take place only through changes in social behavior or some related social process such as attachment. From even this cursory review of the varieties of social organization, it is obvious that the effect of a given genetic change on social behavior will depend on the type of social organization within which it takes place. For example, in groups formed by social attachment, the existence of the group and its component members is dependent on this process, and there should be strong selection for its maintenance and against any weakening of the process.

Mutation and Social Organization

Social organization may result in the formulation of groups ranging from very large ones to small and discrete ones similar to demes. The effect of a mutation is, as with organismic changes, inversely proportional to population size, but unlike organismic change, the effect is on relationships rather than individuals.

At first glance, the effect of genetic change in social behavior appears simple: a change in one individual should affect all members of the group of which it is a member. But since all social behavior is expressed in social relationships, the effect of genetic change is more complex. Each point on the curves in Figure 10.2 is obtained from a ratio, where r = the size of relationship, divided by the size of the group organized in such relationships. That is, the effect of the change is directly proportional to the size of the relationship, and inversely proportional to the size of the group.

There is another limit to such effects, which is the capacity of the species to form multiple relationships. This in turn depends on the capacity to recognize individuals. Thus, a change in this latter capacity would have the tendency to increase the size of functional social groups. Where the limits of this capacity lies is an interesting problem for research, as one would expect it to vary among species.

Relationship theory therefore, has two important consequences for the genetic theory of evolution. One is that it multiplies the effects of genetic change: the expression of such a change in dyadic relationships is twice that of its expression in individuals, and in

triadic relationships three times. The other is that it again emphasizes the importance of moderately small groups for rapid evolution. Given such groups (and their size may be determined by
social behavior), evolution of social behavior should proceed more
rapidly than organic evolution or that of non-social behavior. It
goes without saying that such change must contribute to
survival.

The inverse relationship between population size and mutational change is graphically illustrated in Figure 10.2. The effect
of a mutation falls off rapidly at first and then decreases at a very
slow rate, with the curve approaching a straight line. The graph
also illustrates that the proportion of dyadic relationships affected
is always double the proportion of individuals involved, although
the absolute numbers increase at a much higher rate.

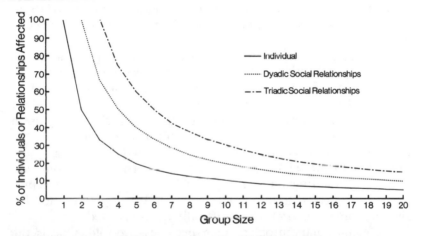

Figure 10.2. Effects of a single mutational change affecting social behavior relative
to group size and social organization. Such a change in a single individual can affect
all other individuals in a group, assuming that it makes contact with all of them.
The effect on social organization as expressed in social relationships is less extreme,
being proportional to the number of individuals in each relationship. Excepting
those relationships involving all members of a group, the proportion of relationships affected rapidly decreases as the group becomes larger, again emphasizing the
importance of small groups relative to rapid evolution. Generally, social behavior
and organization magnify and extend the results of genetic change, whether it
involves a single gene or a combination of genes.

Assuming that a given individual develops a dyadic relationship with every other individual in the group (an assumption that can be experimentally demonstrated in dominance-subordination relationships in a flock of hens), it follows that the change in social behavior of a new mutant individual affects its relationships with every other individual in the population but of course does not affect relationships between other individuals.

This proportion is still further increased if the group develops relationships involving more than two individuals. If a multi-individual group has a relationship involving all the members, as is true in an allelomimetic relationship, the behavior of a mutant could simultaneously affect the whole group.

To return to our example of a group of 4, the change of one individual could affect 100% of the relationships of the entire group of 4, 66% of relationships of 3, and 50% of dyadic relationships. Generally speaking, then, the effect of multi-individual relationships is to magnify the effect of a single mutation affecting social behavior.

When does the effect of a mutation become negligible? Obviously, this is an arbitrary decision, but in a group of 100 individuals, the organismic effect of a mutation is reduced to 1% and its effect on dyadic relationships to 2%. On the other hand, the effect of multiple relationships is to increase the effect, all the way up to 100%. In any case, the effect on multiple relationships is to increase the proportion of individuals affected by a factor equal to the size of the relationship. In the case of triadic relationships, the proportion affected in a group of 100 is 3%. Further, the proportion of affected triadic relationships at any population level is always 3 times the proportion of individuals affected.

The evolutionary problem then becomes two-fold. One is the actual size of the social groups, and here we may point out that many social groups are indeed small, and the size of the breeding group (the animals actually reproducing) may be even smaller. For example, the size of social groups in the California Condor, a species on the verge of extinction, is the mated pair. The consequence of one injurious mutation in the group is to affect the one dyadic relationship, which may mean no reproduction for 2 birds, not just one. This may be a factor in the extinction of these birds.

The conclusion is that social organization, through its effect on population size, magnifies the effect of mutation, whether positive or negative in their results. Positive effects, however, are dependent on gene combinations as pointed out earlier. But if a new combination has a favorable effect, its results may be immediate and widespread, thus favoring the reoccurrence of that combination. Social organization magnifies the effects of gene combinations as well as those of single genes. This has great theoretical importance, in view of the conclusion that positive evolutionary change is predominantly brought about by changes in gene combinations.

It is also obvious that a positive change, because it affects a large proportion of a group's relationships, will favor survival of that group over others in which such a combination does not occur.

The Effects of Sexual Reproduction

The general effect of meiosis and fertilization is to create unique combinations of genes, i.e., unique genotypes. It follows that each sexual relationship created by sexual behavior is also a unique combination of genotypes. Sexual reproduction thus magnifies variation on two levels.

Sexual reproduction produces this effect only to the extent that it is involved in social organization. In the sexual reproduction of marine polychaete worms whose males and females simply discharge their germ cells into the surrounding sea water, the only sexual behavior that is involved is coming together in temporary aggregations. No dyadic or higher order relationships are formed.

In those species whose reproduction involves copulation, the act is necessarily dyadic. Such a dyadic relationship may be of very brief duration, or it may persist throughout a breeding season, or it may last as long as both individuals live, depending on the species. In a group containing more than one member of both sexes, sexual relationships could be formed in all possible combinations of dyadic pairs, usually but not necessarily omitting like-sexed pairs. Or, if there is only one member of one sex and more than one of the opposite sex, there can be polygynous or polyandrous organization. Any regularly organized set of sexual relationships is usually referred to as a mating system.

The mating system is not completely determined by sexual behavior, but cannot exist without it. In single-male-multiple-female groups, for example, agonistic behavior usually results in the ejection of all but one male; thus both agonistic and sexual behavior shape the system.

In summary, sexual reproduction, acting through sexual behavior, produces dyadic relationships, whether brief or long-lasting. Because the behavior of each individual is in part determined by its heredity, the nature of dyadic sexual relationships is determined by the interaction between genotypes, and in any genetically variable population each of these relationships must be unique. As on the organismic level, the effect of sexual reproduction is to magnify variation. It should be added that this magnifying effect should be felt in any dyadic relationship, whether or not it is based on sexual behavior. The same principle can be extended to triadic and higher order relationships: Each relationship should therefore be unique.

Is this variation purely random? It would be, except that certain kinds of dyadic sexual relationships do not result in reproduction. For example, within an inbred mouse strain, where every genotype is identical except for the X and Y chromosomes, mating takes place with equal ease between any male-female pair. But if an experimenter tries to mate them with individuals from other inbred strains, mating in some cases may be difficult or impossible, as Vale and Ray (1971) found in attempting a 6-way diallel cross. The genotypes do not fit, probably because of phenotypic differences in sexual behavior. This involves a sort of mutual selection between genotypes, related to Darwin's notion of sexual selection, but with no competition involved, and brings in the process of Differential Survival.

Inbreeding and Social Organization

As I pointed out earlier, inbreeding depends on sexual reproduction, and mating systems may lead to either inbreeding or outbreeding. But if social organization produces inbreeding, either by limiting the size of the breeding population or by influencing the choice of mates, inbreeding will in turn influence social organization.

The primary effect of inbreeding is to reduce variation. In an inbred population, genotypes and hence the social relationships formed by the resulting phenotypes, will become more similar. As this happens, social organization will become more rigid. Also, as with genes and genotypes, organization in different isolated or semi-isolated populations should become different. Social organization as well as social behavior should be an isolating factor.

Differential Survival and Social Organization

Survival of both the individual and the group depends on social organization. An adaptive form of social organization is one that will protect the existence of its individual members. Consequently, differential survival will favor those forms of social organization that perform this function most effectively. Since social organization always involves more than one individual, and frequently a whole set of individuals, and because it cannot be expressed by a single individual, selection must operate on the expression of social organization involving several individuals. In short, differential survival will favor both an adaptively organized group as a whole and the individuals that best contribute to that organization.

Within an organized group, differential survival in the form of social selection will favor those individuals that adapt themselves best to the social organization. This might either increase variation, as in the cases where individual variation facilitates individual recognition and division of labor, or, more commonly, decreased variation that maintains the social organization.

Interactions between Differential Survival on Different Levels

A particular behavior pattern, defined as a segment of behavior that has a function, may affect survival on different levels. This effect may be positive to a greater or lesser degree, negative in variable degrees, or essentially neutral. As an example, a pattern of sexual behavior in a mallard duck would have neutral survival for the individual (it has no function if emitted by a solitary bird), has strong positive effects on the maintenance of a pair bond, and might have either no effect or slightly disruptive effects on the pair bonding of other birds. To take another example, the feeding behavior of the same species has a strong positive effect on the survival of the individual bird and no effect on the levels of social relationships or of societies except as these are dependent on the survival of the individual.

Theoretically, the survival value of a particular behavior pattern can be positive, negative or neutral in all possible combinations with respect to each level of organization. If a behavior has positive value at all levels there will be strong selection in its favor; if its effects are negative on all levels, there will be strong selection against it. If its effects are positive on one level and negative on another, the result should be some sort of balance or equilibrium between them. An example is the "broken wing" behavior pattern of some ground nesting birds, which has the effect of leading a predator away from the nest. It looks as if the parent bird were endangering her own life to preserve her eggs, but in actuality, little danger is involved. For if the parent sacrificed her life, the eggs or young would also die (Scott, 1968).

In the past, this problem of interaction between levels has been phrased as the evolution of "altruism" (Hamilton, 1964), considering only individual survival and group survival. But this is an oversimplification; the survival value of a behavior must be examined on all levels. This is particularly true of social behavior, whose primary expression is on the level of social relationships. The new concept that I have added here is that there are more levels than "the individual" and "the group." Also, if one examines the survival value of behavior on multiple levels, it may serve to explain the existence of behaviors whose function is obscure.

Social organization and the behavior that produces it are principally affected by selection on three levels: those of behavior, social relationships, and societies. Are they also affected by differential survival on other levels? If an organism does not live, it will never express behavior or be a part of social organization. To this extent, reductionism is justified. But it is also true that one of the major effects of social organization is to promote survival of its constituent organisms; i.e., organization on the highest level feeds back on the lower ones.

One must also consider the effects of genetic variation on social behavior and organization. As I showed at the outset of this chapter, the social interaction of phenotypes representing the expression of different genotypes is extraordinarily complex, so that we must deal with not only combinations of genes but combinations of genotypes.

Interactions between Evolutionary Processes in Relation to Social Organization

From what I have said above, it is obvious that social organization frequently involves the 4-process theory of evolution, including Mutation, Sexual Reproduction, Inbreeding, and Differential Survival. This is not necessarily true in all cases, and the 2-process Mutation-Differential Survival theory may coexist with the 4-process theory in certain special applications. But it is difficult to find an asexually reproducing species that shows any form of social organization other than temporary aggregations. Also, social organization brings with it a new sub-class of Differential Survival processes, that of Social Selection.

With respect to the 4-process theory, social organization, of whatever nature, frequently limits population size, which facilitates inbreeding, which decreases genetic variation within a population and facilitates divergence between populations. At the same time, social organization facilitates the expression of genetic variation within a population, and so should facilitate non-random change within a group. Through the creation of mating systems, sexual reproduction becomes a non-random process, thus contributing to evolutionary change as well as simply maintaining maximum genetic variation.

Indeed, social organization may create the conditions which Wright (1931, 1977) stated contributed to a maximum rate of evolutionary change. Social organization frequently divides a population into small sub-populations within which inbreeding takes place but which also permit occasional transfers of individuals from one social group to another. The degree to which any form of social organization meets these criteria depends on the species involved.

EFFECTS OF SOCIAL ORGANIZATION ON EVOLUTION

One of the major effects of the evolution of social organization is to introduce a new class of selection processes, which I (Scott, 1958; see also Wynne-Edwards, 1962) have called *social selection*. This is a more inclusive term than Darwin's concept of sexual selection, which was based chiefly on competition for mates.

Social selection includes not only sexual selection but differential survival brought about by any kind of factor that originates in the social environment. It may be contrasted with *physical selection*, resulting from factors in the nonliving environment, and *biotic selection*, resulting from factors in the ecosystem. Before we can understand the effects of social selection, we must consider the interaction of social systems with other major systems on different levels.

Effects of Social Organization on the Physical Environment

Even the primitive social organization of temporary aggregations has the effect of modifying the physical environment in a favorable fashion. Among more complex societies, social organization may afford long-lasting protection against selection originating in the physical environment, as it does in the nest building insects and the burrowing rodents. The reduction of physical selection should thus permit greater variation among social populations unless this is in some way counteracted by processes from within the system.

Effects of Social Organization on the Ecosystem

Social organization can have various effects on the biotic environment, depending on its nature and the position of the species in an ecosystem. If in no other way, protection against the physical environment will produce increasing numbers of animals with an increasing demand for food supplies, thus producing pressure on other species and, as a by-product, an increasing amount of wastes.

From the viewpoint of the social system itself, some of its major adaptive effects are as follows. Social organization in a social predator such as the wolf has the effect of increasing the available food supply. A single wolf could not possibly kill a healthy moose, but a sufficiently large pack can live off this species very successfully, as happens in the Isle Royale wolves (Mech, 1966, 1970). On the other hand, social organization of a prey species may provide protection against predators, as in musk oxen that group together when attacked by wolves, forming an outer circle of horns.

As well as these favorable modifications of the biotic environment, social organization may have some negative effects as well. The close and continuous association of animals makes a favorable condition for the transmission of all sorts of diseases and parasites. The rates of negative differential survival of this sort are increased in a social species, balancing to some extent the favorable effects in other directions. Certain kinds of social behavior such as the grooming behavior of most primates may in turn compensate for the otherwise favorable environment for external parasites (Saunders, 1988).

Effects of Social Organization on the Individual Organisms

As well as modifying the external environment and its attendant selection, social organization has direct effects on the individuals that comprise it. A major effect is to stabilize the internal environment of the society, which has the effect, in evolutionary terms, of reducing and stabilizing selection resulting from both the outside world and the society itself. I have already pointed out some of the major consequences of such stability, which generally makes the functioning of the component individuals more efficient. Secondarily, the social environment alters the physiological requirements for survival and should, in the long run, result in internal evolutionary change on the organismic level. Finally, social organization sets up special forms of selection directed toward those individuals that comprise the society, favoring those individuals that adapt well to the organization and maintain it, and tending to select against those individuals that are poorly adapted and by their behavior break down organization.

The nature of social selection depends on the function of the social organization concerned. With respect to reproduction, social selection will favor those individuals whose behavior most effectively results in fertilization and also those individuals who most effectively rear their young. If the function of the social organization is to find food, as it is in wolves, social selection will favor those individuals that are most cooperative in this endeavor. If a wolf does not join the pack hunt, it will get less food.

In human populations, where language is an all important aspect of social organization, there is obvious selection against the survival or breeding success of individuals who are defective in language skills. Very possibly there is positive selection in the other direction for those who can talk well and use the communicative system in other ways.

Effects of Social Organization on Genetic Systems

Genetic systems in the sense of the gene pool of a population are obviously modified in a great many ways by the processes of social selection indicated above. In addition, social organization alters the random breeding structure of large populations. In an animal society the individual no longer has random access to other individuals, but is exposed more frequently to those in his own social group. The most general result is some degree of inbreeding. In the honeybee, a new colony originates in a swarm leaving the old hive. Inasmuch as all the bees in a colony are produced by a single female, the new queen and her mate are likely to be brother and sister, resulting in inbreeding. In an established colony a new queen replacing an old one may make several nuptial flights and so have a chance to mate with males from other hives (Michener, 1974). Also, queens may mate with anywhere from 1-12 males, from whatever colony (Wilson, 1971). One would nevertheless expect that some random drift would take place in this species, with a resulting differentiation of strains. In addition, inbreeding should result in more rapid elimination of injurious recessive genes.

Other kinds of social organization may produce varying degrees of inbreeding, always tending to eliminate injurious recessives but also resulting in genetic drift between social groups, assuming that they are somewhat isolated from each other. On the other hand, if the social structure favors outbreeding rather than inbreeding, this could result in the protection of injurious recessives. In any case, the reduction of certain external selection processes originating in the physical and biotic environments tends to increase the genetic variation in a population. Where social organization depends on individual recognition, as it does in most mammalian and bird societies, there may even be selection in favor of variation of certain anatomical characteristics. In flocks of chickens, for example, individuals recognize each other chiefly by small differences in the shape and color of the comb and wattles (Guhl, 1953).

In general, the effects of social organization on a genetic system vary according to the nature of the particular social organization. It may either increase or decrease variation, and provide conditions that are either conducive to evolutionary change or that may bring it to a virtual standstill. This raises the questions of what actually happens in particular species and how important the effects of social organization may be.

Examples of the Effects of Social Organization on Evolutionary Processes

Among the lower invertebrates whose social organization is confined to the formation of temporary aggregations, we would expect to find relatively little effect of social organization upon evolution. For the most part, these species are composed of very large random breeding populations that fit the requirements of the Hardy-Weinberg principle of genetic stability. At the same time there should be strong selection in favor of those individuals that actually do aggregate under favorable conditions and so survive.

Among the more advanced caste societies of arthropods, the situation is quite different. To take as an example a solitary nest building wasp, there should be strong selection in favor of the offspring of those individuals that provide successful parental care. The young larvae are thus subjected to a different environment from their adult parents, an environment modified by parental behavior. The larvae should, therefore, be subject to selection that favors behavior that is adaptive in this special situation. Thus, young and adults are faced with different problems of adaptation and subjected to different sorts of selection. In these wasps, the solitary existence of the adults and the separation of nests is not highly favorable for the transmission of parasites, but the fact that the larvae live together *is* favorable to parasites. Consequently, selection for resistance to parasites should affect larvae more than adults. Such organization has little effect on the breeding structure of the population except to favor mating between individuals from the same nest, especially if nests are widely separated.

In a more complex insect society such as an anthill, the offspring of a mated pair construct a long lasting microenvironment in which adults as well as larvae are protected from the external envi-

ronment. This reduces the rates of certain sorts of selection emanating from the physical and biotic environments, and increases
other kinds of selection which are related to adaptation for life
within the nest. Since all colony members are descended from a
single pair, selection acts on the social system as a whole and, at
the same time, on the individual level because, from a genetic
viewpoint, the colony and the mated female are identical. The anthill also provides a favorable environment for parasitic and com-
mensal species.

A basic characteristic of such insect societies is the elaboration
of a caste system. Since organization depends on members of a
caste acting in a similar fashion, there should be strong selection
against individual variation within castes. Furthermore, the
method of breeding (Wilson, 1971), in which a swarm of fertile
males and females is released at the same time, is conducive to
inbreeding and so should further reduce variation. But the very
act of swarming makes it possible for colonies within flight distance to crossbreed and so maintain variation, since many adjacent colonies of ants swarm on the same day. Ant species vary
from some parasitic species that only mate within the nest to those
that preferentially mate with non-colony members, thus avoiding
inbreeding. Mating behavior and the resulting social system thus
determines the degree of inbreeding.

A few examples of vertebrate societies will illustrate the contrasting
forms of selection associated with different forms of social organization. Among the nest building fish, the social organization is very
brief and seasonal compared to that of ants. The young in most species are protected only while still in the egg, or for a few days thereafter. Consequently, there should be relatively little effect of the social
environment on the young. For the adults there should be selection
in favor of individual males that can attract females and effectively
protect the nest and eggs. This involves a certain amount of altruistic
behavior. The nest holding male may not be able to feed as effectively
as usual and is more exposed to predators. On the other hand, he
must survive in order to protect the eggs, and so an equilibrium
should be set up between these selection processes.

A major social innovation in the bony fishes is the behavior of
"schooling," a variety of allelomimetic behavior. Almost all species
of bony fishes school at some point in their lives, and some individuals continue this as adults. The adaptive effect in most cases

is to promote survival; that is, a fish that is part of a school is more likely to escape a predator than a solitary individual (Williams 1964). There should, therefore, be strong selection for individuals that are strongly allelomimetic. In some fish species, schooling behavior has the function of increasing the available food supply, as it apparently does in the barracuda, which are, as a group, capable of attacking much larger fish or other prey. Since the bony fishes are the presumed ancestors of the higher vertebrates, it is possible that they share with their descendents the capacity for developing this basic behavioral system.

All birds, being warm blooded animals, must incubate their eggs and thus exhibit this minimal degree of parental care. With a few exceptions, such as the mallee fowl (Frith, 1962), they continue the care of the young after hatching until they become adults, usually within a few weeks. While highly developed, the social life of most birds is also strongly seasonal, with the care of young being exhibited for only a few weeks of the year.

To take a particular example, the sage grouse is a bird that lives in widely scattered groups on the high arid plains of the western United States. A single female and her young may inhabit an area of forty acres or so. As with most precocial birds, incubation and care of the young is done entirely by the female. Aside from a crude nest in which incubation takes place, this involves very little modification of the physical environment. For the young birds, the social environment is each other and the mother, and their differential survival largely relates to their responding effectively to her behavior directed toward keeping the group together, searching for food, and avoiding predators. These behaviors are useful only at this age, and we may state as a general principle that in species that have well-developed parental care, the young face very different problems of adaptation and consequently different forms of selection than those they face as adults. I have named the resulting change in behavior *behavioral metamorphosis* (Scott & Nagy, 1979).

The other major type of social organization in the sage grouse, mating organization, is also seasonal. The mating ground, or lek, is used year after year. The original lek studied by J. W. Scott (1942), still in existence after 30 years, was restudied by Wiley (1973) who found the social organization unchanged. Such a stable system means that these birds, whose adult males and females are ordinarily widely scattered and separated, have a regular way of meeting and ensuring fertilization. The system has the disadvantage of exposing the birds to predation by coyotes and eagles, and to parasitic diseases such as coccidiosis. The possibility of predation probably dictates the fact that the birds assemble in the very early morning before sunrise when few predators are abroad. At the same time, the birds must be visible to each other, and as if to aid in this visibility, the males during the breeding season develop an ornate spangled plumage that is regularly displayed to its maximum. During their displays, the males also produce sounds that are audible at considerable distances, another trait that is presumably adaptive in enabling females to locate the males.

The males set up a dominance order in which the most dominant male occupies a small territory surrounded by the territories of subordinate males. Most of the mating takes place in the center of the lek, and the dominant male may do 80 to 90 percent of the mating. The system should result in a strong selection for the capacity to become dominant, but the overt fighting observed is relatively mild, consisting mostly of buffeting with the wings. Becoming dominant is not only a matter of superior strength and fighting ability but also the capacity of the subordinate animal concerned to become subordinate quickly and easily. Continued fighting would be wasteful of energy and would interfere with rapid mating. Furthermore, the subordinate cocks on the outer fringes of the lek provide warning against terrestrial predators such as approaching coyotes. Most mating thus occurs not only with the dominant cock but also in the safest portion of the lek. Therefore, selection processes act on the system as a whole as well as on the individual. Finally, the social system does result in a considerable amount of inbreeding within local populations, although not enough to eliminate individual variation.

In general, this appears to be a successful and highly stable variety of social organization. In fact, it may be almost too stable because it does not include any regular means for setting up new populations. If the sage grouse population in one area is eliminated by hunting, it may be very difficult to restore it. Social organization has obviously affected the evolution of this species in many ways, one of the most striking being the extreme differentiation of appearance and behavior between the two sexes.

If one applies the simplest theory of sexual selection, it could be argued that male sage grouse have competed for the attention of females and those that were most brightly colored were most successful. However, as observed, the males do not compete for females as such, but rather for places on the mating ground. It is not the most brightly colored male that does most of the mating, but the one who occupies the central position on the lek. The system functions as a whole, with the group of brightly colored birds defining the position of the mating ground in the dim early morning light. Those groups which do this most effectively would be expected to survive; that is, it is the social system as a whole which is being selected as well as the individual. Competition is not merely a matter of individual combat (although this does go on and determines places on the mating ground) but also a competition between populations that are remote from each other and never come into actual conflict. This illustrates the advantages of the concept of social selection, for it permits broader interpretations than does that of sexual selection.

Why then are the males brightly colored and the females so inconspicuous? This can be accounted for on a cost-benefit basis. In this polygynous social organization the loss of males to predators is outweighed by the benefits of conspicuous availability. The loss of a female, on the other hand, means the loss of her descendents. There is, consequently, strong selection in favor of dull-colored female birds with speckled plumage that are difficult to detect in sage brush.

An alternative and more general explanation of this phenomenon is that of an equilibrium between various selective processes both on the same level and on different levels. The limitation of cost benefit analysis is that it leads to a binary analysis rather than one based on the combined effect of many different processes. Also, because it was derived from the concept of monetary costs, cost benefit analysis leads to the assumption of additive effects when, as a matter of fact, most cases involve 3- or 4-way interactions.

We may also take a brief look at the evolutionary effects of social organization in mammals. Unlike insects and birds, they have evolved a physiological rather than social means of protecting their young. The mammalian egg develops within the body of the mother, and correlated with this, very few mammals make extensive alterations in the physical environment, notable exceptions being the dam building beaver and the numerous species of burrowing rodents. Mammals have also evolved a physiological method of feeding the young, the production of milk, which again determines a great deal of the reproductive aspects of social life, particularly the tendency for females to perform most of the care of the infants.

To look at one example in more detail, the social life of wolves is organized around cooperative pack hunting during all of the year and both group and individual care of the young during the whelping season. Usually, only one female in a pack bears young, and there is very little modification of the physical environment. In whelping, a wolf bitch usually enlarges a burrow that already has been dug by a fox or other smaller animal, but she never produces an elaborate structure. Later, when the cubs begin to take solid food, they are fed vomited food by all members of the pack (Ginsburg, 1965, 1975).

With respect to the ecosystem, the social life of wolves is adapted for hunting the large herd animals on relatively level ground (wolves are poor climbers). Individual wolves are too large to live easily on small rodents and not large enough to make successful individual attacks on the big ungulates such as elk or moose. They are capable of modifying their social organization according to the prey involved. Wolf packs that hunt moose are generally bigger than those that hunt deer. Even in their most effective operation, however, wolf packs are unable to catch and kill vigorous adults and generally must eat sick, disabled, and very young individuals (Mech, 1970).

Unlike the sage grouse, social selection has produced relatively small differences in the appearance and behavior of males and females, these being chiefly a matter of larger size in the males. Except during the last stages of pregnancy and during lactation, females are as effective hunters as males. On the other hand, there is considerable variation between individuals within the two sexes. Members of a wolf pack can be easily told apart by a human observer. As dominant predators, wolves are not subject to strong selection by other predators and can tolerate variation within a pack. Indeed, this may be a considerable advantage in the functioning of the group since it may be highly advantageous to have one individual who is extremely alert and wary in response to potential danger as well as others that are calmer and disregard nondangerous signals.

Their social organization also has an effect on the genetic organization of the species. One would anticipate a certain amount of inbreeding in each pack (Wolpy, 1967), but wolves are very wide-ranging animals, and packs probably never become completely isolated from each other. Thus, the species has become spread over all of North America and Eurasia, with the local populations showing a good deal of individual variation and some tendency to vary in size and color according to the climate in which they live, presumably due to selection. Northern wolves, for instance, are larger and more light colored than southern ones.

In general, there is abundant evidence in these two species of the reality of the theoretical predictions that we have made concerning the effects of social organization on evolution. However, each species must be analyzed to determine the relative importance of these different effects, and it is unsafe to generalize from one species to another. To take an obvious example, mammals as a group seldom modify their physical environment by building protective structures, but man has developed this capacity in a manner far exceeding that of any other animal species. To understand this fully, we must consider another kind of evolution, that of culture.

Table 10.2 summarizes the effects of social behavior and social organization on fundamental evolutionary processes. Neither one has any effect on mutation, but both have important effects on variation, which is the raw material of selection. To begin with adaptive behavior, this enormously increases the variation within an individual as it adapts to a changing environment. Because individuals do not meet the same environmental problems, behavior also magnifies the variation between individuals. If, on the other hand, the behavior is modified by learning, it has a different effect on variation. Learning reduces variation within an individual through the process of habit formation, but, again because different individuals form different habits, it magnifies variation between individuals. All this has the effect of reducing the relative amount of variation produced by genetic factors in a population, with the consequent reduction of the effects of either natural or artificial selection.

The social organization of a group also has an effect upon variation. It tends on the one hand to push individuals into similar social roles and so reduces their variation. At the same time, the existence of social roles may enhance variation between individu-

Table 10.2

EFFECTS OF BEHAVIOR AND SOCIAL ORGANIZATION ON FUNDAMENTAL EVOLUTIONARY PROCESSES

	Variation				Sexual reproduction	Inbreeding: random drift	Selection
	Within individuals	Between individuals	Within systems	Between systems			
Behavioral function							
Adaptation	Magnifies	Magnifies			Reduces random nature	Increases opportunity	Facilitates selective survival
Learned organization	Limits	Magnifies			Reduces random nature	Increases opportunity	Limits selective survival
Social organization			Limits	Magnifies	Forms mating systems; decreases random nature	Organizes sub-populations and so determines extent of inbreeding	Modifies selective survival; protects against selection pressures, favours individuals that adapt to the system

Modified from Scott (1981), by permission of Elsevier/North Holland Biomedical Press.

als in different roles. Also, the formation of a social relationship such as that of dominance-subordination may enhance differences between the individuals involved and hence magnify variation between individuals.

A social system also affects variation on a higher level. The organization of a society or social system tends to reduce variation within the system, but since social systems are themselves variable, the result is to magnify variation between systems. In general, the effect of both behavior and social organization is to greatly magnify non-genetic variation.

With respect to sexual reproduction, either sexual behavior or such behavior modified by learning tend to reduce the random nature of sexual reproduction. Under such circumstances, one can no longer assume that mating is a random process. This tendency is still further extended by social organization through the formation of mating systems. Such systems at least partially determine which individuals shall mate with each other, and this again decreases the random nature of sexual reproduction. Since it is no longer completely random, the result is to decrease variation.

One of the ways of reducing variation among individuals is through inbreeding. Sexual behavior, whether modified by learning or not, increases the opportunity for inbreeding simply because neighboring animals tend to mate with each other. Further, individual organisms, unlike the situation of germ cells broadcast into seawater, cannot mate with an unlimited number of other individuals. This, of course, is simply another way of stating the effects of mating systems on the social level. In addition to this, social organization usually organizes individuals into more or less stable subpopulations that are inbred to the extent that the populations are separate and also determines the size of the subpopulation, which again determines the extent of inbreeding.

Finally, behavior and social organization have strong effects on selective survival. An adaptive behavior facilitates survival and thus should be selected. On the other hand, as pointed out above, learned organization of behavior puts a survival premium on learning itself, which may mask genetic differences except those affecting the capacity for learning per se.

Social organization, by bringing about the various processes of social selection, introduces a new process of selection that may either facilitate or work against other sorts of selection processes. In general, the effect of social organization is to protect the individual against biotic and physical selection processes, thus limiting differential survival. It does, however, favor the survival of individuals that adapt and contribute to the continued organization of the system.

All of these phenomena form a long list of independently acting change processes. Consequently, we must conclude that there is no detailed general theory of evolution that applies to all species. There are general categories of change processes, but how these operate depends on the nature of any particular species and hence upon its past evolution and how it has been affected by such processes. A general theory gives us a guide as to what to look for in any species, but does not provide a finite mode of operation for them. This applies particularly to the human species, which has certain unique processes operating within it.

THE NATURE OF SOCIAL SYSTEMS

Physiological Systems and Social Systems

The biological concept of systems was primarily developed by students of anatomy and physiology, and has only been secondarily extended to the study of social organization. It is therefore useful to compare not only the concepts used but also the organization that exists on two levels (Table 10.3).

Both levels of organization conform to the general definition of systems as groups of interacting entities. Beyond this, the nature of the entities and their interactions are quite divergent. The most basic and important difference is that while physiological systems are organized anatomically, i.e., the entities bear fixed spatial relationships to each other, the entities comprising social systems are movable and do not have fixed spatial relationships. Two human individuals who are attached to each other may be in actual contact or thousands of miles apart.

It follows that the concept of social structure as a metaphor, whether derived from physical structure or from living anatomical structure, is best only partially appropriate, and at the worst, completely false. It is at best used for what it actually is, a metaphor. There are spatial relationships among social entities, based on social attachment, site attachment, and features in the ecosystem, but such relationships are flexible and enormously variable and must be analyzed specifically in each case. The concepts of proximity, social distance, and home range are much more appropriate and useful.

A second major difference lies in the nature of the interactions between entities, and is derived from the above. Interactions in social systems are predominantly behavioral, rather than being predominantly chemical as they are in physiological systems. Behavior results in signals, which may be visual, auditory, olfactory or tactile. Olfaction, combined with taste, is the chemical sense, and to this extent there is some overlap between social and physiological communication. Indeed, in some species, chemical signals may produce direct effects on the nervous system and so stimulate behavior. Such substances, called pheromones, are so named because they mimic the internal action of hormones.

Differentiation in function between constituent entities is achieved in different ways on the two levels of organization. In physiological organization, cells become differentially functional as they diverge structurally, and similar cells combine in tissues. In social organization, organisms may also be differentiated according to function with accompanying individual differences in structure, the simplest sort of variation being that among adult females, adult males, and young of both sexes. Among social insects, such organization has been carried further, with anatomical and physiological specializations for the functions of reproduction, care of young, the building of nests, and defense. It is tempting to analogize the resulting "castes" with tissues, except that the members of the castes, while their behavior is to some degree coordinated, still react behaviorally and so with a considerable degree of variation and independence.

Finally, physiological organization is definitely hierarchical, while social organization (from which the concept of hierarchy originally

Table 10.3
PHYSIOLOGICAL AND SOCIAL SYSTEMS COMPARED

Characteristic	Social Systems	Physiological Systems
Spatial Relationships	Movable	Fixed
Unit of Organization	Organism	Cell
Interactions	Behavioral	Chemical
Organization	Relationship	Tissue
	Group	Organ
	Institutions (Humans only)	Organ systems

came) may or may not be organized in such a fashion. This concept of hierarchical organization is one of the least useful metaphors, derived as it was from a special form of human organization based on structural analogy with a pyramid, plus the assumption of one-way control. Humans were divided into classes with each controlling a larger class below it, the largest class being on the bottom.

Superficially considered, there is some similarity with physiological systems. An organ controls the tissues that compose it, for example. But the organ includes tissues and is not separate from them. The same form of *inclusive* hierarchy is found on the social level, especially well developed in human societies, where groups include individuals, and institutions include groups, and so on. But the *exclusive* or priestly hierarchy is something new and does not appear in physiology. There is no one "queen cell" that controls the brain, for example. Even the nervous system, which coordinates a great deal of physiological activity, is subject to two-way interaction and feedback from other systems.

These comparisons lead to the conclusion that no single general theory of systems organization is possible. While it is conceivable that a phenomenon may exist on every level of organization, as does two-way interaction between entities, the nature of such interactions varies from level to level. Indeed, the principle of creativity itself argues against the notion of deriving all phenomena from some one lower level process. Instead, we need to develop bodies of theories appropriate to each level, to relate these where possible but to avoid the assumption that all are derivable from a single unifying principle.

It follows also that the idea of a society as a superorganism, as Emerson (1952) suggested on the basis of his studies of insect societies, is useful as a technique of comparison rather than as a valid concept. Societies do carry on some of the functions of organisms but they also do things which organisms cannot. A society is a *superorganization*, in the sense that it includes organization between organisms, but it is not itself an organism.

In summary, social organization strongly modifies all processes of biological evolution, particularly as they relate to the evolution of social organization itself. It may create conditions that either greatly speed up evolutionary processes or promote extreme stability, with all intergradations between. The elaborate nature of human social organization, strongly affected as it is by cultural evolution, makes the problem of its biological effects extremely important.

Chapter XI

On Cultural Evolution

Evolution, defined as changes in the organization of living systems that persist for more than one generation, includes change processes on three levels of organization: genetic systems, social systems and ecosystems. Corresponding to these are theories of biological evolution, cultural evolution and ecosystem change. Social systems are affected by all three of these processes, which interact with each other. This chapter will deal primarily with cultural evolution, defined as changes in behavior resulting from changes in behavioral information passed along from one generation to another.

CULTURAL EVOLUTION IN NONHUMAN ANIMALS

In addition to direct effects, changes in social systems involve interactions with systems on two other levels. With respect to social-genetic interaction, I have already shown that social systems can produce changes in genetic systems through the process of social selection. Conversely, genetic changes from whatever cause can modify the organization of social systems. The latter is difficult to demonstrate clearly under natural conditions because it is usually impossible to experimentally separate genetic differences from other sorts of population differences. In domesticated species, however, where clear-cut genetic differences in social behavior among strains have been established, it is easy to demonstrate that such differences result in different kinds of social organization. For example, highly aggressive breeds of dogs such as fox terriers, basenjis, and Telomians tend to develop rigid dominance orders, whereas more peaceful breeds, such as beagles, develop much looser systems (Pawlowski & Scott, 1956). Likewise, male dogs develop dominance orders on the basis of physical contests, whereas females tend to do this on the basis of threats and vocalization (Scott & Fuller, 1965).

Modification by Experience

Social organization can be modified as the result of differential experience as well as by genetic variation. Mice can be trained to be either fierce fighters or completely peaceful in their relationships with each other, resulting in the presence or absence of social organization based on fighting (Scott, 1944).

Behaviorally Transmitted Modifications of Behavior

Such experientially-induced changes in social organization can be termed evolutionary only if they can persist for more than a single generation. Such a persistent change is cultural evolution, defined as a change in behavior that is transmitted through behavioral communication rather than by the transmission of genetic information. As defined, such changes must be social in nature and so involve a change in social organization, however slight. Such changes can and do take place independently from genetic change. We may, therefore, speak of cultural inheritance as contrasted to genetic inheritance.

One of the commonly used tests for the presence of cultural inheritance is that of rearing an animal apart from its kind and consequently having only the opportunity for genetic transmission of information. If a certain behavior pattern disappears, we can assume that it was transmitted culturally, but if it persists we can conclude that it is transmitted genetically. However, the results of such experiments are always difficult to interpret, and a result such as the latter does not necessarily prove complete genetic determination.

A much more important problem is whether or not cultural changes actually take place. A few examples will demonstrate that there is evidence that such changes occur in the higher vertebrates and will also illustrate the problems of interpreting such evidence. Bighorn sheep are historically reported to have migrated each year from the high mountain meadows to low buttes and ridges on which they spent the winter, traveling back to the mountains again in the spring (Honess & Frost, 1942). Since stock raisers began to use fences in the western United States, these migrations have ceased, and the sheep have been spending winters in the high mountains under severe conditions where survival rates are poor. It seems obvious (and this corresponds to what we know of sheep behavior (Scott, 1945), that migration routes were learned as younger animals followed older ones and that the information was passed along from generation to generation. However, it also can be argued that those sheep that attempted to migrate were more often killed by hunters and, thus, that a genetic change has taken place. If the latter explanation is correct, it would follow that there must have been considerable genetic variation with respect to the tendency to migrate and that extreme selection through hunting affected only the migrants. It is therefore difficult to support this modification of behavior as a clear-cut example of cultural change.

Geist (1971) has since studied the Rocky Mountain bighorns in the mountains of southern Alberta, where the animals have been little disturbed except by hunters, and where the sheep still migrate between summer and winter ranges, sometimes as much as 20 miles. He concluded, based on the year-by-year distribution of identified individuals, that the young animals inherit the home ranges of their elders by acquiring their movement patterns. The majority of females adopted the ranges where their respective parent flocks had stayed, a minority shifting to other flocks between 1-2 years of age. Young rams leave the female flocks in which they were born and join other groups of males, acquiring the home ranges and migration patterns of these flocks instead. Strong observational evidence thus supports the hypothesis of cultural transmission of migration patterns to individuals during a time period when overall patterns of the flocks had not been altered.

We have already mentioned the change in the habits of the English blue tit, which rapidly adopted the behavior of opening milk bottles (Hinde, 1969). This again appears to be cultural change, but an alternate explanation is simply that these birds had a surplus capacity that came into use in response to an ecological change, namely the advent of milk bottles with paper caps. To show that the change was truly cultural, it would have to be demonstrated that birds who saw other birds feeding in this way adopted this habit faster than those that did not observe it. In short, behavioral transmission of behavior must be conclusively demonstrated before we can speak of cultural evolution.

The necessary unambiguous evidence for cultural transmission was provided by Kawai's (1965) detailed observations of changes in behavior among Japanese monkey troops. In one troop, the behavior of washing sweet potatoes, furnished as food, was first seen in a female in 1953. By 1962 this had been acquired by all the troop members except young infants and adults more than 12 years old. A change as rapid as this could not be a genetic one, since over the nine years many of the troop members remained the same. If the new behavior was acquired individually as a result of a common surplus capacity (as suggested in the genetic explanation of the bottle-opening behavior of the tits), then it should have occurred more or less simultaneously in all members of the troop and at random with respect to social relationships. The trait actually spread slowly throughout the troop, with those animals that were closely associated with each other acquiring it first.

Cultural transmission probably occurs in less social species of mammals but is less obvious. Mainardi (1980) experimentally demonstrated the social transmission of information in laboratory house mice who learned an escape route from others. The capacity to receive information from a preceding generation should exist in any species that has the capacity to learn and in which there is some form of sensory contact with older individuals. On the other hand, transmission of information either through behavior or pheromones should occur constantly, whether received or not. Teaching, or the purposeful transmission of behavior to particular individuals, is harder to demonstrate and probably occurs rarely.

Another example of non-genetic intergenerational transmission of behavioral information is the acquisition of song patterns in the perching birds. First described in the oriole by W. E. D. Scott (1901), this phenomenon has since been verified in many other songbirds (Marler & Mundinger, 1971). A male bird reared in isolation will in adulthood produce a song unlike that of its parent, but if it has the opportunity to hear the parent it will reproduce the same song pattern a year later. The phenomenon has special interest because of its resemblance to the transmission of human language, albeit of only a single signal.

Such birds have locally distinct song patterns ("dialects"), and Mundinger (1980) has studied the origin of such dialects in the house finch, a species that was released in the Long Island areas of New York in the early 1940's. The species gradually spread, and as it did so the songs of new local populations differentiated from those of their parents, producing a branching pattern of change, except that where branches later came into contact they might influence each other and produce a mixed song pattern. Mundinger concluded that he was observing a case of ongoing cultural evolution.

He also listed nearly 50 other reported cases of cultural transmission of behavior, 17 of them occurring in chimpanzees and other primates, but also in other mammals, birds, reptiles, fish, and even some insects. Galef (1976) had compiled a similar but shorter list. Many of these cases are based on purely descriptive and sometimes anecdotal evidence. In others, the behavioral information is transmitted indirectly, as when young salmon acquire the information that leads them to return as adults to breed in the rivers in which they were spawned. The young salmon never see their parents, who pass along information merely by laying eggs in particular streams. The young salmon as they develop organize this information as a memory of the taste of the water in their native stream, which enables them to find it years later. Information of this sort, however, seems more likely to lead to stability than to cultural change.

With all these limitations, there are now solid grounds for concluding that cultural evolution of various simple sorts is possible in some other animal species than man. Therefore, such evolution must always be considered as one of the possible explanations of observed behavioral changes in a nonhuman species.

HUMAN CULTURAL EVOLUTION

While one can find occasional instances of cultural change in nonhuman animal societies, these involve relatively minor processes that usually affect only local populations and which may easily disappear. The evolution of verbal language capacity in humans, on the other hand, has produced a sort of culture and cultural change that is unique and that can only be understood as a separate phenomenon.

Relationships to Biological Evolution

While human culture is dependent upon the biologically evolved capacity for language and the associated changes in neurological organization, both the acquisition of language and the information it transmits are largely independent of genetically transmitted information. It follows that cultural evolution is similarly independent of biological evolution. Even under the most favorable circumstances, biological evolutionary changes in a population may take dozens of generations, and major changes are likely to take millions of years. Cultural change, on the other hand, may take place in a single generation or less, as it did in the American Plains Indians when they were introduced to horses and guns, and in our own culture with the invention of the automobile. We must conclude that cultural change for the most part proceeds independently of genetic change.

But not entirely. Cultural change must operate within the limits of human biological capacities. Humans race with each other, on foot, on horseback, and in automobiles, but nobody tries to race on all fours. Or to take a more extreme example, cultural change that attempts to eliminate sexual behavior cannot persist.

Also, cultural evolution affects the processes of biological evolution. The most profound effect is that on Differential Survival. All human cultures attempt to prevent or cure illness and so postpone death, and modern cultures have succeeded in doing this to a remarkable degree, although there is still no way to permanently alter the biological aging process. In this respect, cultural evolution extends and supplements a similar trend in biological evolution.

Livingstone (1980) points out several instances in which cultural selection may have influenced the distribution of genes or gene combinations in human populations, one being the persistence of the enzyme lactase in most adults in cultures that have long used milk products from other animals, in contrast to the situation in cultures that have not done this. Presumably a person in a culture having milk producing animals had a better chance of survival if she/he could digest milk and avoid lactose diarrheas. Other cases are less clear-cut; while there are average differences in physiological responsiveness to alcohol between populations that have historically been high and low consumers of alcoholic beverages, such as persons of European vs. Oriental ancestry, the variation among individuals in both populations is much greater than the overall population differences (Reed & Hanna, 1986). Thus culture may affect the process of natural selection in opposite ways, by introducing new selective processes and at the same time protecting individuals against them.

All known human societies attempt to regulate sexual reproduction through some form of marriage system that prescribes who shall mate with whom. Thus we have polygynous, monogamous and (rarely) polyandrous mating systems, with endless variations. In our own current culture we commonly have serial monogamy which in effect combines polygyny and polyandry, both sexes having multiple mates.

These mating systems usually have some effect on reproductive rates. For example, the marriage systems of many tribal societies insure that every female is early married, which should have the effect of maximizing reproduction. Other systems, such as that in present day Ireland, may involve late marriage and unmarried females, thus lowering the birth rate. Some cultures may regulate reproduction directly through infanticide, abortion and contraception.

Marriage systems may enhance inbreeding, as in the cases of villages in India where marriages usually take place within the members of a small community; or they may attempt to enhance outbreeding, as in our own cultural rules against the marriage of close relatives.

Finally, culture may even influence mutation, as ours has done by increasing exposure to radiation and chemical mutagens. The effect is to increase genetic variation, usually of an undesirable sort.

Overall, the effect of human cultural evolution is to induce major modifications in the processes of biological evolution. These effects can change and fluctuate with cultural change, which means that the modifications may not persist long enough to produce persistent biological changes. The reciprocal effects of biological evolution on cultural evolution are likely to be minor at the present time, but must have been extremely important during the evolution of language capacities.

Human Origins

It now seems clear that our remote ancestors came from Africa. Furthermore, the fossil evidence shows that they were plains living primates from extremely remote times and were small, slightly built, but erect creatures who ran and walked on two feet (Johanson & White, 1979). Why did the early hominoids develop a bipedal locomotion? If we look at other mammals that have evolved in this way, such as kangaroos among marsupials and kangaroo rats among rodents, we find them all living in arid desert-like regions. Various adaptive explanations have been suggested, including the fact that an erect posture ensures that there will be only two feet instead of four touching the hot sand or rocks and also that an erect posture gives a much wider range of vision, which could be important for survival in a more or less empty landscape. At any rate, these facts and speculations suggest that man was not only a plains living primate but a desert living one. Indeed, it is hard to see how these primitive men and women, with few or no tools or weapons, could have survived in any other habitat because of their vulnerability to the large carnivorous mammals. The large carnivores cannot survive in desert or semidesert regions where today we see only such smaller forms as coyotes, desert foxes, and jackals, which could not resist threats from even moderately sized primates such as the early hominoids.

Leakey and Lewin (1977) speculated that the early hominoids may have lived in savannah areas similar to those in parts of present-day Africa, with moisture enough to support occasional trees together with luxuriant grasses in the rainy seasons of the year. Such areas also support herds of antelopes and various carnivores, including hyenas, Cape hunting dogs of the family Canidae, and leopards and even lions among the cats. The association of leopard remains with early hominoids supports this idea, but I suggest that hominoids could have co-existed with these larger carnivores only after they developed tools (weapons), expertise in their use, and became hunters themselves. I would also suggest that, if hominoids were anything like people today, they would have moved into any area that was open to them. That is there would be a trade-off between the more abundant food supplies of the savannah, and the greater safety of the desert, the latter situation being that in which the African Bushmen live today.

A second anatomical feature from which we can draw inferences regarding behavior was their teeth. These, together with the jawbones that support them, are always the best preserved of humanoid remains. They are the hardest bones in the body and so are less likely to be destroyed by weather, predation, or accidental crushing. Even a superficial inspection of these teeth shows us that they are primarily suited for an omnivorous diet and do not show the dietary specializations of the carnivores or the grazing ungulates. Even gorillas, which are the primate attempt at a herbivore with a purely vegetarian diet, have teeth of the same general kind.

Our ancestors thus could have eaten anything. But teeth that have been used show signs of wear depending on the type of food. Johanson and Edey (1981), after reviewing the then available evidence, concluded that their specimen, which they named *Australopithecus afarensis* or Lucy for short, was indeed an omnivore, eating a variety of vegetable foods and probably some animal food when it could be caught. If these early humanoids also had a digestive tract of intermediate length, as does modern man, they could never have subsisted on foliage, as do gorillas, but must have lived on anything they could pick up: concentrated vegetable foods such as seeds, nuts, roots and berries, together with such small animals as they could pick up or catch. They could have scavenged parts of the bodies of large animals left by carnivores, as Louis Leakey once suggested, but any hunting of these large mammals must have awaited the invention of hunting weapons.

Then there are the jaws. These projected in an ape-like fashion, but were more rounded, similar to those of modern humans. One of the major changes in human skeletal evolution has been a reduction in the length of the jaws and a change in shape so that the chin, rounded in ancient men, now projects further than the teeth in most humans.

Along with this has come a reduction in the size of the teeth. Brace has made extensive studies of ancient remains in all parts of the world and concludes that this has been a general tendency. From the late Pleistocene until approximately 10,000 years ago, the change was a gradual one, then became more rapid (Brace & Rosenberg, 1986). This last change was associated with a change in diet as indicated by the appearance of blackened stones that might have been used in ground ovens, and latter of pottery cooking dishes (Brace, 1979). That is, large teeth were no longer necessary and because of relaxed selection they became smaller. This conflicts with genetic evolutionary theory, by which the absence of selection should simply halt change. The two views can be reconciled if it is assumed that the change in tooth size was associated with some other change in the skull such as the increasing size of the cranium, development of the vocal apparatus, or even social selection toward a more attractive facial appearance that might have involved facial expression. Selection of such positively adaptive characters would, after the cultural discovery of cooked food, no longer be opposed by selection for large teeth. In any case, this is an example of the interaction of cultural and biological evolution, with cultural change speeding up a biological one.

A third anatomical feature was the cranium. The early hominoids had relatively small brains and low-crowned skulls compared to modern man, and the distinction between the genus *Australopithecus* and that of *Homo* is generally made on the basis of cranial size. It is tempting to assume that this change was associated with the development of the capacity for language.

Unfortunately, the speech-producing organs do not fossilize. The larynx, pharynx and vocal cords are soft tissues. The closest we can come is to look at the attachment points of muscles to the skull and the shape of the corresponding bones. On this evidence Lieberman (1975) concluded that *Homo* has had a fully developed voice box for only 50,000 years. Even Neanderthal Man did not have a fully developed pharynx. This does not mean that earlier humans could not talk; only that they could not talk as well as modern humans.

Lieberman (1984) also points out that in nonhuman mammals, including chimpanzees and other primates, the position of the larynx or windpipe is high enough in the throat that it can form a continuous airway with the nasal passage. Thus a dog can breathe and drink water at the same time without choking. The larynx of the human newborn infant occupies a similar position with similar results: it nurses and breathes without choking. But the human adult larynx is much lower, leaving a large resonating chamber in the back of the throat through which sound waves pass as they leave the vocal cords in the larynx. Thus the capacity for producing modulated sound increases as an infant's vocal apparatus becomes more like that of an adult. And an adult cannot talk and ingest food at the same time.

The relative sizes and positions of the bony hard palate and basicranium (skull floor) reflect these changes, and on this basis also Lieberman concluded that Neanderthals could not have had a fully developed vocal apparatus, although the numerous cultural artifacts associated with their remains indicate that they must have had speech. They could talk, but not as well as modern man.

Lieberman analyzed the measurements of some of the more primitive hominoids and concluded that, with the possible exception of *Homo habilis*, all of them were similar in their suprapharyngeal airways to the plan of chimpanzees and other mammals. On the basis of the then available evidence he was not prepared to say when and where the new model vocal apparatus appeared in the *Homo erectus* line (the presumed ancestors of modern man). All these fossil hominoids are represented by usually unique and often fragmentary specimens rather than populations of complete skeletons. For this and other reasons, Lieberman's conclusions must remain tentative until supported by other evidence.

Most importantly from the viewpoint of this chapter, Lieberman concluded that the early divergent humanoid lines were replaced by others having superior language powers. He also suggested a new adaptive function of language powers, that of group problem solving. Because a problem can be communicated to many others through language, there is a greatly increased chance that some person in the group may find a solution, or that two or more may interact to find the solution. This is reminiscent of Corning's synergy hypothesis, and indeed Lieberman used the term. "The synergetic effect of rapid data transmission through the mechanism of encoded speech and the cognitive powers of the large humanoid brain probably yielded the full human linguistic system" (p. 329). Finally, Lieberman pointed out that neoteny, the retention of infantile characteristics in adulthood, will not explain the evolution of the human voice box; the vocal apparatus of human adults is not like that of infants.

In Darwin's day, it was common to speak of a "missing link" between man and other primates because there appeared to be literally no fossils of the remote ancestors of human beings. The reasons for this are now becoming clear. Africa had not yet been explored and studied by paleontologists. The dry areas in which the humanoids lived were unfavorable for the formation of fossils, and it is only after lifetimes of searching that these have been found. Further, a moderately large animal living in a semiarid area can never become numerous simply because of the scarcity of food. Rare animals leave few fossils.

Our ancestors became successful in terms of numbers only a relatively short time ago. We shall probably never know exactly when the capacity for human language first appeared, but we can surmise that it was responsible for this increase in numbers because of the immense advantages it confers for the transmission of information. Thus the capacity for language must have had an enhancing effect upon the development and use of tools, particularly fire, clothing and weapons used in hunting, all of which have enormous advantages for survival.

Why did no other species evolve the ability to communicate in this way? Any answers that we can give are speculative. The basic capacities that other primates lack are quite simple, namely the ability to make sounds voluntarily and the ability to modulate them. It is possible that such capacities were useful on barren plains as a means of keeping in contact. In such areas, which have few landmarks and where it would be necessary to spread out to find food, vocal calls would be useful for keeping the members of a group in touch with each other and in coordinating their activities. Also, most predators react to loud noises as if they were unpleasant, perhaps because they warn prey animals, or perhaps because they interfere with attention to an activity that must be highly coordinated to be successful. The ability to make such noises at will could have been useful as a defense against predators. But many other species, including the rest of the primates and animals living in a great variety of habitats, have evolved the capacity to produce vocal signals.

The ability to mimic vocal signals made by other species has independently evolved in various species of birds, probably as a surplus capacity arising in connection with the evolution of individual recognition signals and local song dialects, but no bird species has ever progressed to the further point of symbolic language. We can only conclude that the origin of human language capacity was probably accidental.

Biological Evolution and Language

However our original language capacities may have evolved (and they may have first appeared in a purely accidental fashion as a result of mutation or surplus capacities), it is obvious that language as such is useful only within a social system; that is, it is not an ability that confers adaptive advantage for one individual alone. But, once the ability appeared in a social group, that particular group would have an almost immediate advantage for survival over other groups that were unable to communicate well. Hence, it should have produced differential survival at the level of social groups. Further, in any social group where communication by language is practiced, the individual with poor language abilities is at a strong disadvantage compared to the individual who has superior language ability and thus has strong abilities both in accumulating information and in the ability to influence his or her fellows. Even in modern civilized societies, persons with poor language ability (the so-called feebleminded) are at a strong disadvantage with respect to reproduction (Reed & Reed, 1965). Consequently, there should always be strong social selection in favor of language ability. Thus, physical and biotic selection directed at the level of the social group should combine with social selection within the group to produce changes in the capacity for language. None of these classes of selection necessarily involves violent competition, either between groups or between individuals.

Finally, language tends to change and diversify independently in different small groups, not only as a result of isolation but also tending to further isolate such groups from each other. The stranger who cannot make himself understood is not likely to change tribes. Thus, language should act as an isolating mechanism maintaining separation of local groups and so contributing to genetic as well as cultural changes.

Because the use of language facilities survival within a social group, it produces some relaxation of external selection directed against characteristics other than language, as well as positive selection toward improvement in language itself. Hence, more variation is possible within the social system, again introducing a condition favorable to genetic evolution.

One of the direct ways in which language contributes to survival is that it facilitates the use of tools by speeding up communication and contributing to the storage of information. Once our humanoid ancestors had acquired certain tools, especially fire, clothing, and weapons that could be used in hunting, they began to enter new physical environments, moving out of the desert and arid plains and eventually spreading all over the world with the exception of Antartica. Tools resulted in the relaxation of selection from certain outside sources; but at the same time, by entering into new ecosystems, humans were subjected to a variety of new selective processes. This, again, would contribute to rapid biological evolutionary change. It also involved men, women, and children, now truly members of our own species, *Homo sapiens*, in the phenomenon of adaptive radiation, observed whenever a group of animals enters a new habitat, resulting in the diversity now seen between members of our species in different parts of the world. However, this diversity never reached the point of division into new species before the evolution of culture made humans so numerous and mobile that these local groups came back into contact to form a continuous worldwide breeding structure (Scott, in Scott & Fuller, 1965).

In short, all theoretical considerations lead to the conclusion that once minimum capacities for the use of language appeared, human evolution should have proceeded very rapidly in the direction of maximizing this ability.

Bigelow (1975) has argued that selection between groups may have been augmented by warfare; i.e., one local group could literally exterminate another. While this may have happened occasionally, it is difficult to see warfare as being a major factor among early gatherer-hunter groups. Nor is it a necessary condition. All that is necessary is for one group to outbreed another.

Agonistic behavior probably had a more profound effect within groups. Freedman (1984) has suggested, on the basis of observed behavior in certain nonhuman primates and human tribal organization, that there is a tendency for such groups to reproduce by fission. When the group divides, it does so along family lines, with a group of close relatives leaving together. This of course would increase inbreeding and the chance that the departing group would carry different and possibly more beneficial combinations of genes.

Thus, the biological evolution of the capacity for cultural evolution should have produced a strong feedback effect, increasing its speed. It is likely that this interaction produced the extraordinarily rapid rate of human organic evolution as well as that contributing to behavior and culture. Even though hominoid ancestors can now be traced back nearly 4 million years, the change is still rapid compared to those of other species.

This brings up the problem of what language actually does for a social group. We now use language in enormously sophisticated fashions, but we should remember that it has taken at least 50 thousand years (Lieberman, 1975, 1984) to achieve our present sophistication, and probably a great deal longer. A great many of these language skills, particularly those associated with science, have been developed within the past few centuries.

Aside from its highly specialized functions, language has some obvious simple and general ones. One is social control and coordination, as language is used as a tool to manipulate others, beginning developmentally with a mother's efforts to control the behavior of her infant and the infant's efforts to control her. Second, language results in the transfer of information from individual to individual. As we have seen, such transfers do occur in nonhuman species, but the process is enormously speeded up by verbal language, which also facilitates transfer of information from one generation to the next. A major advantage of such transmission is the ease with which the use of tools and perfection in their use can be taught. Finally, language has order and organization and hence tends to impose order (however artificially and unrealistically), especially on social systems but also upon people's ideas about the physical and biotic world. That is to say, language is a special sort of symbolic system which can not only be used to represent other systems but also may influence them.

Grammar, Logic, and Social Customs

The order which is inherent in any system of language was first discovered by grammarians, who were able to demonstrate that languages tended to be organized in similar fashions, especially if they appeared to have a common origin.

Thus, the linguists found that languages might use similar terms for objects or even social relationships that were presumably shared (English "brother"; German *Bruder*, Latin *frater*, French *frere*, Russian *brat* and so on). And so they grouped these languages into a common family, the Indo-European. To illustrate the organizational basis of a language, the English language is organized into units called sentences which can be reduced in their simplest forms to a subject, verb, and object. To use the language of systems, an entity (subject) acts on (verb) a second entity (object). Such an organization is consistent with the general law of causation, which states that when event A always precedes event B, A can be considered the cause of event B. Even nonhuman animals act as if they were aware of this principle, which introduces predictability into the world. Such a simple formulation, however, is not consistent with reciprocal causation (although this concept can also be expressed by language by using more complex arrangements of symbols), and it is therefore consistent with mechanistic theories of causation and may have suggested such formulations. It is possible also that it may have led to the concept of hierarchical organization and status; i.e. the subject comes first and ordinarily acts upon the object, and thus is superior to it, whatever may be the case in the nonsymbolic world.

Another way in which language affects social organization is through the establishment of rules of behavior. Studies by cultural anthropologists demonstrate that each culture tends to set up its own rules that may vary widely even with respect to such fundamental matters as the sex roles (Mead, 1939). Further, each culture usually organizes its rules into logically consistent codes stemming from a small number of general principles or assumptions.

The reasons given for such tendencies are somewhat speculative, but there are at least two reasonable explanations. The first is that logically related codes of behavior are easier to remember, and hence more likely to persist than a collection of unrelated rules. A second explanation that does not conflict with the first is that people are emotionally disturbed by conflicting or noncongruent statements which imply that they should be acting in two opposite ways.

In any case, such codes of behavior are symbolic systems that purport to represent social behavior and organization in a particular culture. Being developed intuitively and largely based on deductive logic, they tend to be noncongruent with real organization. While they may act as guidelines for behavior and so affect it, they may in some cases be so far removed from reality as to be impossible to live by. Also, they lack many of the properties of the living systems which they attempt to represent. They frequently assume one-way causation or are derived from a single general principle. In either case, they do not represent the interaction and feedback that occurs in living systems. The entities (symbols) that compose such logical systems are nonliving and do not, in fact, interact with each other, and thus cannot portray a real living system. Finally, and also because they are nonliving, they tend to be even more stable than living systems, and this is especially true if the codes have been preserved in writing. Once a code has been written down, anyone can refer back to the original, even though many generations and tens or thousands of years may have elapsed.

Cultural Change

There are some fascinating analogies between genetic inheritance and cultural inheritance. In recent years it has been fashionable to think of genetic transmission in terms of information theory, which was originally developed in order to explain cultural phenomena. For example, there is an analogy between genes, which are the units of genetics, and words, which are the units of cultural heredity. Both can be considered to transmit information. A new word can be considered the equivalent of gene mutation, and so on. However, these are only analogies, i.e., resemblances in function, and we should remember that words and genes are not only distinctly different structurally but also that they show certain important differences in organization.

The chromosomal system for the transmission of heredity is a binary one, that is, genes are always associated in pairs, and in sexual reproduction each parent can only transmit one of a given pair to any particular offspring. The system of language transmission is not binary, although it can be reduced to this in dichotomous classifications and in binary computer systems. The use of words presents not only multiple alternatives but in some cases an almost infinite choice of alternatives.

Second, the genetic system is essentially a noncumulative one, in the sense that no individual normally has more than two genes at one locus. In the process of bisexual reproduction the system automatically discards genes, this being one of the processes that result in genetic evolution. The genetic system has cumulative properties in that variant genes can be accumulated in the gene pool of the species, but limitations upon this are imposed by the total numbers in the population and the nonsurvival of mutations that interfere with successful living. On the other hand, cultural systems are indefinitely cumulative. There is no theoretical limit to the amount of information that can be stored and transmitted in cultural fashion except that imposed by available space in the physical world.

Both language itself and the culture which it transmits can evolve. In the case of language, new units are continually being introduced by local social groups. In our own English language we particularly notice the formation of slang, but new words constantly come in also from such sources as scientific research and foreign languages. Along with these changes, if groups of people are somewhat isolated from each other, they tend to develop their own vocabularies, ways of pronunciation, and even grammatical usages. Such changes can develop into local dialects, and if isolation continues long enough, dialects can evolve into separate languages. This change process goes on most rapidly in spoken rather than written language, which is more readily fixed. It is similar to genetic evolution in that isolation is conducive to differentiation between local groups. The results of this process could formerly be seen in the Indian tribes of California, each of which spoke a different language not understood even by relatively close neighbors (Kroeber, 1961). Similarly, hundreds of languages have survived on the continent of Africa, and in the subcontinent of India there are dozens of languages and dialects.

While the processes that produce change in language are still operating, there are two factors that slow these down in modern cultures. The first is the existence of written language that indefinitely preserves words in their older forms. The second factor is the increasing use of modern means of transportation and mass communication that make isolation between local groups virtually impossible. A third factor is cultural dominance. A politically dominant culture tends to extend its language while obliterating those of others, as occurred with the extension of Arabic during the Arabian conquest, the extension of Russian in the Russian Empire, and the extension of English to various parts of the world as the result of imperial expansion. A more classical example is the Roman Empire, which laid the foundation for "Romance" languages in Italy, Romania, Spain, and France.

With respect to the evolution of human culture, it likewise carries within it processes that inevitably produce change. If for no other reason, human culture changes because it is cumulative. Each new generation of people tends to accumulate additional stores of information. Furthermore, since culture is not inherited biologically, each child must accumulate its own store of information, and because he starts at a different point in time than did his parents, there is a different mass of information available to him. He (or she) never absorbs it all, and so something is inevitably lost. In the process of organizing its cultural inheritance, a child may do this in new ways and consequently produce a reorganization of culture. Without written records we would expect that cultural change would proceed relatively rapidly, contrary to a favorite myth that in the "old" days human social conditions were stable.

As we stated in our consideration of genetic evolution, reorganization is impossible unless preceded by disorganization. The ultimate disorganization in human life is death: all the cultural information accumulated by an individual is dissipated at his death unless he or she has been able to transmit it in some form. No one is ever able to transmit all his accumulated information simply because of inherent difficulties in communication. An even more important factor is that each new individual must accumulate and organize information anew (in this sense, a child really is a "tabula rasa," or blank slate). Compared to genetic evolution, the essential disorganizing process lies not so much in the process of transmission – which can, under favorable conditions, be extremely accurate – but in the preservation of developmentally unorganized material in the germ cells followed by the destruction of organized material in death. Thus, cultural evolution also is basically dependent on biological processes, but of a different sort. The possibility that unorganized portions of both individual and social organization may be maintained suggests some interesting possibilities concerning the conscious planning of organization on both these levels.

Written records greatly extend the amount of information that can be stored by a culture and the range of time through which it can be transmitted. People are still responding to the Bible more than 2000 years after it was written. Theoretically, all information could be stored and made available to later generations over infinite periods of time. Nevertheless, much information is discarded or lost. In the first place, the culture itself dictates what shall be written. In earlier civilizations records were chiefly kept concerning the lives of kings and their accomplishments. Today we still stress political records, but the storage of scientific information is considered equally important. We store more information than cultures in the past, but nevertheless much is lost. Not only is there selective storage and destruction, but there may be accidental loss as well, as when the library of Alexandria was burned, resulting in the destruction of much of the recorded Greek culture. Such catastrophic accidents are rare today, but they can occur. Furthermore, under modern conditions the capacities for storage in libraries are so great that they result in a sort of cultural overload. Even with the aid of computers, much of this information becomes irretrievable and so is lost.

Thus, there are several ways in which cultural evolution takes place. Many of these are analogous to the processes of biological evolution, especially in that the rates of cultural and biological changes are both related to the size of the group; small populations are more favorable to rapid change than very large ones. However, there are certain very important differences. One is the cumulative quality of cultural change, and the other is the fact that, unlike the genes, bits of lost cultural information are much more readily replaceable. Knowledge can be rediscovered.

This brings up the question of whether there is anything in culture corresponding to biological death and extinction. The answer is that cultural death can occur, but does not occur regularly and inevitably. With small cultural groups such as the California Indian tribes, the culture disappeared as the tribes died out as a result of contact with diseases borne by Europeans and slaughter by settlers (Kroeber, 1961). Small human populations can be wiped out by disease, starvation, and warfare, and their cultures perish with them. However, the wars of the past have seldom completely wiped out large populations. What they have done is to introduce a new culture which merges with the old to a greater or lesser degree. For example, the Mayan Indians of Yucatan formed a relatively large population that was reduced but not eliminated by war with their Spanish conquerors. They no longer had access to the written records of their cultural ancestors but retained their own language and maintained many of their basic ways of life except for religion and the religious hierarchy. In China the Mongolian conquerors left few traces behind them. The Norman conquerors of England eventually lost their language but modified that of the conquered Saxons, eventually producing an essentially unified culture.

The Future of Human Cultural Evolution

Because of the creative nature of cultural evolution, there is almost no way that one can precisely predict its future. Even an all-knowing scientist, if one had lived contemporaneously with *Homo erectus* in Africa, would have found it difficult to anticipate that the descendants of this creature would be playing in symphony orchestras or conducting figure skating contests. The best that we can do is to look at the past and infer what we can from historical trends. From these we can conclude that there are at least three major ways in which cultural evolution has altered the human condition.

The Relationship of Humans to Ecosystems

The first change of this sort was that resulting from the discovery or invention of tools and artifacts: tools for hunting, fire, and clothing. Hunting weapons permitted humans to metamorphose from gatherers and scavengers to gatherer-hunters and thus to occupy the position of a predator in an ecosystem, competing with some of the group hunting social carnivores such as the Cape hunting dogs of Africa. While there was some very early migration out of Africa into tropical areas, it was fire and clothing that permitted human social groups to move out of ecosystems similar to those in the Great Rift Valley of Africa (whence all the earliest hominoid remains now known have come) into all terrestrial ecosystems in all continents with the exception of Antartica. In so doing, humans altered these ecosystems to greater or lesser degrees. Some authors believe, for example, that the extinction of the large Pleistocene mammals (Martin, 1984) came about largely because of the hunting of these early men.

A second major change came with the dawn of agriculture, which occurred independently in Mesopotamia (and adjacent regions), in Central and South America, and in China and the Far East. Agriculture involves the domestication of plants and animals. From an ecological viewpoint, raising farm crops alters the ecosystem in two ways: Cultivation halts the process of plant succession, so that conditions are always favorable for the desired plant species. More generally, cultivation holds plant succession in a highly productive stage. Domestication of animals produces another sort of modification of the ecosystem, again favoring certain species and enabling man to become almost the sole predator upon them, as well as to use animals as sources of energy to operate tools and machines.

At any rate, agriculture resulted in a large increase in human populations, and people began to live in cities about 7000 BC in the Middle and Near East. This in turn set the stage for the cultural evolution of more elaborate and complex forms of social organization.

The third major change has been recorded historically, one based on the direct utilization of physical energy rather than its indirect use through plants and animals. This change has not been sudden; wind power has been used to propel boats since ancient times. Water power began to be used extensively in the late Middle Ages to operate grain mills. But the greatest change came with the use of coal to operate steam engines beginning in the 18th century. This change has been called the Industrial Revolution, corresponding to the agricultural revolution some 9000 years earlier.

Coal, and its related fuels, oil and gas, are fossil fuels and so originally derived from plants. Their supplies are limited and this will eventually force some new change in man's relationship to his ecosystems. Enthusiastic proponents of nuclear energy once held it to be a cheap source of inexhaustible power, but it has so far not lived up to their promises. It is far from cheap to control its potentially dangerous energy, and no one has yet found a satisfactory way to dispose of nuclear waste. Will we see a new revolution in the human place in the ecosystem, or will we experience a slow reversion to our former place?

Cultural Change in Social Organization

A second major aspect of cultural evolution is that concerned with social organization and social systems, resulting in an uniquely human phenomenon, the *institution*, defined as social organization maintained without face-to-face contact. The most primitive of these institutions is based on family organization, originally maintained in small face-to-face groups of up to approximately 50 individuals, as it is in present day primate groups and human gatherer-hunter societies. But with language it can be extended to larger groups, as it is among tribal societies organized into clans, which may include several thousand people. The primary feature of family organization, both in face to face groups and as institutions, is that each member of the organization is related to every other one, with the behavioral interaction in each relationship defined at least to some degree.

The second human institution to arise was probably that of religion, an institution whose most obvious activity (though not the only one) was the conduct of ceremonies with respect to supernatural beings. Closely following, or perhaps originating from it, were governmental or political institutions, creating a class of individuals whose function was to regulate the behavior of other individuals, usually through real or implied force. Also growing out of religious institutions and finally separating from them were educational institutions, whose function is the transmission of information from generation to generation.

Finally, and probably most recently, we have economic institutions, groups of people that were at first devoted to trading tools and other human artifacts and later took over the processes of production as well.

Each institution (those above being the major ones), not only has a special set of functions in any human society, but also a special set of verbal rules describing and regulating behavior in the institution. These rules are logically related to each other and so may be called a code of behavior, or they also may be called a belief system. These are an intrinsic part of institutional organization; no institution can function without them. Both verbal and functional organization can and does change with time; i.e., this is one of the processes of human cultural evolution.

There are no social institutions in nonhuman animals. There are face-to-face family groups but no verbal rules describing them and integrating separate family groups. There are no churches, no schools, no governments, and no businesses in nonhuman animal societies. Institutions are a higher level of social organization peculiar to human societies and their changing development is a major feature of human cultural evolution.

These more complex institutions over the centuries have evolved in the direction of depersonalization of the interactions between members of the institution, increasing specialization of social roles and, along with the latter, the multiplication of such roles. This has had several consequences. A major effect is that one individual can replace another without disrupting the system (although it is always disturbed to a greater or lesser degree, depending on its organization). Another consequence is that the institution becomes potentially immortal; as long as replacement of entities occurs, there is no dissolution of the system. Still another is that the same individual can have roles in two or more systems simultaneously. Perhaps most importantly, institutions of this sort, not based on individual recognition, can become much larger than the 5,000 or so members which seems to be the upper limit of size in tribal organizations based on the family.

As human history shows, the process of evolving these large-scale institutions has been a long and difficult one, and is not yet over. People in many parts of the world are still living within tribal organizations and we have still to develop effective worldwide institutions.

What is the future of human institutional evolution? There are signs that institutional organization may be reaching biological limits, at least in present forms. People need the satisfactions derived from face-to-face contacts, and while television and similar communicatory devices provide some of these, most, like television, lack the feedback function.

Nevertheless, political institutions have been extended over very large areas of the world: China, India, Russia and the United States. But political institutions, based on force as they are, typically expand only with the use of force, as in warfare. And subject peoples, especially if they belong to a different language and culture are notoriously rebellious. Political organizations based on force are inherently unstable.

Economic institutions extend beyond the boundaries of political institutions to which they bear close relationships. The world is now often supposed to be divided into two major types of economic institutions: capitalistic and socialistic. Actually, they almost never exist in pure form, but in a variety of mixtures and modifications, none of which are completely independent. Perhaps worldwide institutions will eventually emerge from economic organization, but this has not yet occurred nor will it necessarily be desirable.

Like all living systems, institutions tend to become increasingly complexly organized, and as they do so become extraordinarily stable. Here again we see the operation of the principle – No reorganization without disorganization. When an institutional change takes place, there is usually some destruction of existing organization, often accompanied by violence. The change is usually called a revolution, and one of the major problems of the social sciences is that of bringing about desirable institutional change in a nonviolent fashion, not only to avoid excessive destruction, but in order to bring about desirable changes that are often only partially realized by violent revolutions.

Revolution is a vast and complex phenomenon which almost necessarily arouses emotional responses; I shall therefore treat it only in the broad context of cultural evolution. In order for a revolution to take place in any sort of institution, there must be widespread dissatisfaction with its operation. Second, some person or group of persons must have ideas concerning its improvement or replacement. Since institutions are founded on common belief systems, additional people must be converted to these new beliefs. Notable examples are the founding of new religions by prophets who preach a new way of life, new systems of economics such as that of Marx, and new systems of government as advocated by the early American leaders involved in the American Revolution. Campbell (1975) has suggested that cultural evolution of institutions is shaped by a process analogous to Natural Selection. That is, when two or more institutions come into competition, the one that is most satisfactory will survive. He concludes that, considered over long historical periods, human institutions have evolved in ways that are increasingly satisfactory to their members.

But the important point is that institutions are based on shared belief systems, which are in turn based on another cultural evolutionary process.

The Evolution of Ideas

Changes in the places of the human societies in ecosystems and changes in organization of their constituent institutions are both affected by what people think; i.e., how they symbolize in words what they experience in the world around them and within themselves. Again, like revolution, cognition is a vast and complex subject that is one of the major concerns of research psychologists. I shall therefore call attention to only one or two aspects of thinking that are relevant to cultural evolution.

The most important is that thinking, although it may lead to a stable organization of ideas such as a belief system, is constantly being destabilized by a little studied process, that of fantasy. Far from responding directly to outside stimuli, most of us spend the majority of our waking hours thinking about other things; things that happened in the past, things that might happen in the future, plus a liberal admixture of things that never existed and may never happen. In short, this is the intrinsic creative process of cultural evolution. Amplifying on this theme, Etkin (1985) has asserted that "projective consciousness," meaning the ability to fantasize the past and future, was a critical factor in the cultural evolution of tribal organization.

The process of fantasy may involve any sensory or motor aspect of experience. One can visualize new scenes, hear new music, even imagine new smells and tastes. Or one can put words together in new combinations, as one does in writing. Words also permit people to transmit their fantasies to others in ways that are impossible with other forms of symbolization.

The adaptive value of the process is obvious. Fantasy allows us to solve problems in ways that would be impossible to discover by simple trial and error. In fact, the capacity is so valuable that there must have been, and may still be, strong social selection in favor of those individuals with strong capacities for fantasy (also called imagination). Because this capacity is so valuable and so widespread, I suspect that its precursor may exist in nonhuman animals, although this would be hard to establish directly, as no one can ask an animal what it is thinking. The work of Koehler (1927) on insight learning in apes supports this. He and others have found that animals can solve problems without previous experience, as if they have solved them in some form of imagination. And, as all dog owners know, dogs act as if they have dreams. If a dog can have sleeping fantasies, why not waking ones?

It is tempting to analogize the function of fantasy in cultural evolution with that of mutation in biological evolution, in that both are sources of variation and hence the basis of change. There is, however, a major difference. Gene mutation is completely random, but idea formation frequently arises from and is related to stimulation from external and internal sources. Furthermore, we have over the past several centuries evolved a process for generating ideas relating to the real world, which we call the scientific method. Like any organized system (in this case a symbolic one), science tends towards stability, but also retains unorganized aspects that permit change and creativity. Nor is this the only way of consciously generating new ideas. There is the older method of religion, based on meditation and testing an idea by the internal satisfaction it generates. Other processes of human creativity, such as those employed by artists, may have less to do with social organization, but produce a cultural evolution of their own.

It is organized creativity which permits some degree of conscious control over cultural evolution, again an element that does not ordinarily enter into biological evolution except as humans attempt to control it through cultural means. And so there is always hope for the future, even with respect to such apparently insoluble problems as international warfare. But since the process of cultural evolution is based on a creative process, the future of the cultural evolution of ideas is never precisely predictable. It would be a dull world if it were.

Thus far I have attempted to develop theories of cultural evolution without reference to the work of others along similar lines. I shall now briefly review some of the more prominent and influential theories of other authors and relate them to my own formulations.

BIOLOGICALLY BASED THEORIES OF CULTURAL EVOLUTION

Analogies with Biological Evolution

Biologists interested in cultural evolution have usually analogized and extended the concepts of biological evolution rather than objectively describing cultural phenomena, examining their properties, deriving whatever theories seem appropriate, and finally comparing and contrasting the two sorts of theories. Thus Mundinger (1980) equated the gene with the "meme," or internal memory in the nervous system of a particular transmitted behavior pattern. The genetic concept of a character or phenotype thus became a "model".

With respect to the four general processes of biological evolution, he replaced mutation with invention, insight and copy-error, the last of which occurs in the transmission of bird song. He found no equivalent of sexual reproduction, which he called meiotic drive, and thus no equivalent of inbreeding. But he did postulate the equivalent of random drift as "random memetic drift", and replaced natural selection by psychological (purposeful) selection.

Mundinger also postulated the cultural equivalent of a species, which he called an "institution", which he defined as a population of models (instead of organisms) ancestrally descended through a single lineage and maintaining its identity from other similar populations. The single lineage concept is a difficult one to maintain, in view of the ease with which behavioral information can be exchanged between human populations; such exchange also occurs even in his bird populations. And the term "institution" was an unfortunate choice, since it already has a well-established meaning in sociology to describe certain forms of human social organization such as the family, political institutions, etc., none of which are much like a species. A better term would be that of a society, already used to describe socially organized animal and human groups. Perhaps a better biological equivalent would be that of the deme, or local population, but even these may or may not be socially organized.

Cavalli-Sforza and Feldman (1981) independently developed a set of analogies similar to those of Mundinger but with some variations, more specific applications to human cultural evolution, and more attention to genetic theory. They considered that cultural differences between human groups are caused by 1) mutation, including innovation and random copy error, 2) transmission, but by different processes than in biological evolution, 3) cultural drift, or sampling fluctuations, 4) cultural selection based on decisions by individuals, and 5) natural selection where culture has consequences at the level of Darwinian fitness.

The principal differences from Mundinger's formulation is that Cavalli-Sforza and Feldman did not postulate an analog of the gene and phenotype, that they analogized sexual reproduction, the process through which genetic information is transmitted and which is also a change process, with teaching and learning, and that they retained natural selection as one of the change processes in cultural evolution. They further reasoned that since the mode of transmission of genetic information is basic to biological evolution, the mode of transmission of behavioral information should be similarly basic to cultural evolution and they developed a mathematical theory of such transmission in considerable detail. They then applied some of the techniques devised by geneticists to analyze biological heredity to the analysis of the process of transmission of learned information through language, such as that from parent to offspring. This led them to a binary model of information and its expression in terms of probability ratios. This approach has interesting possibilities but is limited by the fact that neither learned information nor its sources are confined to the binary mode.

Such analogies are interesting and insightful, but can be valid only insofar as identities can be established between the concepts and processes involved. The weakness of reasoning by analogy, i.e. resemblance in function, was long ago established by the comparative anatomists, who made a distinction between analogy and homology and noted that similar functions can be performed by very different organs.

Furthermore, analogizing is likely to blind one to the differences and unique qualities of each set of processes. Genes reproduce themselves in exact copies (except for accidents), but a meme, or neurological memory trace cannot reproduce itself and pass the replica along to another individual, although humans (and possibly some nonhuman animals) may attempt to pass such memories along to the next generation by teaching. As any teacher knows, teaching rarely if ever produces exact replication. The process of learning is inherently different from gene replication in that it takes place in another individual and is not a process of replication but of organizing behavior in relation to experience, part of which may include contact with behavior of a parent and other individuals.

Finally, the theories of biological evolution used as a basis for analogy usually have not included the concept of systems, and particularly that of genetic systems and the corollary that gene combinations and the resulting organisms are the major units of selection rather than individual genes, although selection (differential survival) may occur on any level of organization. A more exact analogy suggests that behavior patterns might be related to each other, and psychological selection might be done on the basis of combinations

of behavior patterns as well as single ones. For example, the agonistic behavior of a mouse includes several alternate behavior patterns, and its adaptive behavior includes the capacity to use these
appropriately, singly or in succession. But these physiobehavioral
systems are quite different from genetic systems in that a genetic
system once formed tends to be constant and invariable, whereas
the essence of behavioral adaptation and learning is variability.

In contrast to the above efforts to develop theories of cultural
evolution as analogs of biological evolution, Lumsden and Wilson
(1981) have attempted to apply a theory of biological evolution
directly to human culture, arguing that culture is in part a product
of basic biological evolutionary processes.

Such an effort is only as good as the evolutionary theory on
which it rests, and the authors limited themselves to a two-process
theory, mutation and natural selection. A further limitation was
their neglect of the concept of genetic systems, leading to the use
of the single-gene substitution model. While they recognized that
polygenic inheritance may affect the behaviors that they presume
to have been evolved, they did not realize the importance of gene
combinations as the basis of selection.

Still other limitations arise out of the neglect of the more general
aspects of systems organization. They recognized that culture has
an effect on genetics, conceptualized as the organism acquiring a
behavior, object or idea from the culture which would then affect
its biological fitness. But such fitness depends not only on the individual but the social systems of which it happens to be a part.

They did, however, employ analogy in at least two ways. One was
the use of the term "culturgen," defined as transmissible behavior,
mentifacts and artifacts, as an analogy with the concept of the
gene, the transmissible unit of biological heredity. Along with this,
they tended to assume that culturgens also occurred in pairs as do
alleles; although behavioral variation is not limited to a dichotomous distribution.

Their general argument was that the genetic makeup of individuals would lead them to choose one culturgen, behavioral or otherwise, in preference to others, and since this might affect survival,
the genetic makeup of individuals should be subject to evolution
through natural selection. They then calculated the effects of selection, again based on single gene replacement, and concluded that

major effects could be produced in 50 human generations, or roughly 1000 years following the occurrence of a favorable mutation.

The results of selection have been known to geneticists for years. When any complex character is selected, the result depends on the genetic variation present in the population, the degree of genetic determination of the character, the severity of selection, accidental selection of undesirable effects, the size of the population, and so on. Generally speaking, the major effect of selection under stable environmental conditions occurs within the first few generations, with very little change after six or seven generations. When selection is discontinued, the phenomenon of genetic homeostasis (Lerner, 1954) appears, and the population tends to move back to its original state. Thus the "Thousand Year Rule" developed by these authors is virtually meaningless, based as it is on unsound assumptions. Further, as I have shown elsewhere, the present conditions of human population structure, resulting in large part from cultural change, are such as to bring the general processes of biological evolution nearly to a halt (Scott, in Scott and Fuller, 1965).

Nevertheless, Lumsden and Wilson have produced some interesting ideas. One is an attempt at theoretically defining the biological restraints on human cultural evolution. They conceptualize these as "epigenetic rules" meaning the ways in which human genes interact with the environment to produce an organism. Thus they conceived as a primary rule the peculiar human neurological basis of sensory perception, which determines how individual humans generally perceive themselves and the external world. Certainly this should affect the ways in which humans organize their behavior, although even these abilities are subject to genetic and environmental variation.

Curiously, they do not list the primary basis of human culture, the capacity to speak. There is considerable evidence to the effect that infants are strongly motivated to produce language, as well as to imitate what they hear.

Lumsden and Wilson also postulated a secondary set of constraints. In contrast to the first, these are a very mixed bag. One is the process of attachment, which is, as I have shown, basic to the maintenance of a long lasting social group. It occurs universally among humans, except in certain pathological cases, and can take place at any time in life, albeit at different rates and with different consequences. If anything, this should be a primary phenomenon rather than a secondary one. Maternal-infant bonding which the authors list separately, is merely a special case of the above.

Other listed constraints are facial recognition in infants, non-verbal communication, fears and phobias, incest avoidance, the mental processes of valuation and decision making, and possibly the process of verification, or the formation of verbal rules.

When examined, all these phenomena turn out to be a miscellaneous collection of things which the authors believe are genetically determined to a greater or lesser degree. Some of them, like the non-verbal social signals may well have been evolved in the remote past, but all the studies on emotional expression indicate an enormous amount of individual variation in the abilities for sending and receiving such signals, as well as cultural modification of these signals. Others, like incest avoidance, have numerous alternative explanations. Certainly in our culture, the facts indicate that incest is a rather common phenomenon.

Finally, the authors have overlooked a very general phenomenon, that of the contribution of variation to the process of problem solving. Far from forcing behavior into a mold, this phenomenon dictates that behavior, and hence culture, will differentiate. The only constraints are the results.

Overall, this was a theoretical attempt to demonstrate that biological evolution has an important effect on cultural change. While this has undoubtedly been true in the past, e.g., the evolution of basic language capacities, it is by no means necessarily true at the present.

Other interesting ideas included the use of the term co-evolution in a different sense from that in which it is ordinarily employed, namely the evolution of separate genetic systems that affect each other (see Chapter XII). Rather, they used it to describe coordinated change on two levels of organization. They also concluded, on mathematical grounds, that culture slows the rate of biological evolution, a conclusion that I have reached on grounds of modification of selective processes. Finally, they conclude as I have done, that the grammatical and semantic structure of language exceeds the capacity of the genome to encode it.

Socioeconomic Theories

Data from Archeology and Cultural Anthropology. The data on which concepts of cultural evolution are based come from two main sources, one dating from remote prehistory up to the present, and the other from observations on contemporary human societies. Archeologists study human remains whether they be bones, broken pieces of pottery, or ruined buildings, while cultural anthropologists observe living people and their belongings, and what they do and say. By combining the two sets of data it is possible to infer what people did before the dawn of written history, and also what they probably did but did not write down during historical times. Most authorities now agree on the following general account of human cultural evolution.

After the hominoids discovered fire and clothing, they gradually spread all over the world, not reaching its remote corners until relatively modern times, as in the settling of Iceland by the Vikings and the migration of Polynesians into the Hawaiian Islands. In addition to the evidence of the artifacts they left behind, there are two sorts of traces of these movements in contemporary humans. One includes the differences of physical appearance among various local populations. These are the traces of the adaptive radiation referred to above, and had these human populations remained separate, they might have in the course of millions of years become several different species. Partly because of continued migration and partly because of the enormous growth in populations which resulted from cultural evolution, these local populations have not remained separate and still belong to the one species *Homo sapiens.* The second sort of evidence is provided by the differences and resemblances between languages in these various populations although this is not very reliable evidence because of the capacity for learning new languages.

The hominoids spread all over Africa, and they must have left that continent via the land bridge with Eurasia, spreading out in all directions from that point. Going eastward, some of them took a southerly route, becoming the dark skinned people we call Melanesians, who now inhabit some of the Pacific Islands. Some of them entered Australia, perhaps as recently as 30,000 years ago.

Another group of people took a more northerly route across Asia, settling in the northern and eastern parts of that continent and becoming the modern populations that we call Orientals. Some of them crossed the Behring Strait and entered North America, eventually settling as far south as Tierra del Fuego and becoming the cultures called American Indians. This may have happened as little as 30,000 years ago, and perhaps as long as 50,000 years.

Then there were the people who moved north and westward into Europe into its adjacent islands and became the cultural ancestors of most of the people who now live there as well as those who in modern times migrated to the Americas and Australia. Some of them probably went to India; others to Southwest Asia.

Peoples were still migrating during historic times, as when the Gauls from France attempted to occupy Italy and indeed took the northern part, which the Romans called Cisalpine Gaul. Later the Mongols from northern Asia moved into China and attempted to move into Europe. Eventually the Turks occupied Southeastern Europe, where they remained until the last century. But these were invasions of areas already occupied. The result of such invasions was usually a mixture rather than a complete replacement of cultures, although the latter did occur in areas that were sparsely inhabited.

The major human migrations must have occurred prior to the dawn of agriculture, which is usually dated about 7500 B.C. in Mesopotamia and nearby regions. Therefore, these early migrants must have been gatherer-hunters and perhaps more hunters than gatherers, subsisting on the Pleistocene megafauna, the large mammals that flourished in that era and became extinct in relatively recent times, perhaps helped by the human hunters.

Then agriculture appeared in Mesopotamia, Egypt, the Indus Valley, China, and independently in Central and South America. With it came the rise of urban civilization as populations increased and moved into cities. In each of these areas the residents domesticated plants of whatever species were available (Moore, 1985). Of these the grains were the most important, probably because they were portable and could be easily stored over long periods. Thus rice was domesticated in China and the Far East, maize in Central America, other grains in India, and wheat and similar grains in Mesopotamia and Egypt. A different sort of food plant, the potato, was originally cultivated in Peru, probably because it grew in and was suitable to a high altitude.

Animals also were domesticated, and in some parts of the world, particularly in arid plains regions and semi-deserts, these animals made possible an alternate life-style, that of the herdsmen, who occupied an ecological niche similar to that of a predator. Carnivores can never become more numerous than their prey species and the populations of herdsmen never became as numerous as did those people who cultivated plants. One animal, the dog was domesticated before the agricultural revolution and was probably used in hunting and later in herding activities (Scott, 1968).

All these centers of early agriculture were similar in climate. They occurred in warm climates in areas that had plenty of rainfall or, as in Egypt, access to plentiful water in a river. They did not occur in the tropical rain forest, nor in the colder parts of the temperate zone, nor in deserts and other highly arid regions. The common factor appears to be a climate permitting high plant productivity.

Once agriculture was adopted, certain general cultural changes followed in all these areas: great increases in the size of populations, the building of homes and other structures in cities, and the erection of large buildings for religious purposes. Most importantly from the viewpoint of cultural evolution, each of these cultures developed some form of written language. Along with this they developed various forms of theocratic polities, then militaristic polities, and then conquest states (Adams, 1966).

Descriptive Theories

To many 19th century thinkers it appeared that humans had progressed through a series of set stages in their rise from savagery to civilization. These stages were: 1) Hunting (with little emphasis on gathering), 2) Nomadic Herding, and 3) Agriculture and the rise of cities. They further assumed that humans must go through these stages and, as a corollary, that present day peoples who were found in any of the earlier stages must be biologically inferior. Such ideas as the latter quickly became racist doctrine, with all its deplorable results, and were still widely held through the first third of the present century. They have still not totally disappeared.

Meanwhile, anthropologists began to accumulate more and more objective information about the so-called primitive peoples. From these facts it became obvious that what people now do or have done in the past is strongly related to the climate and ecology of the areas in which they live. For example, Steward (1955) studied the lives of the various tribes of Shoshone Indians that formerly lived in the high arid plains of the Rocky Mountains in the United States. They lived by hunting and gathering, and because food was so scarce, the only way that they could exist was to spread out in small family groups, occasionally coming together for a communal drive of rabbits or antelope. Other than this, tribal organization was almost nonexistent.

Similar limitations bound the Aborigines living in the deserts of Central Australia, where it rains on the average of once every 18 months and the vegetation is extremely sparse. Eskimos living in the Arctic lived within another set of climatic restraints; there was no way that they could have domesticated plants and built cities.

On the other hand, agriculture and urban civilizations arose in all parts of the world where climatic conditions were favorable, and this suggested theories based on various aspects of the environment: physical climate, ecology and the use of energy, and the human uses to which they were put. The earliest of these theories involved economics, the ways in which humans used and distributed environmental resources.

Economic Theories

Adam Smith produced the first major economic theory in his *Wealth of Nations* (1776), but Karl Marx was the first to look at economics in the context of cultural evolution. His general thesis was that humans must first produce the means of existence before they can pursue politics, science, religion, art, etc., rather than the reverse (Harris, 1979). This of course agrees with the historical facts that such civilized pursuits showed their great development after the agricultural revolution (Adams, 1966). But Marx lived long before the concept of systems came into general use, and with it the concept of reciprocal causation. Today it is easy to see that ideas and productive work interact and so modify each other, rather than posing the problem as a contest between two philosophies, materialism and idealism, as did Marx and Engels. But it is not within the scope of this chapter to critique Marxian theories; suffice it to say that his ideas, ironically enough, became the foundation of a worldwide political movement of enormous importance.

Economists have traditionally concentrated their attention upon the processes of production and exchange of goods, but as the physical and biological sciences developed, scientists began to look at culture in respect to different levels of organization. Energy is a key concept in both physical science and the biological science of ecology, and Cottrell (1955) used changes in the utilization of energy to explain cultural change. As he put it, "Energy available to man limits what he *can* do and influences what he *will* do" (p. 2). In the same era, anthropologists began to develop more inclusive theories.

General Theories

White, a cultural anthropologist, produced one of the best developed general theories (1959). He defined culture as things dependent on symboling, including tools, clothing, customs, art, language, etc. and stated that culture so defined is both accumulative and progressive. Its general functions are to make life secure and to serve the needs of humans, including inner organismic or spiritual needs.

Culture is extra-somatic and behaves as if it were non-biological. White was one of the first theorists to make extensive use of the systems concept, stating that the culture of all mankind is a closed system but that subcultures are open systems affecting each other. Human culture cannot be a closed system, as defined by Bertalanffy, as all living systems must take in external energy. But it is closed to outside cultural information; we have yet to contact cultures in other worlds.

Cultural systems have four classes of components: technological, sociological, ideological and sentimental or attitudinal. Of these, the technological component is basic to all the others and is a major determinant of culture, but not the only one. Technology involves the use of energy, and in early human history there were two stages. In the first of these, all energy came from human effort, and the chief changes came from the improvement of hand tools, such as knives, needles, and paddles for boats. In the second stage, additional energy came through the technological innovation of agriculture. On this basis White proposed a general Law of Cultural Development (p. 56): "Culture advances as the amount of energy harnessed per capita per year increases, or as the efficiency or economy of the means of controlling energy is increased, or both." He thus postulated that a major change process in cultural evolution is change in the utilization of energy.

One can make minor criticisms of White's theory from the vantage point of a quarter of century of further scientific work. It is not true that culture is entirely non-biological, nor that it does not appear in nonhuman animals. And his use of the systems concept was somewhat loose: he included ecosystems within social systems rather than the reverse. But it was a basically sound approach and led to numerous interesting ideas and hypotheses.

Corning's more recent (1983) sociocultural theory was an attempt to develop a general theory that incudes all the major aspects of the above theories. As with his theory of genetically based evolution (see Chapter VIII) he emphasized functional synergism, or combinatory processes, as "the underlying cause of the progressive evolution of sociocultural evolution in higher mammals and especially in the hominoid line" (p. 259). In his view, the changes produced by combinatory processes are self-evident, especially in changes involving economic organization.

He listed four basic cultural change processes, without in any way attempting to relate these to genetic change processes, as follows:

1) *Innovation*, including discovery and invention. A major example was the first use of fire, and any number of such discoveries since.

2) *Selective Diffusion*. When a new invention arises, it is not immediately adopted nor necessarily by all people who hear of it. Rather, an innovation will be adopted (if at all) because it appears to satisfy social or psychological needs. That is, it diffuses or not because of its apparent function.

3) *Selective Reproduction*, or transmitting an innovation to the next generation. This is accomplished by teaching, imitation, and selective reinforcement, positive or negative. The result is to stabilize the use of the innovation and thus inhibit further change.

4) *Selective Replacement.* This process largely applies to artifacts, such as the replacement of gas lights by electric ones. Not all artifacts are replaced, as in the retention of sailboats for special uses.

Finally, Corning related sociocultural evolution to biological evolution by concluding, as did Lumsden and Wilson, and Feldman and Cavalli-Sforza, that cultural practices may have fitness consequences and so be involved with natural selection. For example, culturally determined health practices, including dietary ones, may influence selective survival.

Comparisons of Socioeconomic Theories

Contemporary socioeconomic theories of cultural evolution differ principally in matters of terminology and emphasis. There are few disputes concerning the nature of the phenomena concerned. Disagreements chiefly concern which change processes are more important. Thus White suggested that changes in technology and the resulting use of energy are most important, whereas Corning emphasized innovation and discovery. It is obvious that discovery can lead to changes in technology, and there is no real disagreement.

At one time cultural anthropologists disagreed concerning the mode of descent of culture, one school arguing that each item of cultural information must have come from one source, diffusing from such centers into all others; the other school holding that cultural descent is multilineal (Steward, 1955), with information being discovered and passed along down separate and sometimes parallel lines. Actually, neither of these theories is mutually exclusive, and both can take place at the same time. In prehistoric times human cultures were much more separate than they are today; the Eastern and Western Hemispheres were cut off from each other for thousands of years, to take an extreme example. Today there is much more contact, but people still inherit the languages of their own cultures, and along with it a great deal of traditional information. In short, multilineal cultural descent was once more important than it is today, but is still with us.

Another theoretical disagreement concerns the relationship between biological and cultural evolution. Social scientists in the past have often assumed that cultural evolution is entirely independent. At the opposite extreme, biologists such as Lumsden and Wilson have argued from mechanistic-reductionist theory that biological evolution determines cultural evolution. But from the viewpoint of systems theory, the two processes must affect each other, and I have shown how this occurs. If anything, present-day cultural evolution has a much more profound effect on biological change processes than the reverse.

Table 11.1
PROCESSES AND PRODUCTS OF CULTURAL
EVOLUTION

A. Change Processes
   1. Primary Intrinsic Processes (within organisms)
      a. Fantasy and projective consciousness
      b. Learning
   2. Group Processes
      a. Language change: Concepts and organization
      b. Synergic processes: Combinatory processes and synergic problem solving
      c. Invention, innovation, discovery
   3. Storage Processes: Accumulation of information
   4. Directive Processes
      a. Psychological selection: Teleonomy
      b. Differential survival: Natural selection
      c. Death and birth
B. Transmittal Processes
   1. Modeling, Imitation
   2. Lingual Communication: Teaching, Learning
   3. Diffusion and Reproduction of Artifacts
C. Products of Cultural Evolution
   1. Lingual Products
      a. Language itself – vocabulary and grammar
      b. Ideas: Symbolic representations of non-verbal phenomena, including
         concepts
      c. Records
      d. Rules for behavior
      e. Ceremonial behavior
   2. Non-lingual behavior
   3. Social Organization, including Institutional Organization
   4. Tools, machines – artifacts related to the use of energy
   5. Symbolic artifacts
      a. Religious
      b. Artistic
   6. Constructions – buildings, etc.
   7. Manufactures – food, clothing, etc.

CONCLUSIONS AND SUMMARY

Theories of Cultural Evolution

In Table 11.1 I have listed the processes and products of cultural evolution as developed in this chapter and have grouped these processes according to resemblances in function. The overall category of change processes includes the primary processes intrinsic to individual organisms; fantasy, projective consciousness, and learning.

Through language these are transformed into group processes: change in language itself, its concepts and organization; synergic processes that involve some sort of combinatory functions among individuals; and the results of individual creativity expressed as invention, innovation, and discovery.

A third category of change processes is that of accumulation of information which I have labelled as a storage process.

Finally, there is a group of directive processes: psychological selection or teleonomy, differential survival or natural selection, and the general change process produced by death and birth involving the destruction of learned information through death and its reorganization through birth and development.

The second major category is that of transmittal processes. Modeling and imitation occur in nonhuman animals without speech, and in humans accompanying both spoken and unspoken behavior. Lingual communication includes conscious instruction and learning. Then there is information provided by the diffusion and reproduction of tools and other artifacts.

It is obvious that this classification is somewhat artificial, in that there is some overlap in function between processes, much of which is due to the fact that they may go on at the same time. Nevertheless, any satisfactory theory of cultural evolution must be a multiprocess theory. No single process will provide more than a partial explanation of the facts.

In a third section I have listed the more important kinds of cultural products. The list is only partial; a complex industrial culture produces an almost infinite number of objects and artifacts and the behavior resulting from them. As might be expected from systems theory, these products feed back through the transmittal processes and affect the change processes. One-way causation is very rare.

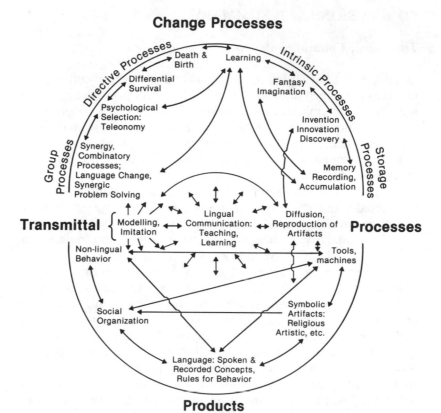

Figure 11.1. Processes and products of human cultural evolution. This diagram illustrates the principal causal-interactive relationships between these processes and their products. In every case there is two-way interaction. Except for Differential Survival (Natural Selection) I have not included the processes of either biological evolution or ecosystem change, partly because this would make the diagram too complex for clarity, and partly because these can be related to cultural evolution as a whole rather than to its specific processes (as Natural Selection can also). The action of processes of cultural evolution is much more complex than that of biological evolution (see Figure 4.2), but even this diagram does not depict its full complexity.

In Figure 11.1, I have indicated some of the causal relationships between the major processes of cultural evolution. No change processes are exempt from feedback; even birth and death are modified by culture. The general effect of such interactions should be to produce stability, but this can only result in the slowing of change processes, not stopping them.

The large number of processes and products contrasts strongly with biological evolution, which has only four major processes and can only directly affect living material. There is one transmittal process instead of three, and biological evolution has its immediate effect confined to one product, physiological organization.

An even greater contrast lies in the fact that three out of four of the biological change processes are random in nature, only Differential Survival having some degree of directive effect, while the numerous change processes of cultural evolution are almost always modified by purposiveness and attempts at adaptive functions. As Corning would put it, teleonomy is much more general and immediate than in biological evolution.

Interactions of Biological and Cultural Evolution

As I indicated earlier, culture can affect all four of the fundamental change processes of biological evolution. Mutation rates may be altered by man-made changes in exposure to radiation and chemicals. Even before the era of scientific discovery, the decision of a human society to live at high elevations or lower ones resulted in differential exposure to cosmic radiation.

Cultures regulate sexual reproduction through sexual behavior and the choice of mates in a variety of ways, none of which produce random mating. The degree of inbreeding is also regulated, both by verbal rules and by the size of the society within which mating takes place.

But the most profound effects of culture are on Differential Survival (Natural Selection). The general effect is to reduce mortality and so reduce survival differentials arising from physical sources and ecosystems. In addition, culture directs and modifies the effects of social selection. Even in nonhuman animals there is selection for those individuals that best adapt to the social system of which they are a part. Among human cultures, social selection can be modified in a great variety of ways, as the following examples illustrate.

Among tribal cultures, the usual arrangement is that every girl shall be married, usually soon after puberty. This means that every female has an opportunity to reproduce, so that differential survival chiefly depends on physiological variation: differential fecundity and differential mortality. There should be selection for those females capable of reproducing healthy and fertile offspring. The situation of males, on the other hand, is quite different. Particularly in polygynous cultures, all males do not mate, and the culture determines which ones are allowed to marry and reproduce, frequently on the basis of economic assets. Since infantile mortality is usually high in tribal societies, the longer such a man lives, and the more wives he has, the better his chance of finding gene combinations that produce survival. An obvious effect of such a culture is to select for longevity, and among prehistoric tribes this may have contributed to the evolution of a long-lived species.

A more modern example was provided by Galton's (1869) study of the British aristocracy. Marriages were arranged in order to increase power, as represented by land and other forms of wealth. The cultural ideal, then, was a marriage between two wealthy young aristocrats. But an heiress was likely to be wealthy because she had few relatives, and the genetic effect was to select for infertility. Many of the noble families died out, as Galton pointed out. He feared that "genius" was also selected against but he based his ideas on the then inadequate notions of genetics (this was before Mendel's rediscovery), and had no inkling of the importance of gene combinations and their effects on variation in complex characters.

In order for a culture to produce important changes through social selection, several conditions must be met:

1) The selection must be continued consistently across many generations. This means that the culture must be stable for hundreds or thousands of years. Otherwise, selection might operate in very different directions that cancelled each other out.

2) The favored sort of individual must actually have a differential opportunity to reproduce. If the culture rewarded bravery in battle, individuals of this sort would be likely to die young and so have little opportunity to produce offspring.

3) The reproductive differential must be strong enough to produce a reasonably rapid effect.

4) The society and the mating population of which it is composed must be small enough so that there is some chance of a uniform genetic basis for the selected trait being brought about. In a very large population, selection is likely to result in a variety of gene combinations producing similar phenotypes. As I have pointed out, cultural evolution in recent times has produced very

large populations within which the opportunity for rapid biological evolution is quite limited (Scott, in Scott and Fuller, 1965).

Considering the reverse sort of effect, that of biological evolution on cultural evolution, biological evolution made human cultural evolution possible, particularly through the evolution of the capacity for language. This, combined with the presumed social organization of early prehistoric peoples into small but not entirely separate groups, should have made unusually rapid biological evolution possible. Cultural evolution, through the production of conditions favorable to large populations with increasing possibilities of genetic interchange has since produced conditions that inhibit rapid change.

This does not mean that biological evolution of the human species has come to a complete halt. Like cultural evolution, biological evolution operates through processes that make continual change inevitable. One of these is mutation; its function is to increase variation. The weakening of differential survival and the consequent enormous growth in populations likewise increases variation. Also, the larger the population, the greater the chance for unusual gene combinations to occur.

What effect does this have on cultural evolution? As I have pointed out, the result should be a synergistic reaction between biological diversity and increasing complexity of social organization. The greater the biological variety of humans the greater the possible variety of cultural roles that they may fit.

Otherwise, as Lumsden and Wilson (1981) have argued, the principal effects of biological evolution on cultural evolution are constraining ones. These hangovers from past biological evolution, however, are in part negated by the present trend toward increasing variation. Because they vary, the biological constraints no longer affect all individuals consistently. I conclude that the principal current effect of biological evolution is to facilitate cultural variation.

Applied Cultural Evolution

As I have demonstrated, social change is inevitable, but need not be unguided. One of the basic characteristics of humans is that they are clever, and when they work together on the solution of problems, they are capable of synthesizing adaptive and useful forms of change (Lieberman, 1984).

Cultural evolution is far easier to guide than is genetically based biological evolution. Altering the gene combinations in the gene pool of even a small population is difficult to bring about and can only be accomplished over many generations, thus requiring some sort of continuity over centuries. To accomplish such a change in all of the several billions of individuals comprising present world-wide human populations is virtually impossible. Genetically, we are a variable but highly stable species, and the one direction in which biological evolution is likely to go, or even can go, is toward increased variation.

Further, gene combinations act directly on physiological processes and only indirectly on behavior. In contrast, cultural evolution is a process of behavioral change and behavioral transmission, and thus is far more accessible for conscious modification. Currently, the best possibilities for controlled genetic change lie in molecular genetics, but even with these techniques it is difficult to work with gene combinations, and even more difficult to bring about changes in whole populations. The best possibilities are to work with the modification of single injurious genes that affect health of individuals, not the overall organization of individuals. The result, again, is to negate the effects of natural selection. That is, any controlled genetic change primarily affects biological evolutionary processes, not cultural ones.

In contrast, cultural change can come about very rapidly, with direct effects on behavior. Such changes may take place in one generation or less, as has been the case in our culture with the spread of television viewing. Furthermore, cultural changes can spread rapidly across cultural boundaries, and affect the majority of human populations, as seems to be the case with television. A few years ago, I visited Mexico, when the government was attempting to improve economic conditions among the poverty-striken Mayans of Yucatan by providing them with access to electric power. One immediate result was that almost every home acquired a television set.

General Principles of Cultural Change

From the theories of cultural evolution, it is possible to derive several general principles. I have already stated one of these: that *cul-*

tural change is inevitable. A second principle, based on observation is: *the rate of change varies according to the product changed.* Thus, tools and artifacts (such as the television sets mentioned above) may change very rapidly, while social organization changes very slowly as do the verbal systems associated with such organization.

Third, the rate of change depends on the nature of the underlying system involved. Any living system tends to become stably organized and to maintain that stability. Also, any change in such a system is more likely to be disruptive of the system than to improve its function. The immediate effect of any change, however beneficial, is social disorganization. Verbal systems, especially the codes of behavior that explain and guide social organization, are likely to be unusually resistant to change simply because they are nonliving. This is especially true of written codes of behavior. The Mosaic laws are still with us in unchanged form after several thousand years. The verbal economic systems developed by Adam Smith and Marx and written down by them are similarly persistent. Such verbal systems are likely to be considered sacred (i.e., they represent eternal truth with which it is dangerous to tamper).

Nevertheless, both *social systems and the associated verbal systems can vary in their degree of flexibility.* Those that permit changes are those that have change processes built into the organization. For example, the political system of the United States permits change in its constitution (a verbal system) through the processes of amendment and judicial interpretation. Our economic system is unusually flexible in that it permits any change that will make money. At the same time, the theoretical explanations of such behavior are considered sacred; scientific research on economic behavior (except such superficial research as that on marketing a product), is discouraged for fear that it might destroy people's faith in the system.

Finally, the basic change processes of cultural evolution go on within individual organisms: fantasy, and organization of behavior through learning and experience. Without such variation, social change would be impossible.

Given these principles, how can inevitable cultural change be guided into desirable channels, be brought about rapidly or slowed down according to the nature of the desired change, and accomplished with a minimum of harm? There are few people who believe that our present culture is perfect, however better it may be than it was in the historical past. Even the most ardent conservatives, who are dedicated to maintaining a culture unchanged, are usually trying to change culture back to some real or imagined culture of previous times. But in every age, there has been disagreement as to what changes are desirable.

In fact, no one can predict the exact outcome of cultural change. Modifying a large and extremely complex system always produces some unforeseen effects. The best solution, from a scientific viewpoint, is experimentation. Try it out: if it produces desirable effects, save it; if it fails, discard it. Of course, it is unethical to deliberately manipulate the lives of individuals, but people are constantly initiating their own experiments by setting up new forms of organization. Such experiments frequently lead to violence, as happened between the supporters of various forms of Christian religions who fought wars for hundreds of years. Eventually, the United States solved this problem by establishing the principle of religious toleration.

Indeed, toleration is a major problem in social change. Today there may be riots, violence and even wars between followers of different religions, and religious sects as in India and the Middle East, but the major conflicts concern economic institutions. The world is divided into two armed camps concerning competing economic systems, and within many countries there are constant armed struggles between the followers of these systems. But no two cultures react in the same way, and the result has been a number of economic experiments. If one examines the results dispassionately (and this is not easy), one must conclude that the most successful experiments, whatever the labels that are attached to them, have been those with mixed economies. Stated in simplistic terms, capitalistic economies have been more successful in solving problems of productivity, whereas socialistic economies have been more successful in solving problems of distribution, and a mixed economy has the possibility of solving both.

Whatever the merits of the competing systems, the attempt to solve economic disputes by warfare is extraordinarily costly and wasteful to either system. If there is any sort of cultural change that should benefit mankind universally, it is that of reducing war and enhancing the processes of peaceful change. The problem here is one of changing a primitive method of bringing about cultural change into a method based on scientific knowledge. But we must admit that our current scientific knowledge is incomplete. We need to find out more concerning why people accept some sorts of social change and reject others. If there is a central problem of cultural evolution, it is that of bringing about nonviolent social change.

Chapter XII

On Eco-evolution: Change in Ecosystems

As implied by our definition of evolution (changes in organization persisting over more than one generation), changes in the organization of ecosystems can be called evolution and are of equivalent importance. There is, however, no commonly used term for this type of change in organization; therefore, I shall call it eco-evolution, or ecosystem change.

Definition of an Ecosystem

In accordance with the general definition of a system, an ecosystem is a group of interacting plant and animal species inhabiting a particular area. The term was first used by ecologists in the 1930's (Tansley, 1935), but similar concepts were employed long before that. Particularly in the older literature, groups of interacting species were called communities, implying that the animal and plant species in a habitat had something in common. Whatever the terminology, the group of interacting entities (or system) must be a functional unit that is more or less discontinuous with other units and should have all of the general properties of living systems, including a tendency to achieve stability.

Ecosystems are never independent of the physical environment, as the kinds of plants and animals that can live in a particular place are dependent on soil, water, and climatic conditions. One might anticipate that marine ecosystems would be more independent of soil, but not entirely so. The ecosystem of the Georges Banks, one of the world's best fishing grounds off the New England and Canadian coasts, depends on upwelling currents that bring with them mineral nutrients for the plants on which marine animals feed.

A good example of an ecosystem is the plant and animal species that inhabit a fresh water lake. They interact with each other and are cut off from similar ecosystems in the same general area by land barriers. They are not, however, completely independent because some individuals belonging to the same species, such as water birds, may live in more than one lake. Also, lakes are connected to streams that may bring in new individuals and new species. Ecosystems, then, consist of subsystems within larger systems. The most inclusive ecosystem is composed of all living plants and animals inhabiting the biosphere, or that part of the globe in which living organisms exist. In some ways, this inclusive system acts as a unit, particularly with respect to the exchange of energy.

ORGANIZATION AND FUNCTION OF ECOSYSTEMS

Organization

Considered as a component entity of an ecosystem, a total species population is organized as a unit in two principal ways. The first of these arises from the definition of a species as individuals that have access to a common store of genes, i.e., the gene pool. In animal species having sexual reproduction, the necessary interaction between system entities (genotypes) is usually accomplished through sexual behavior. Consequently, for many animal species, sexual behavior is equivalent to species organization. Exceptions are those marine species that reproduce by broadcasting germ cells into the water. In this case, the common organization for reproduction is achieved on the physiological level.

A second major way in which species act as units is also found on the physiological level, since all members of a species tend to utilize energy in a similar fashion. This involves a basic concept in ecology, the analysis of relationships between species with respect to energy.

Ecosystems as Energy Systems

Because there are limited amounts of certain kinds of physical matter on earth that can be organized into living material, these substances must move in cycles in order for life processes to be maintained. Some of the most important cycles are those involving oxygen, nitrogen, and carbon. Oxygen is produced by plants as a by-product of the process of photosynthesis. A certain part of this oxygen is reused by plants in their metabolism, and the excess is breathed by animals and converted into carbon dioxide, which in turn is used by plants to produce more oxygen. Similarly, nitrogen, which is an essential element in protein compounds, is fixed by plants in compounds that are eventually eaten by animals. Finally, by decomposition processes, nitrogen is returned to the atmosphere. However, only a few living organisms have the ability to fix free nitrogen, with the result that nitrogen compounds are often in short supply. This is one point where modern science has successfully intervened to facilitate a major cycle, by synthesizing nitrogen compounds for use as plant fertilizer.

Carbon seldom occurs as a pure substance, and when it does, it cannot be used directly by plants, which can use it only in the form of carbon dioxide to synthesize proteins, carbohydrates, and fats. Plants tend to store carbon compounds in relatively stable forms, and these have in the geologic past been converted into coal and petroleum, removing large amounts of carbon from the cycle. This carbon becomes available only by burning (oxidation), with the result that human use of these sources of energy should produce at least a slight increase in the amount of carbon dioxide. Since modern human societies also facilitate plant growth by the use of fertilizers, such an increase may be counterbalanced by increased use of carbon dioxide. Similarly, certain marine animals have a tendency to lock up carbon as calcium carbonate in their shells, which by geologic processes have been converted into limestone, another form in which carbon is difficult for plants to utilize.

In general, the ecosystems that are involved in these cycles are so large, and include so many species (indeed, all species living on the earth), that they are highly stable; and it would require enormous changes before the alterations would become obvious. Nevertheless, such changes can occur, especially over long periods of time. Conditions were probably much more favorable for plant life in the remote past than they are now, and even the relatively small amounts of newly available carbon dioxide produced by human industry and heating may change this situation again. In addition, even a relatively small increase in atmospheric carbon dioxide should increase the retention of solar heat (the greenhouse effect), again favoring plant growth and wider distribution.

The situation is quite different with respect to another form of ecological organization, that of the exchange of energy through food chains. The energy for life processes comes originally from the sun and is stored by plants by the process of photosynthesis. This stored energy is, in part, used by herbivorous animals, which in turn are eaten by carnivores, who finally dissipate the energy at the end of the food chain. This is a much simplified scheme compared to actual chains, many of which could be described as networks. The organization of any such chain is vulnerable to changes in species numbers or in the relationships between them. Because of their smaller size and specific interspecies relationships, food chains are much more easily disrupted than are the general chemical cycles. We should also remember that food chains are true systems, with two-way interactions between species all along the line.

A food chain, while primarily based on physiological organization, also involves a major behavioral system, ingestive behavior. Elaborate special behavioral relationships evolve between predators and prey and, in many cases, between hosts and parasites. Much grooming behavior, for example, is adaptive in the control of external parasites.

Food chains do not necessarily involve species-wide organization, as the diet of a species may vary from locality to locality, depending on the available food species. Accompanying this there may be variations in predator-prey relationships and, in the case of herbivorous species, variations in the patterns of ingestive behavior. Thus, in ecological organization of this sort, the local population rather than the entire species comprises the unit of system organization.

Analysis of Energy Systems

H. T. Odum (1983) has developed methods for analyzing the function of ecosystems in terms of the flow of energy through their components. In order to do this, it is necessary to include nonliving materials through which energy is transmitted, or within which it may be stored. Thus he defines an ecosystem as follows: "An organized system of land, water, mineral cycles, living organisms, and their programmatic behavioral control systems is called an *ecosystem.*" (p. 17).

From a theoretical viewpoint, the effect is to relate living and nonliving systems in terms of functional relationships. These are far more complex than the relationships within either living or nonliving systems considered separately, but their description and analysis is possible because definite sorts of organization are developed. And because living systems are involved, the characteristics of such systems, such as the tendency to develop stability, are evident in the whole ecosystem. At the same time, the physical systems involved are not passive, are not entirely predictable, and in many cases are not controllable (e.g., solar radiation, sun spots, etc.), and living systems must adapt and accommodate to them.

Viewing ecosystems in terms of energy flow, storage, and dissipation has the merit of greatly simplifying the analysis of such systems. As Odum demonstrated, the effects of human cultural systems are readily incorporated into such an analysis. An objective scheme of the functioning of any cultural system can be depicted, both in terms of current operation and long-term effects. In the future, such analyses will probably become one of our best guides for policy decisions on any level of cultural organization from local to international.

ECOSYSTEM CHANGE

Succession

This phenomenon, which is defined as the orderly change of an ecosystem in a particular area, was first observed on the sand dunes on the shores of Lake Michigan (Shelford, 1913). Because of the action of the wind and water, dunes can be observed in many stages, starting with a new blowout consisting of bare sand that has been blown free of protecting vegetation, and continuing to dunes that are completely covered with forest trees. The first plants to move onto the bare sand are beach grasses, cottonwoods, and willows. As they live, grow, and die, they build up enough humus on the sand to provide an environment in which jack pines can grow. These, in turn, eventually produce an environment favorable to black oaks, which are succeeded by a combination of oaks and hickories. The final stage is the beech-maple forest, the typical climax forest in that region of temperate North America. Each stage of vegetation, or sere, is accompanied by certain kinds of animals that either live on or find shelter in that particular kind of vegetation. Animal species, therefore, play a comparatively passive role in this form of ecological change but can contribute to it in minor ways by grazing, browsing, and by the feeding of insects.

The final, or climax, stage is one of great stability but also one of low productivity of both animals and plants. Beeches and maples are long-lived, slow-growing trees that cast dense shade and inhibit other plant growth by their root secretions and by using up most of the available soil nutrients. Their leaves and trunks provide relatively little food for animal species, and the result is a stable but barren environment for other species.

The phenomenon of plant succession is thus based on physiological processes which result in an area becoming less favorable for the survival of a particular species and more favorable for other species adapted in different ways. Animal species have somewhat the same tendency through the accumulation of waste products and the destruction of food plants, but the effects are less serious because the animals can move, either migrating to new localities or finding food in other places.

The basic physiological change processes in succession involve differing metabolic requirements, patterns of growth, and means of dispersal. They are limited and guided by climatic factors and the availability of seeds from the various species involved.

Given a particular set of climatic and soil conditions and knowing the species available for recolonization, succession becomes a very predictable phenomenon. In the north temperate zone of North America each case of succession recapitulates (with some modifications) what happened after the last ice age when great stretches of land were covered with barren sand and gravel by the retreating glaciers. However, such long time changes in ecosystems are slow enough that they may be accompanied by genetic changes in the component species; thus, ecosystem change of the sort involved in plant succession may be paralleled by evolutionary changes in genetic systems.

The eventual result of plant succession is stability, which inhibits further ecological change. There is no regular way in which a stable ecosystem is disorganized and reorganized, but various accidents such as fire, floods, volcanic eruptions, or climatic changes can produce the necessary breakdown of the system.

Ecosystem Development

E. P. Odum (1969) has suggested that the processes of ecological succession may be included in a broader concept of development. He defined an ecosystem as "a unit of biological organization made up of all the organisms in a given area ...interacting with the physical environment so that a flow of energy leads to characteristic trophic structure and material cycles within the system." The animals and plants so organized thus interact with each other as a community.

To summarize, succession, or ecosystem development, is an orderly and predictable process, it results from modification of the physical environment, and it culminates in a stabilized ecosystem involving a maximum biomass per unit of energy flow.

Like organismic development, ecosystem development is an organizational process, but it cannot be defined in the same way. The organization of a single animal or plant persists for only one generation and hence cannot be a process of biological evolution. The process of ecosystem development, on the other hand, extends over many generations, and the final ecosystem may persist for thousands of years. Consequently, biological evolution goes on during the development of an ecosystem, with reciprocal interaction between the two processes, as will be shown later.

Agriculture and Ecosystems

Examples of human interference with succession are numerous, but the major one is agriculture, as ecologists were quick to point out (Odum, 1969). A few years ago the University of Kansas attempted to preserve a natural tract of virgin prairie covered with grass. Fenced in and protected, the area within a few years began to grow up to small trees, leading to the conclusion that the long-grass prairies were preserved by repeated fires, set either accidentally or deliberately by the Indian inhabitants long before white settlers appeared.

An example of the deliberate use of fire to control succession is the milpa, or slash-and-burn, agriculture practiced in many parts of the tropical world. It received its name in central America, where it was used by the ancient Mayas and is still found in many places. In a new stretch of tropical forest the farmer destroys trees and other plants by girdling and fire, leaving an open area where there is plenty of sunshine and rich soil. Crop plants can be raised for a few years until the soil is exhausted, after which the farmer moves on to a new area and repeats the process, while the old area slowly grows back up to forest again.

Grazing and browsing, whether by wild animals or domestic ones, also modify plant succession. At a moderate level these activities tend to hold plant succession in check. Overgrazing tends to destroy the most edible plants and preserve those which are least edible, with the result that the land becomes less and less productive. Overbrowsing, which often occurs where goats are extensively used in agriculture, eventually results in killing all edible bushes and trees. In dry or hilly country, this has the effect of increasing erosion. More and more rapid runoff of rainfall results in water shortage and a general change toward desert conditions.

As the above examples show, agriculture may take many forms. We usually think of it as the practice of plowing and planting row crops, a technique developed in western Europe and transplanted to various parts of the world, including the United States. In recent years, farmers and agricultural engineers have modified this practice by the introduction of machines and artificial fertilizers, both largely dependent on the availability of fossil fuel. By these means the productivity of the process has been increased approximately ten times over more primitive agriculture.

Properly used, this form of agriculture can be maintained for centuries, as it has been in Europe. It is not, however, suitable for all soils and climates, as experience in semiarid parts of the world indicates. Even with irrigation, the water poured on the land may leach out alkalis from the subsoil that eventually make plant growth impossible.

In general, plow agriculture attempts to disorganize the ecosystem every year by turning over and killing all plants, then sets succession going again on essentially barren soil, controlling the plants that colonize it by planting selected species such as wheat, maize, or soybeans. Economically, their products are highly useful to humans. Ecologically, they are highly productive in terms of organizing nonliving material and so storing the energy of sunlight in forms utilizable by animals.

More recently, there has been a tendency to modify plow agriculture by the use of plant poisons that selectively kill weeds and undesirable plants. The net effect, however, is still the same, to hold plant succession at one stage.

Climatic and Genetic Sources of Change

As indicated above, the most important change processes in succession are physiological in nature, but change can come from other sources as well. In any case, changes in the organization of ecosystems are reflected as changes in the absolute and relative numbers of animals in each species involved. For example, if a species that is intermediate in a food chain becomes extinct, all species dependent upon it must either change their food habits or become extinct themselves. Or if a primary food source does not prosper, the whole chain may be threatened.

Other than succession, the most important causes of changes in numbers in species populations include climatic changes affecting entire ecosystems, and genetic evolutionary changes in each of the component species. Climatic changes may be very long term, as in the cases of the recurrent ice ages in the northern hemisphere, or they may consist of short term fluctuations that produce corresponding fluctuations in numbers from year to year. Genetic evolutionary changes tend to be very slow and gradual since they involve changes in the organization of systems on a different level. Such genetic changes may result in more successful adaptations with resulting increases in numbers of the species concerned. A current example – although the genetic basis is still to be established – is the change in nesting habits of red-winged blackbirds, which formerly established breeding territories only in marshes, but in recent years have begun to nest in cultivated fields, such as alfalfa, with corresponding increases in numbers to the point that they have become pests in many Midwestern areas of the United States.

On the other hand, a change that results in less successful adaptation can produce a reduction in numbers and, in extreme cases, extinction. More successful adaptation on the part of one species requires that other interdependent species in the ecosystem adapt to this through their own genetic changes. Failure to adapt successfully may result in extinction, whereas successful adaptation introduces a new balance of organization between species.

As with other systems levels, ecosystems become more stable as they become more highly organized, with the result that each species tends to occupy a particular ecological niche in one ecosystem with little direct competition with other similar species. For example, when the white settlers arrived in North America, there were two carnivores that occupied the ecological niche of predators on the large hoofed animals: the cougar, or mountain lion; and the wolf, sometimes called the timber wolf. These two species hunted in quite different ways, the cougar by individual hunting and lying in wait for passing prey, and the wolves by pack hunting and long pursuit. The former method works best in broken or mountainous country, the latter on relatively flat areas, with the result that the two species usually preyed on different populations and thus almost never came into direct competition. Nevertheless, ecosystems never become as stable as some other types of systems and are particularly vulnerable on a microlevel where an entire system may be easily wiped out by climatic changes or human intervention.

In summary, ecosystems show the same tendencies to develop stable organization as do other living systems, but such stability is much more easily upset by random factors than at lower levels. The so-called "balance of nature" is quite fragile in many ecosystems. And unlike genetic and social systems, there is no regular process by which ecosystems are disorganized and reorganized.

INTERACTION WITH GENETICALLY BASED EVOLUTION

Since all animal and plant species are entities within ecosystems, part of ecosystem change consists of the simultaneous biological evolution of each component species. Such changes must inevitably modify the relationships between species, and since differential survival is largely dependent on biotic factors and processes, the overall process of evolution must include all ecologically related species. This genetic aspect of ecosystem change is currently receiving a great deal of attention under the name of coevolution (Futuyma & Slatkin, 1983; Nitecki, 1983).

Coevolution

Here we must consider evolutionary processes in plants, as ecosystems always include both plants and animals, and animals are directly and indirectly dependent on the existence of plants, as well as the reverse.

I shall not try to describe the entire scope of plant evolution, but only point out certain ways in which its processes differ from those of animal evolution. In the first place, the movement of plants is very limited and they consequently lack organismic behavioral adaptation and its outcome, social organization. (Some plants can move certain parts, such as petals that open and close, but they usually remain "rooted" to a particular spot.) Plant adaptation is almost entirely limited to physiological processes based on structural organization. But, through coevolution, plants can make use of animal behavior for purposes of fertilization and dispersal. A well-known major case is the coevolution of insects and the flowering plants. A specific example is the yucca moth, which cross-fertilizes the yucca flowers but whose larvae live on yucca seeds. It is to the yucca plant's advantage to provide this food, so that there will be a new generation of moths. But the yucca moth larvae must not eat too many seeds, or there will be no more yucca plants.

The function of dispersal is illustrated by the relationship between several species of pines and nutcracking birds such as Clark's nutcracker (Tomback, 1983). Pines are fertilized by wind-blown pollen, but their heavy seeds are eaten, carried about, and occasionally dropped elsewhere by nutcrackers. It is to the advantage of the pine tree to evolve good nutrition for nutcrackers, and to the advantage of the latter to carry the seeds about and occasionally (wastefully, from the viewpoint of the individual) drop them. As Tomback points out, one must demonstrate that the evolution of each species actually affects that of the other in order to verify the existence of coevolution.

Theoretically, there is no such difficulty. Evolutionary change in one species must inevitably affect those species with which it has ecological relationships, and vice-versa. If the yucca plant became extinct, the yucca moth would have to evolve in other directions or to become extinct also.

So far, ecologists have tended to study limited cases between two species or several species connected by similar relationships. Further progress demands that all related species be considered, if we are to develop a general picture of eco-evolution.

In some cases, however, limited study of relationships is justified. For example, an endoparasite may have only one important ecological relationship, that with its host. But, as May and Anderson (1983) point out, the host usually harbors an entire community of parasites, and its evolution will be affected by all of these, as well as its relationships with non-parasitic species. And this will in turn affect the evolution of each specific parasite.

Further, the processes of plant evolution differ from those of animals on the genetic level. The major processes are common to both: Mutation, Sexual Reproduction, Inbreeding and Differential Survival. If anything, inbreeding is of greater importance in plants, because of their immobility, and many plants exhibit the most extreme degree of inbreeding, self-fertilization, which is impossible for most animal species.

More than this, new species in plants can be created immediately and without isolation through gross chromosomal changes (See also Chapter VI.) Ordinarily, fertilization is impossible unless both gametes carry the same chromosome number. But if the complete set is doubled or tripled, and a similar double or triple set is found in another germ cell, fertilization is possible, and a new species has arisen. Such aberrations of meiosis occur in all species, but because of the enormous numbers of gametes produced by many plant species, such occurrences are far more likely in plants than animals and have been observed in many cases.

Further, if a gamete bearing a double set of chromosomes is fertilized by a similar gamete from another species, the result can be a fertile, pure-breeding hybrid that potentially is the foundation of an instant new species with characteristics differing from both parents. Because the complexities of behavioral adaptation are not involved, such a species is more likely to succeed in plants than animals.

If it occurs at all, speciation by hybridization should be most likely to occur in animals living in marine environments. Many species reproduce by broadcasting enormous numbers of germ cells into the water. If two species that were reasonably compatible reproduced at the same season, there would be at least some chance of viable double-diploid hybrids being produced. This could be one possible explanation of the saltatory changes described by paleontologists such as Gould and Eldredge (1977). Unfortunately, fossils leave no chromosomes, and the hypothesis cannot be tested unless related surviving forms are available.

Thus, the theory of coevolution must embrace the genetic evolutionary processes of both plants and animals. To be complete, it should include the evolution of entire ecosystems. Since this would require the development of theories at least as complex as the ecosystems themselves, it would be extraordinarily difficult. The most useful theories, therefore, will be those that apply to specific relationships. Since most species have many important relationships, it follows that many theories should apply to a particular species, corresponding to its various relationships. For example, the same animal species could be involved in host-parasite, predator-prey, and plant-dispersal relationships. To me, the most fruitful approach would be to analyze one species at a time in all its aspects.

Research in this area, moreover, could be undertaken along lines varying from a consideration of ecosystem evolution to the genetic evolution of a particular species and its ecologically related species, as well as the evolution of classes of ecological relationships. In any case, any study of biological evolution must involve genetics and the consideration of the genotype as a system.

Unlike many areas of evolutionary thought, the evolution of ecological relationships, or coevolution, has direct practical applications. For the human species and similarly long-lived animals, biological evolution is ordinarily so slow as to be of little practical use. But we are associated with other species, such as viruses, that run through enormous numbers of generations in a human lifetime and undergo rapid evolutionary changes that are of great importance to medicine. Given enough time, the human species can respond with the evolution of resistance. The end result should be the coevolution of a disease that does not kill its host.

EFFECTS OF ECOSYSTEM CHANGE ON BIOLOGICAL EVOLUTION

There are two principal kinds of ecosystem change. One is the modification of the physical environment by the processes of living, as in plant succession, marine island building by corals, or the building of limestone by the deposition of calcareous skeletons of mollusks. Some of these processes may be very slow, and others relatively rapid, but the general effect is to alter the environment in which the species itself lives, as well as that of other species. Such changes can occur without genetic change.

The second kind of change is that of biological evolution itself. This is going on simultaneously in all members of an ecosystem, each species affecting some of the others directly and some indirectly.

With respect to biological evolutionary processes, ecosystem change of either sort should have little effect on mutation except possibly as certain life processes might produce mutagenic chemical substances. But the major cause of mutations, aside from human culture, is radiation. Plants do provide some protection from ultraviolet radiation for other species by creating shade. If anything, ecosystems probably decrease the rate of mutation.

Ecosystems should have no direct effect on the ongoing process of sexual reproduction, although that of the flowering plants has evolved in connection with the ingestive and reproductive behavior of insects.

The process of inbreeding could be affected by ecosystem changes resulting in the division of species habitats and resulting semi-isolation of small populations. If an animal species lives off one food plant, and the range of that plant becomes divided, the animal species must also become divided.

But the major effect of ecosystem change is upon the process of Differential Survival. Ecosystems are the source of biotic selection, which is correspondingly modified by both genetic and non-genetic changes.

If a species is confined to a single ecosystem, the normal process of ecosystem development (succession) could totally wipe it out. Therefore, such species can only survive in the stable or climax stage of an ecosystem. Indeed, such a species must always be on the endangered list, irrespective of human cultural evolution which deliberately and accidentally frequently destabilizes ecosystems.

This is a neglected aspect of biological evolution, that ecosystem change is a regular source of species extinction. No competition is involved; the species simply eliminates itself by destroying its environment and is overwhelmed by its successors. The long-range result should be the survival of species that are widely distributed and are adaptable enough and that they can accommodate themselves to a variety of ecosystems and ecosystem stages. Ecology thus gives a clear answer to the old evolutionary problem of why overspecialization leads to extinction.

The implications for human survival are obvious. The greatest threat to human existence is the human species itself. Like other species, humans have a tendency to increase and multiply under favorable conditions. The larger the population, the faster we render the environment unfit for survival, in a variety of ways. We cover fertile farmland with houses and pavements. We use up water stored in aquifers and render the land above it unproductive. Our waste products accumulate so fast that in some areas people can only dispose of them by creating mountains of garbage, not to mention toxic wastes that destroy all forms of life including our own.

At the same time, humans can foresee the future and so can modify it through cultural evolution; we need not go the way of successful species in the past. But unless enough people have the knowledge, and unless enough people are willing to sacrifice short-term gain for long-term advantages, we are likely to reduce ourselves to a level of barren survival.

Plant succession brings about the local extinction of certain plants and their replacement by others with similar effects on the animal species dependent on them, so that the survival of a given species is favored at one time and not at another. Different sorts of selection for individuals must be going on when the species is just coming in, when it is flourishing, and as it goes out (MacArthur & Wilson, 1967).

They developed these ideas from a consideration of a special form of succession involving the repopulation of small islands in which either the animal or plant species, or both, have been wiped out. They point out that in the early stages of succession Differential Survival will favor species and individuals that have a very high reproductive rate, no matter how wasteful, because resources are unlimited ("r selection", r being the intrinsic rate of increase).

Later, as the area becomes crowded and resources limited, those individuals and species will be favored that have a small but efficient rate of reproduction, perhaps amounting only to replacement levels ("K selection", K being the carrying capacity of the environment).

It follows that a similar rule should favor the success of different species colonizing the island, and that it should end up with species that replace themselves most efficiently with a minimum of waste. Also, although the authors do not discuss it, when the animals but not plants are extirpated on an island, and later recolonize it, the above ideas suggest a form of succession that could primarily involve animal species instead of the more common emphasis on changes in vegetation.

Further, the animal species in an area undergoing succession are affected by selection processes emanating from different plant and animal species as they succeed one another. We would expect that under these conditions, selection would favor characteristics, including behavior, that were adaptive under a variety of conditions. That is, the overall process of succession is itself a source of selection.

Thus there is a reciprocal relationship between ecosystem change, or ecoevolution, and the processes of genetically based evolution. Genetic change results in ecosystem change, and ecosystem change affects the processes of genetically based evolution, particularly that of Differential Survival. Since genetic change involves a large random element, and since a large portion of ecosystem change is not based on genetics, the resulting interaction is a dynamic and continuing one; i.e. evolution of either sort never achieves a condition of stasis.

INTERACTION WITH CULTURAL EVOLUTION

Effects of Culture on Ecosystems

Modern human culture seeks to dissociate humans from ecosystems and has been extraordinarily successful in some respects, especially in the control of many infectious diseases. One of these, smallpox, has recently been eliminated from the whole world. But large and dense populations provide ideal opportunities for transmission of airborne viruses such as colds and influenza. These viruses evolve so rapidly that they are always a little ahead of cultural change.

Cultural evolution has been particularly successful in changing or eliminating the human-animal and human-plant ecological relationships. Some species have become extinct, and some have been deliberately modified. Still others have adapted themselves to human culture. Urban dwellers now have to protect their garbage against raccoons, and molds grow on the plastic calking of their bathtubs. Thus the changes produced by culture rarely achieve stability; attempts to control the biotic environment must respond to ever-evolving ecosystems and thus involve continuing effort.

Contrasting to these attempts at dissociation, there is the esthetic pleasure of contact with unmodified and unspoiled ecosystems. At the present time, the United States' population has a majority in favor of preserving ecosystems as opposed to a powerful minority who would modify and destroy them for short-range benefits. We must remember that humans evolved for millions of years in close daily contact with ecosystems, and even the most confirmed urban dwellers often seek to restore this contact through their pets and house plants. Thus there is a strong movement not only to conserve but restore ecosystems.

As described in the earlier part of this chapter, the agricultural revolution basically consisted of modifying the ecosystems of which human societies were a part. Such modifications drastically altered the biotic and indirectly the physical environment, which in turn changed the kinds of selection to which surviving animal and plant species were subjected. This gave a new direction to evolution, a process that one can still see going on in the United States where, except for relatively small areas cultivated by Amerindians, row agriculture was suddenly introduced in the 17th century and spread over the whole country in about 300 years.

The industrial revolution has produced further changes which are still proceeding, especially as human habitations and pavement cover land so that much of it can no longer support an ecosystem. The degree to which this process can be controlled will determine much of the future quality of life in this country.

Reciprocal Effects on Human Cultural Evolution

Ecosystems have always been a major determinant of the material aspects of human culture. As *Homo sapiens* spread to different parts of the world the species entered a variety of ecosystems, each of which demanded different sorts of adaptation. Thus Eskimos developed boats and weapons for killing marine mammals, tools for processing furs, and shelters appropriate to the severe Arctic climate. At an opposite extreme of climate, the native Australians developed tools for dealing with the desert ecosystem in which many of them lived, wore almost no clothing, and used shelter only for shade.

The above cases are ones in which human societies culturally adapted themselves to ecosystems without seriously modifying them. This appears to have been true of many of the contemporary hunter and gatherer-hunter societies. It was probably not true of hunter societies in prehistoric times, which may have exterminated the large American mammals (Martin, 1973) which were slow to reach maturity, had low birth rates, and were vulnerable to slaughter by groups of human hunters. Assuming this to be true, the hunters were then forced to live on other prey animals.

As I pointed out above, the present trend in human cultural evolution is to isolate human societies from ecosystems. Much is gained in safety and health, and much is lost in terms of pleasure in adaptive behavior and esthetic enjoyment. The net effect is to largely remove cultural evolution from the influence of ecosystems and the changes that they undergo but at the price of continuing effort which itself is a change in the direction of cultural evolution.

CONCLUSIONS

The highest level of organization among living systems is the ecosystem; consequently, ecosystems are the largest of all living systems. Their basic entities or units are species populations which, as we have shown, are themselves often organized into subpopulations of societies or social systems, which in turn are composed of organismic systems based on physiological systems and finally on genotypes, or genetic systems. A reductionistic philosopher might argue that because genotypic systems are basic to all, everything can be understood in terms of genotypes. This is obviously not the case: there are reciprocal causal relationships between higher and lower levels of systems organization, some direct and some acting through successive levels. An important part of living organization can be understood through genetics, but only a part.

Moreover, the organization of systems at different levels is inclusive, and one can argue that the functions of the most inclusive system, the ecosystem, is therefore most important, affecting as it does hundreds or thousands of different species. Also, there is a certain degree of hierarchical organization. While causation between levels is always reciprocal, it can be argued that more control is exerted by the upper levels on the lower, than vice-versa; for example, that Differential Survival, proceeding in a large part from ecosystems, outweighs the genetic response to the ecosystem. Or perhaps it would be fair to say that the issue is always in doubt, varying according to the phenomena involved. In any case, the concept of hierarchy is too simple to explain more than a limited part of the operation of a complex system.

In the past, biologists interested in more basic levels have sometimes denigrated the Science of Ecology, calling it loose and not subject to their strict technique of controlled experimentation. I am saying that the study of ecology is the biologist's greatest challenge, leading to the discovery of the most complex and all-embracing of biological truths.

To summarize, ecoevolution is the product of three major change processes. The first of these, coevolution, includes the combined processes of genetically based evolution of all the species in a given ecosystem. It would be an error, however, to assume that these processes are additive and therefore that coevolution can be understood by simple extension of the processes that proceed in a single species. Evolutionary processes among the members of an ecosystem are interactive, and we must assume that they may produce non-additive and hence novel or creative results. Understanding coevolution is one of the major challenges facing evolutionary theorists.

The second process, that of succession or the development of ecosystem organization, is in part the product of coevolution, but also has major feedback effects through local extinction and changes in the process of selection. Also, because it operates by the tendency of organisms to render an environment, both physical and biotic, unfit for their own survival, succession will proceed independently of genetic change. In most cases, the processes of succession will proceed much more rapidly than genetic evolution. Consequently, the best forms of adaptation to succession are those which permit flexibility and adjustment to a variety of environments. In the case of animals, flexible behavior provides an ideal form of rapid adaptation to changing conditions.

The third process, that of climatic change, involves the operation of nonliving systems such as the solar system and the geophysical system which is slowly changing as the continents move about in response to physical forces, and quite rapidly in daily and seasonal fluctuations of weather. Many of these changes are independent of living matter, as in the case of solar storms resulting in fluctuation of solar radiation. Such is not the case in the geophysical system. The climate does depend on ecosystems and their activities, as in the green house effect and the regulation of moisture. Coral Islands and much of the geological strata of continents are the result of the activities of marine organisms.

Thus the processes of ecosystem change include some that are non-genetic in nature. They present the possibility of developing a much more comprehensive and definitive theory of genetic evolution through the more precise understanding of the processes of biotic and physical selection, and they help to define its boundaries. Further, they make it possible to depict the overall relationships between the three major evolutionary processes.

It is relatively easy to diagram the reciprocal relationships between biological, cultural, and ecosystem evolution (see Figure 1.1). It is also easy to describe the relationships between ecosystem change and the four major change processes of biological evolution. But the relationships between the complex processes of human cultural evolution and eco-evolution are correspondingly complex.

The major effects of cultural evolution upon ecosystem change are produced by the products of cultural change (see Table 11.1). Tools and machines change the use of energy, which inevitably disturbs ecosystems, whose dynamics depend on the use of energy. The end results of tool use are constructions and manufactures, altering the physical environment and through this altering the function of ecosystems.

The reciprocal relationships between ecosystem change and cultural change processes are not so obvious and measurable. Ecosystem changes stimulate the intrinsic change processes of fantasy and imagination with all the unpredictable outcomes of these creative processes. They stimulate the group change processes of synergic problem solving, including science, and they lead to invention and innovation.

Hopefully, these changes may result in changes in ideas and codes of behavior that will change the tendency of the human species, shared with all other living organisms, to render the environment unfit for survival. The process of developing new codes of behavior is proceeding rather painfully and slowly in the United States at the present time.

If there is ever to be a general theory of evolution, it should be based on ecosystem change as the most inclusive and all-embracing form of biological organization. The students of coevolution are making a start in this direction. To my mind, however, it is equally plausible to argue that a general theory will be a collection of special theories, not reducible to simple generalization. This being so, the most profitable approach will be to examine single species and those that are closely related, either genetically or ecologically, to determine which evolutionary processes are going on, and to study the interactions between them. Biological organization is too complex to be described in terms of any one simple principle.

Chapter XIII

On the Future of Evolutionary Theories:
The Evolution of Evolution

Scientific thinking in the biological and social sciences is undergoing a slow revolution away from mechanistic metaphors borrowed from early concepts of the physical sciences toward the concept of living systems which embody two-way causation or feedback, and creativity resulting from the development of higher levels of organization. Along with this there is a trend away from conceptualizations based on dichotomous thinking and bipolar opposites and toward concepts based on continuous variation and multi-dimensionality as exemplified by complex systems.

The concept that all phenomena can be symbolized in terms of bipolar opposites was first strongly expressed by Descartes, but is also inherent in Western European language and culture. We like to think in the simple terms of black and white, light and dark, good and evil, and this was going on long before Descartes. So we are dealing not just with a scientific revolution, but a cultural one as well, with all the difficulties involved in such revolutions.

With respect to evolutionary theory, this revolution was essentially accomplished and recorded in the 1960's in the volumes entitled *Evolution after Darwin*. (Tax, 1960) For example, the 4-process theory is clearly outlined in Dobzhansky's (1960) paper in which he stated that evolutionary-genetic change is affected by two deterministic factors, mutation and selection, and by two sources of randomness, sexual reproduction and inbreeding. He also emphasized the creative principle: "Evolution is a creative response of living matter to environmental opportunity...there are good reasons to think that evolutionary histories are unique and nonrecurrent." Further, the "...biological theory of evolution...

visualizes a creative process resulting in the emergence of real novelties..."

I may add that while mutation is a deterministic process, it is also a random one. Thus, three of the four genetic-evolutionary processes are random and non-directional. The random nature of evolutionary change is in part responsible for its creativity. Similar views were expressed by other contributors, who included the major thinkers of that day. One can only conclude that the genetic theory of evolution was already well-developed by 1960. But cultural change, even among scientists, is a slow process; many theoreticians who have dealt with behavior and social organization since that time either were not aware of these developments or failed to appreciate their significance.

In these chapters I have attempted to link modern genetic-evolutionary theory with behavioral and social adaptive processes, using the conceptual framework of systems. Each time a new form of adaptation has arisen, the process of evolution has been modified. If I were addicted to metaphorical thinking (and who is not?) I would say that the phenomena of behavioral adaptation and social organization have each created a new evolutionary ball game.

But this is not the final word. I have sketched out only the main implications, and much remains to be filled in. In addition, geneticists are beginning to describe the operation of genetic systems at the level of genes themselves.

New Developments in the Genetic Theory of Evolution

New technical developments, especially in the field of molecular genetics, are throwing fresh light on the systems changes that are the primary source of change in biological evolution.

The discovery that enzymes are directly related to genes plus new biochemical methods that permit the easy identification of enzymes, has made it possible to compare genotypes across species without going through the laborious techniques of breeding experiments and, indeed, make possible comparisons of species that cannot be interbred. Results of these studies show that mammalian species share a very large number of genes, so that it appears that genotypes are more similar than phenotypes. Two explanations have been offered. One is that these "structural" genes (structural in the sense that they produce proteins with definite biochemical structure) are not as important in evolution as are "regulatory" genes, that turn structural genes off and on at different times in development (Ayala, 1976). This is, of course, gene interaction. The other and more general explanation is that gene interaction multiplies variation in ways impossible to explain by simple gene addition.

Supplementing and extending these techniques are some even more remarkable ones by which it is possible to compare and identify genes by analyzing the sequences of amino acids within them. The results again show a large number of identical genes in distantly related mammals such as mouse and man.

Retroviruses (Varmus, 1983) are a group of viruses remarkable in that a single stranded RNA genome is replicated through a double stranded DNA provirus which penetrates a chromosome within a cell of the host. Thus the virus is passed along with the chromosomes to daughter cells. In addition, it produces viruses within the cell which are capable of penetrating the cell membrane and infecting other cells.

One of the first retroviruses to be discovered was that causing mammary tumors in mice. Since then, such viruses have been implicated in tumors and cancers of a wide variety of vertebrate animals including man. Working within a cell, such a retrovirus stimulates it to grow, thus providing more living space for itself.

A remarkable property of these viruses is that when two strains are present in the same cell they may show recombination; i.e., exchanges of material so that the elements of the strands are present in new combinations. The result is the same as that of sexual reproduction in higher organisms, except that the exchange takes place within a gene, not among them, but with a similar result, increase in variation. Like other viruses, retroviruses also mutate, producing variation in still another way.

Furthermore, analyses of mammalian genes show that some are identical with certain retroviruses. One can argue that the virus is a "wild" gene or, more likely, that mammals have incorporated these viruses into their genomes where they produce new effects. If so, it is probable that the viruses were living symbiotically prior to incorporation.

From the viewpoint of evolutionary theory, this means a new source of variation supplementing that of mutation of the species' original genes. Also, while a mutant gene is a modified old one, these viruses represent entirely new ones. It follows that the evolution of a species may depend on its coevolution with viruses and possibly be facilitated by it. Still another discovery regarding primary gene action (and this is true of some retroviruses also) is that of numerous position effects; i.e., the effect of a gene may depend on its being next to another one on the chromosome. There are even cases where certain sequences of genes appear to be mobile, moving from one part of a chromosome to another and producing different effects in each place.

The first major evidence for this phenomenon was obtained by McClintock (1951, 1956), working with the genetics of maize. She demonstrated the existence of "controlling elements", genetic material that could appear on different chromosomes or different parts of the same chromosome, but producing different effects at each locus: gene mutations, and a variety of chromosomal rearrangements.

Some of the best evidence among animal organisms comes from Drosophila, founded on the technique of studying the giant polytene chromosomes of the salivary glands. These chromosomes are banded in ways that correspond to the genes that they carry. Detailed studies in recent years have shown that dispersed, moderately repetitive sequences of these bands occur in highly variable places in different stocks and different species (Rubin, 1983). Furthermore, the effects of these groups of genes differ according to the site on which they are inserted, modifying their expression and producing mutations. The exact modes in which they act have not been determined, but one possibility is that two genes in close proximity may modify each other's activity and so produce new gene products. Or they may disturb the composition of a structural gene itself. This suggests that these effects may be produced by the same processes of genic exchange as in the retroviruses. Rubin concluded that about 10% of the genome in Drosophila is composed of these transposable elements and hence that a large fraction of spontaneous mutations and chromosomal rearrangements are caused by them.

The evolutionary effects are twofold. One is to increase variation; the organism itself increases the rate of mutation by interactions between its own genes that are not dependent on outside factors such as radiation. The other effect is to provide direct evidence of genic interaction on the molecular level. Such interaction takes place not only outside the cell (as a good deal of physiological genetics would indicate), but within the chromosomes themselves.

The evidence again supports the importance of gene combinations in evolution rather than single genes. The genes are not independent, nor are their effects additive.

The general significance of these discoveries is to reinforce the theory that the genotype is a complex interacting system whose effects depend upon gene combinations. It should be possible to monitor evolution at the genotypic as well as organismic levels, and to chart the relationships between the two in ways that have previously been possible only by inference from the organismic level. We can anticipate the development of new and more complex theories of genetic evolution in the future.

Among these is the "neutral theory" of Kimura (1982) which addresses the importance of mutation as a change process. It is based on the finding that many of the genic polymorphisms discovered by electrophoretic methods have little or no effect on phenotypes, either positive or negative. Prior to the development of these methods, the only way that genic variations could be discovered was through variation in phenotypic characters whose adaptive or maladaptive nature could be assessed directly. Kimura concluded that each species should have a large reservoir of neutral genic variation.

The theory falls into two parts. One is that many enzyme polymorphisms are selectively neutral and are maintained by the balance between mutational input and random extinction, the latter being the result of random drift, which can occur even in large populations through occasional reductions to small numbers, producing a genetic bottleneck through which only part of the genic variation can pass.

The selectionist argument against Kimura's position is based on the assumption that Natural Selection is the only change agent and therefore that every existing variation must have some function. The only way that the issue can be settled is through empirical evidence in each particular case. The neutralist and selectionist hypotheses are not necessarily universal, and either one may apply to a given instance of genic polymorphism. As I have pointed out, every variation that exists does not have to be adaptive; consequently its adaptive value, if measurable, can be placed on a scale ranging from strongly adaptive through neutral to strongly maladaptive.

The second part of Kimura's theory deals with the slowness of genetic change through mutation, which I have described in Chapter III. He points out that even with very large but finite populations, random drift and fixation of neutral mutations should occur during the millions of generations that have occurred in geologic time. Thus, the incidence of corresponding genes and their enzymes in distantly related animals should reflect the gradual accumulation of differences, irrespective of whether these are related to the adaptive differences between the species concerned. Obviously such figures will not give exact measures of relationships, as differences in generation time and fluctuations in population size may differ between the two species. Kimura concluded that, however slow the process may be, mutation can still bring about evolutionary change.

FUTURE OF GENETIC THEORY

The new developments in molecular genetics will inevitably have further effects on evolutionary theory. At present this is most evident with respect to the process of mutation. Kimura's theory relates to long-time effects of mutation and the accumulation of excess capacities for variation, but the new developments with respect to mobile genes suggest that there are sources of variation within genotypic systems and even raises the possibility that variation may not be entirely at random in some systems, i.e., that changes in the system could be self directed.

The other area where molecular genetics is having an important effect is in taxonomy, where a new revolution may be underway. It is now possible to chemically compare DNA in related species and from this make estimates of the degree of relationship in a highly precise way. Some of the limitations of this method are first that it depends on good techniques of sampling species populations (a sample of five or six from a local area might involve an unrepresentative deme and give a false impression of the species as a whole) and second that as now developed, the technique does not measure gene combinations, or gene interaction. While the great majority of DNA molecules might be similar in two species, a few different combinations or new interactions with regulatory genes could produce large differences in phenotypes. It will always be necessary to compare the molecular evidence with that from comparative anatomy, physiology, and behavior.

A similar technique is based on measuring similarities and differences in the DNA carried by mitochondria in animals and chloroplasts in plants, cytoplasmic bodies that are passed along only through maternal lines and are not subject to the reassortment of combinations as produced by meiosis, although alterable by mutation. This may turn out to be another place where the two process theory of evolution has an application.

With respect to the inter-related processes of inbreeding and sexual reproduction, these are so well understood that it is unlikely that their roles in genetic-systems theory will change.

The same is not true of selection theory, and I have in this volume indicated a few places where it is being modified. Selection, or more properly, Differential Survival, involves processes of many different sorts, the main categories being physical, biotic, and social, each including many sub-processes that are often independent of each other. The result is that any species population is always undergoing selection from many different and often opposing sources, so that it is difficult to define the fitness for survival of any individual or kinship group except at a particular moment in time. At such a moment, there should be some groups that are well adapted and others that are less so, their fitness shifting as situations change. As selection experiments show, species tend to evolve genetic systems that are buffered against the effects of recurring selection. And in animals with highly developed social organization, the most constant source of selection is the social one.

From the viewpoint of systems theory, most of the major evolutionary processes operate independently, and their interactions must always be included in any general theory. Perhaps the most general evolutionary phenomenon is the production and maintenance of variation; in a changing world, the best adapted species population is a variable one, just as the individual best adapted for survival is one with the best capacity for varying its physiological and behavioral responses. As an example, one important genetic systems phenomenon that is too often neglected is that once a species population becomes separated from others, its evolution proceeds independently, except for ecosystem interactions.

This means that there can never be any completely general theory of evolution except perhaps for the principle of variation: that each species will be unique.

Contributing also to the uniqueness of species is the fact that three out of four of the major evolutionary processes are random and non-directional in nature. This means that much evolutionary change is dependent on chance and hence non-predictable. A phenomenon may or may not be adaptive, and one would predict that any species would carry a share of non-adaptive or even maladaptive phenotypic characteristics, just as every species carries a load of injurious genes. If this load becomes too heavy, a species may be on the road to extinction.

Returning to the process of variation, behavior magnifies the variation and hence the adaptive capacity of individuals. An animal that can behave can adapt itself to a great many situations to which a non-behaving organism cannot. At least in the more complex vertebrates, two subsidiary behavioral capacities have evolved: that for learning from experience and forming habits of those behaviors that are most effective and, opposed to this, the tendency to vary behavior, no matter how strong the habit. This feeds back on selection processes, blunting their former effects and leading to new directions of selection, namely for those individuals having a demonstrated capacity for learning balanced by variation. Because such capacities are always developed, the selection must take place in later life and favor older individuals if competing with younger ones that have not yet developed these capacities.

Development itself should play a strong part in future evolutionary theory. Developmental processes are organizing processes and so are the ones through which evolutionary change is manifested. Further, extending or curtailing developmental processes may be the easiest way that the organization of a system may be changed in a non-disruptive fashion.

SUMMARY OF GENETIC EVOLUTIONARY THEORIES

Any sound theory of biological evolution must be based on sound genetic theory. The essence of biological evolution is genetic change. The theories presented here are based on two general principles:

1) *A gene always functions as part of a genotypic system*; and its effects on organization are always dependent on other genes. The one apparent exception is that of viruses, but even a virus can only function within the genetic system of another organism.

Further, genes are almost always pleiotropic and interact with other genes in a non-additive fashion. Therefore, *any genetic theory of evolution must deal with combinations of genes as well as individual genes.*

2) Evolution consists of change processes acting on the organization of complex living systems organized in sets of nested systems and subsystems, ranging from ecosystems to genetic systems, and whose entities interact not only on the same level but between levels. Therefore, *evolutionary theory must include systems theory*, or, as I have named it elsewhere, polysystemic theory.

The Processes of Organizational Change in Biological Evolution

There are four such processes: Mutation, including all forms of genic change; Sexual Reproduction, including the processes of meiosis and fertilization; Inbreeding; and Differential Survival or Natural Selection. Mutation has the function of producing genetic variation, without which evolution would be impossible. Sexual Reproduction has the effect of magnifying variation by breaking down genotypes and reassembling genes in new combinations. Inbreeding reduces the number of possible gene combinations in a population and thus brings about change. Differential Survival likewise reduces the number of gene combinations but in ways that promote the continued existence of the living systems involved and thus are directional with respect to other living and nonliving systems.

Theoretically, these four processes (or classes of processes) could operate in all possible combinations of one or more at a time. Actually, there are only four of these that have or can be seriously considered.

1) *One-Process Theory*. The only possible theory of this sort is Mutation Theory, long since abandoned as a general theory but applicable in the special and artificial case of highly inbred laboratory strains largely protected from natural selection. Its speed is inversely dependent on the size of the breeding population.

2) *Two-Process Theory*. Here the only possibility is that of *Muta-*

tion + Differential Survival. This is the equivalent of Darwin's Variation + Natural Selection, and is also the basis of Fisher's (1930) theories. It applies to any species that lacks sexual reproduction, such as most (but not all) viruses and other asexually reproducing organisms. This theory has often been combined and confused with the single-gene replacement theory.

3) *Three-Process Theory.* The only possible combination is that of *Mutation + Sexual Reproduction + Differential Survival.* This theory applies to organisms that have sexual reproduction but not inbreeding. It should apply to some of the marine invertebrates that produce enormous numbers of germ cells but have little opportunity for inbreeding.

4) *Four-Process Theory.* This consists of *Mutation + Sexual Reproduction + Inbreeding + Differential Survival* and should apply to any species that shows sexual reproduction and inbreeding; i.e., any species population that is divided into demes. It should apply to the vast majority of terrestrial animals.

Single-Gene Replacement and Shifting Combination Theories

Either of these theories can be combined with any of the above as is appropriate. The shifting combination theory (Wright's shifting balance theory) is confined to those organisms having sexual reproduction and hence can be associated only with the Three-Process and Four-Process Theories.

The single-gene replacement theory, on the other hand, is entirely appropriate in organisms consisting of a single gene, and also in species that reproduce asexually. The theory has only limited applications within the Three-Process and Four-Process Theories, because it depends on two assumptions that are seldom met: 1) that the new gene has the same effect in all possible combinations (i.e., a "major" gene) and 2) that successive mutant genes have additive effects on a character that is selected. The first assumption is clearly met in the case of lethal or other injurious genes, but major genes that have positive effects are virtually unknown. Likewise, additive effects of genes that modify the same character are virtually unknown. The single-gene replacement theory is therefore important in sexually reproducing organisms only in the case of negative selection against major injurious genes.

GENETIC-SYSTEMS THEORY AND THE EVOLUTION OF BEHAVIOR

In its simplest form, behavior is movement, a capacity that makes it possible for an animal to move from an environment that is unfavorable for its survival into one that is more favorable. Presumably from this beginning, every species has evolved more highly organized behavior that promotes living processes and deals with recurrent environmental situations. The smallest segment of behavior that has a function is the behavior pattern or modal action pattern (Barlow, 1977). It is, therefore, a unit upon which selection can act.

Although each species evolves independently and hence the evolution of their behavior diverges, it is possible to classify behavior according to function, and so to make comparisons between species. I have identified some eleven categories of behavioral function, five of which are found in all species and hence are presumably basic, plus six others that are predominantly social and have been evolved only in more complexly organized animals.

Since each behavioral category in any species usually consists of several different patterns of behavior, it can be considered as a system. However, such a form of organization is so different from other living systems that I have concluded that it is more useful to consider them as physiobehavioral systems, a form of organization that coordinates internal and external functions.

Behavioral evolution takes two general forms that comprise a continuum. One is the evolution of a special pattern to fit each environmental situation that the organism faces, a trend that is seen in its most extreme form in some of the one-celled animals. At the opposite extreme, a species evolves a few general patterns that are highly modifiable by experience, an example being the human capacity for developing spoken language. In between these extremes, most of the highly organized animals have evolved combinations of both trends. It is obvious that the modal action pattern is adaptive only in a stable environment, and in the usual case, most of these stable patterns are social in nature, correlated with the fact that social organization is often the most stable part of the environment. Surprisingly, there have been few theoretical arguments over the evolution of behavior. The instinct theorists assumed that modal action patterns were genetically determined, but offered no detailed genetic theory to support this. But they do offer an opportunity to test the alternate theories of gene combinations and single gene replacement through species crosses where hybridization is possible. There must be a genetic explanation of why such patterns are so stable. The limited data that are available support the gene combination theory, but there is still much to be done.

Several theories have been offered to explain the evolution of behavior, such as the Baldwin effect, surplus function, preadaptation, and ritualization. None of them are mutually exclusive, suggesting that the evolution of behavior may take a variety of pathways. But all of them involve the concept of transformation of function, avoiding the problem of creating a behavior pattern *de novo*.

Effects of Behavior and Social Organization on Genetic Change Processes

Behavior introduces a new form of adaptation. Up to and including the level of organismic systems, organization is largely based on structure; i.e., fixed spatial relationships between constituent entities in a system. Behaving organisms can move about, changing spatial relationships. Further, behavior makes possible a new level of organization, that of social systems dependent on behavioral interaction.

Both of these phenomena have effects on genetically based change processes that are summarized in Table 10.2. While neither behavior nor social organization affects the basic process of mutation (except in the case of human societies producing mutagenic agents), they have profound effects on organismic (phenotypic) variation. Behavior introduces a large element of non-genetic variation, which in turn modifies (usually reducing) the process of differential survival. Social organization accentuates behavioral variation between societies, but limits it within a society.

Sexual behavior and social organization both modify the process of sexual reproduction so that it becomes less random. Social organization may affect the process of inbreeding, either positively or negatively. Finally, both behavior and social organization modify Differential Survival in important ways, usually by decreasing the differential. This in turn has an effect on genetic variation, which should tend to increase.

In conclusion, while the same biological processes of evolutionary change operate at all levels, their actions and their interactions are modified in the higher levels of organization. Evolution as a whole is a different process on the behavioral and social levels from that on the organismic level, which in turn is different from that on the genotypic level.

GENETIC SYSTEMS THEORY AND THE EVOLUTION OF SOCIAL ORGANIZATION

Many of the early theoreticians in this field began with an overly-simplistic set of assumptions such as 1) mechanistic-reductionism which in its most extreme form argues that all living phenomena can be explained in terms of genetic elements, 2) that Natural Selection is the only evolutionary change process, 3) that Natural Selection only operates through competition between individuals, 4) that the only process of genetic change was that of single-gene replacement, and so on. It has been the central task of this book to reconcile the theories so produced with modern genetic-systems theory, a task that has in part been accomplished by the theoreticians themselves.

A major contribution was Hamilton's (1964) concept of "inclusive fitness" that pointed out that evolutionary change depended not only on the survival of an individual but his/her ability to produce surviving offspring that carried similar heredity. From the viewpoint of gene combination theory, gene combinations in a sexually reproducing species are produced by a mated pair, and it is the ability of such pairs to produce individuals with combinations adapted for survival that is important. Therefore, "inclusive fitness" must always involve at least two individuals as a mated pair, and more if the individuals are involved in several matings.

Hamilton's concept was almost simultaneously extended by Maynard Smith (1964) as the hypothesis of kin selection, namely that the survival or fitness of a group of related individuals might depend on an inherited pattern of behavior that favored the survival of offspring. This and Hamilton's work suggest that social animals should behave in ways that are helpful to other individuals in proportion to the degree of genetic relationship between them. This has led to a great deal of research on the relationships of animals in social groups, and also on the ways in which they recognize kin, as opposed to non-related individuals. One result of this has been the discovery of many new cases of "helpers", related individuals that are not themselves currently reproducing (Emlen, 1984).

Another important concept (Maynard Smith, 1977, 1982) was that of the "evolutionarily stable strategy", defined as a phenotype, behavioral or otherwise such that no competing strategy could replace it in a species population; in short, a characteristic in which there was little variation except of a deleterious sort. As experimental studies show, many social behavior patterns are very stable, varying only in frequency and intensity under artificial selection (Scott & Fuller, 1965). The underlying genetic basis of such stable organization is yet to be discovered, but may be experimentally analyzed in species crosses. Evidence so far obtained suggests gene combination inheritance, but this in itself will not produce stability, which poses a fundamental problem.

I have suggested four hypotheses that have their roots in systems theory, all of which are compatible. The first is that the internal functioning of a living system is efficient in proportion to the stability of the system; therefore living systems should evolve in the direction of greater stability. Second, the organization of systems cannot be changed drastically without altering or destroying functions essential to life. Therefore, organization can become more complex only if it maintains necessary function. Third, a stable system is most adaptive in a stable environment, social, biotic, and physical. Because for many species, the social environment is the most stable of any, social behavior patterns tend to become stable. Finally, strong selection in a stable environment will lead to a survival of only the most adaptive combination of genes in the population.

The combination of all these factors could produce stability great enough to bring evolution to a standstill, and may explain the great stability of some organisms in the paleontological record. Corning (1983) has offered a theory that provides escape from this situation, namely, that of combinatory processes on higher levels of organization. Thus, individual organisms could remain stable while combining on the social level to produce new phenomena.

Maynard Smith (1982) also used the concept of strategy as used in games theory to predict the sorts of behavior that two animals might exhibit in a conflict situation. As applied to the analysis of agonistic behavior, it chiefly leads to a detailed examination of such behavior in animals without previous contact, and is probably most applicable to semi-solitary species that do not form dominance-subordination relationships.

Axelrod and Hamilton (1981) used games theory to explain how cooperative behavior may have evolved out of competitive behavior. This theory arises out of the assumption that all evolutionary change results from selection through inter-individual competition, an assumption that is not warranted either by genetic-systems theory or that of cooperation based on physiological function. In short, this is not the only way in which cooperation necessary for social organization may have been evolved. To my mind, the concept of strategy is most useful as a device for describing and analyzing the overall operation of a social system of a particular species. Any complex animal society obviously employs dozens of strategies, behavioral and otherwise, and the problem is to discover how these interact with each other.

The most productive lines of future research on the biological evolution of social organization should lie in the direction of describing the social organization that has been evolved and attempting to explain its evolution rather than trying to work out the logical consequences of some preconceived theory. In this respect systems theory is particularly useful as a way of describing and comparing social systems from an overall viewpoint. Thus, many current theories are concerned primarily with the behavior of the individual entities within a social system rather than dealing with the system as a whole. For example, a major phenomenon of social organization is the development of social relationships out of which relationship theory has been developed. Aside from Vehrencamp (1979), little attention has been paid to the evolution of the capacities to develop such relationships.

Further, more attention should be paid to functional or physiologically based theories of social evolution. A major paradox of systems theory is that while organismic systems may compete, there is ordinarily no competition within the systems, and many philosophically minded biologists have wondered why social systems are not similarly organized. The answer is also provided by systems theory, namely the principle of creativity, that on the level of social organization, it is possible for the entities (organisms) to be both cooperative and competitive.

Obviously, there can be no social organization without cooperation, defined as regular and mutually beneficial interaction between entities. I have outlined several functional theories of social evolution, all of which have their bases in physiological function, beginning with Allee's theory of aggregations resulting in physiological benefit and the furtherance of physiological function.

For example, sexual aggregations and sexual behavior make sexual reproduction more efficient. Sexual reproduction can be made still more efficient by the protection of fertilized eggs, at first physiological and then behavioral. This in turn can be extended to immature offspring and related adults and eventually to unrelated individuals. Thus the evolution of altruism can be explained by the extension of care-giving behavior without direct competition except in that groups showing such behavior should survive better than those that lack it. This avoids the difficulties imposed by Hamilton and others who were attempting to derive altruism directly from competition.

Another example is the evolution of agonistic behavior. Instead of competing in a random fashion, social animals have evolved systems which have the special function of organizing behavior involved in conflicts between two or more individuals. The result is that the animals spend less time and energy in competing and so can spend more on productive activities, and also that the risk of death or physical injury is reduced in most cases. Physiobehavioral agonistic systems appear to have evolved independently in the different major phyla, but in every case the most plausible theory is that it arose from primitive defensive behavior, some form of which exists in every phylum that exhibits behavior.

Seen in this light, Maynard Smith's (1982) games theory is an attempt to explain the behavior of individuals within an agonistic system. In common with similar theories, this is a microtheory that leads to the detailed study and analysis of behavior, instead of a general systems theory approach that leads to macrotheories. Needless to say, both have their usefulness.

The macroevolutionary theory involved is that of transformation of function. It is consistent with systems theory in that it avoids the problem of drastic reorganization of a living system, something that inevitably produces serious dysfunction. It is also broadly applicable to the problem of the origin of social behavior and organization, for which I have suggested the following functional roots: 1) shelter seeking, 2) sexual reproduction and its derivative, the care of others, 3) defense against injury and derived agonistic behavior and, very importantly, 4) the capacity for site attachment and derived social attachment. The theory does not lend itself to mathematical formulation, except where numerical figures are involved, as in population studies, but it is entirely consistent with genetic-systems theory. One advantage is that the transformation can occur either gradually, or quite rapidly where alteration of the form of behavior is not required, as in cases of preadaptation and surplus function.

ECOEVOLUTION AND COEVOLUTION

Another area that should develop rapidly in the future is that of the related phenomena of ecosystem change and the biological changes of species within an ecosystem. From the systems theory viewpoint, this is evolution on the grandest scale, and the possible interactions between the constituent entities, the species, are so complex that their analysis would be impossible except that we already have a well developed ecological concept and associated theories, that of tracing the flow of energy within a system. This technique (Odum, 1983) can be applied either to a single social system or to an entire ecosystem.

From the viewpoint of social organization, an animal society may replace the species as the unit of organization within an ecosystem. If all the societies within a species are identical, the theoretical problem is a simple one, but there is evidence that social organization, at least in mammals, may vary within a species depending on variation between ecosystems, that is, a species may be part of more than one ecosystem and play different roles in each.

Energy theory has already been fruitfully applied to social organization as the investment theory of Trivers (1985), and there is much more that could be done. Why is it that animal societies so often seem to waste energy rather than using it efficiently? Animals and the social organizations that they produce must have energy in order to survive as living systems, but they do not seem to evolve in the direction of becoming energy efficient machines. The relationship of energy to complex systems should be a fruitful field for research in the future.

Then there is the problem of analyzing the evolutionary consequences of interaction between species. Most of the current work is based on examining the relationships between pairs of species, but it is obvious that any species has relationships with many others, all of which should interact.

Finally, there is the problem of the reciprocal relationships between social organization and the ecosystems of which they are a part. If an animal society becomes successful, it inevitably modifies the ecosystem to which it belongs, sometimes destructively. This is particularly evident as human societies develop and expand.

CULTURAL EVOLUTION AND BIOLOGICAL EVOLUTION

Some cultural (non-genetic) transmission of information occurs in non-human animals, but human verbal communication has no counterpart in other species. While it has biological roots, it is a different phenomenon from biological evolution. What has evolved biologically is the *capacity* for language and with it the capacity for a new variety of symbolic thought.

Attempts to develop theories of cultural evolution by analogy with the processes of biological evolution have been relatively unsuccessful because of fundamental differences between the change processes in the two. Biological inheritance is non-cumulative; offspring always have the same number of chromosomes as their parents, and much genetic information is therefore discarded in each generation. Cultural inheritance, however, is cumulative, limited only by the capacity of individuals to receive and store it, and there are no theoretical limitations to the amount of information that can be stored by written or mechanical means.

Language also has more capacity for variation. DNA is based on only four amino acids, and while these can be associated in almost infinite numbers of ways by differences in order and sequencing, a language may have twenty or so different sounds that can be grouped in combinations that are limited only by difficulties of pronunciation. This is another example of the systems principle of creativity.

Because the human infant's memory is a genuine *tabula rasa*, enormous changes in cultural information are possible (though not inevitable) in large numbers of individuals from one generation to the next. In contrast, changes in genetic information are much slower to spread through a population.

The most promising theories of cultural evolution are therefore based on culture itself rather than biology, although biological evolution and variation in capacities must always be included in such theories. I have assembled some of these theories, all of which appear to be compatible, with the result that cultural evolution appears to be an extremely complex process.

Its importance to human practical affairs cannot be overestimated. If we really want to improve the human condition with respect to the ever-present problems of poverty, disease, mental illness, violence and warfare, this is the way to go. We need to know how to bring about desirable social change, and we need to know how to predict the outcomes of such changes. We need to discover why it is relatively easy to bring about technological change, and so difficult to change social organization other than by the traditional destructive process of revolution.

This brings me back to the problem posed in the first chapter of this book: how to avoid the misuse of biological evolutionary theories to justify harmful cultural practices. The overall principle is relatively simple: Scientists themselves must state the cultural implications (in other words, the practical applications) of their theories and discoveries. In order to do this, they must be sufficiently broadly trained to be able to do this accurately, and they should check their conclusions with other scientists from many disciplines. Some of the worst misuses of evolutionary theory have come from badly informed scientists themselves.

I can suggest a few generally agreed upon propositions that are justified by our current knowledge of the genetic systems theories of evolution. People should be trained to respect individual and population differences; genetically based variation is inevitable. Genetic variation between human populations is relatively slight, consisting of average differences with a great deal of overlap. Further, differences between local populations are disappearing as these populations merge with each other. Biological evolution goes on, but in the direction of increasing variation among individuals rather than population divergence and overall species change. The result should be increasing numbers of unique gene combinations, facilitating increasingly complex social organization (Scott & Fuller, 1965). Ranking human populations in terms of superiority and inferiority is for these reasons genetically unjustified. Therefore, racism should be abandoned.

Perhaps the most important positive cultural implication from this book is derived from systems theory. The existence of a living system at any level is dependent on cooperation, defined as supportive, integrative and mutually beneficial interaction between its constituent entities. Without it, no organization could exist, only chaos such as we see in a group of non-living gas molecules, each colliding with the others at random.

This is particularly important in a culture that places a high value on competition, such as that of North America and Britain, whose major unifying concept is that everything is a fight. The institution of marriage is viewed as contests for personal power between husband and wife and parents and children. Religion is a struggle between good and evil. Politics is a contest between two parties, and the system of justice was originally derived from trial by combat. Education is interpreted as a contest for grades, and economic life as a competition for monetary rewards.

Such a culture could not exist without compensating cooperative institutions. In order to have winners there must be losers, and someone must take care of the losers. In the past, family members took care of their less fortunate members, and religious groups encouraged charity for the poor. Most importantly, the care-giving function was organized on the basis of sex roles. Women were supposed to give care and support, while men were supposed to compete. In the competition for power in the family men were always supposed to win.

In the modern industrial societies of Europe and America, these functions have been increasingly taken over by governmental institutions in the form of unemployment insurance, health insurance, income insurance (social security), and so on. More informally, at least in the United States, a slow cultural revolution is taking place, divorcing the two functions from the sex roles, so that a woman has freedom to become a competitor, and a man has freedom to become a care-giver. This change arises out of the cultural ideal of equality, first stated in the United States in connection with the American Revolution against the hereditary class system of Britain, and that has been slowly extended ever since.

Here is another place where an appropriate cultural application can be made. Cultures are in part verbal or symbolic guidelines for social organization, and no one single principle will suffice. A symbolic system is inevitably a simplified and non-living version of the living system that it represents. In practice belief systems of a culture must include interaction between and elaboration of such beliefs if they are to be effective. Put negatively, beware of over-extension of cultural concepts, beliefs, and principles. Even the broad and inclusive concepts of systems theory are not perfect.

Applied to the subject matter of this book, which is an attempt to discover symbolic systems that will describe, explain and predict the operation of change processes in the organization of living systems, the future trend should be in the direction of developing more complex theories. I see no hope that a single universal theory will ever be discovered, no matter how glorious (for the discoverer) such a prospect may be.

The picture would not be complete without including science as a cultural system. Once seen as a search for absolute truth distinct and separate from the process of ordinary living, science is now viewed as a social institution, consisting of a group of individuals who work together to discover and transmit symbolic systems that explain and describe the operation of the non-symbolic world; i.e., living and non-living systems. In a culture such as ours, competition will always play a part in the scientific process, but we need to remember that science is essentially a cooperative endeavor devoted to group problem-solving, as Lieberman (1984) put it. All our work rests on that of others.

Because scientists and their creations are part of human culture, they will undergo cultural evolution. Each new generation of scientists will act upon the information it receives from former generations and its current members and create something new. Thus the evolutionary theories of a generation hence will bear some relationship to those of today, but will not be identical nor entirely predictable. Whatever the members of the next generation do, I hope that they will take up what I see as the most important task of evolutionary science, to learn how to control and direct constructive cultural change.

References

Adams. R. McC. (1966). *The evolution of urban society in early Mesopotamia and Prehispanic Mexico.* Chicago, IL: Aldine.

Alexander, R. D. (1971). The search for an evolutionary philosophy of man. *Proceedings Royal Society of Melbourne, 84,* 99-120.

Alexander, R. D. (1979). *Darwinism and human affairs.* Seattle, WA: University of Washington Press.

Allee, W. C. (1951). *Cooperation among animals, with human implications.* New York, NY: Schuman.

Allee, W. C. Emerson, A. E., Park, O., Park, T., & Schmidt, K. P. (1949). *Principles of animal ecology.* Philadelphia, PA: W. B. Saunders.

Axelrod, R., & Hamilton, W. D. (1981). The evolution of cooperation. *Science, 211,* 1390-1396.

Ayala, J. F. (1976). Molecular genes and evolution. In J. F. Ayala (Ed.), *Molecular evolution.* Sunderland MA: Sunderland Associates.

Baldwin, J. M. (1896). A new factor in evolution. *American Naturalist, 30,* 441-451, 536-553.

Banks, E. M., Pimlott, D. H. & Ginsburg, B. E. (Eds.). (1967). Ecology and behavior of the wolf. *American Zoologist, 7,* 220-381.

Barash, D. P. (1982). *Sociobiology and behavior* (2nd ed.). New York, NY: Elsevier.

Barlow, G. W. (1977). Modal action patterns. In T. A. Sebeok (Ed.), *How animals communicate* (pp. 98-134). Bloomington, IN: Indiana University Press.

Barlow, G. W. (1988). Has sociobiology killed ethology or revitalized it? *Perspectives in Ethology, 8,* (in press)

Bentley, D. R. (1971). Genetic control of an insect neuronal network. *Science, 174,* 1139-1141.

Bentley, D. R. & Hoy, R. R. (1974). The neurobiology of cricket song. *Scientific American, 231* (2), 34-44.

Berke, R. E. (1977). *The relationship between co-operation and competition in social life: A general systems theory analysis.* University of Southern California Dissertation.

von Bertalanffy, L. (1968). *General systems theory: Foundations, development, applications.* New York, NY: G. Braziller.

Bigelow, R. (1975). The role of competition and cooperation in human evolution. In M. A. Nettleship, R. D. Givens, & A. Nettleship (Eds.), *War, its causes and correlates* (pp. 235-261). The Hague: Mouton.

Blanchard, R. J., & Blanchard, D. C. (1977). Aggressive behavior in the rat. *Behavioral Biology, 21,* 197-224.

Blaustein, A. R. (1983). Kin recognition: Phenotypic matching or recognition alleles? *American Naturalist, 121,*749-754.

Brace, C. L. (1979). Krapina, "classic" Neanderthals, and the evolution of the human face. *Journal of Human Evolution, 8,* 527-550.

Brace, C. L. & Rosenberg, K. R. (1986). Late Pleistocene and Post-Pleistocene changes in human tooth size: a case of evolutionary gradualism. (Private communication.)

Bradt, G. W. (1938). A study of beaver colonies in Michigan. *Journal of Mammalogy, 19,* 139-162.

Brain, P. F., & Parmigiani, S. (Eds.). (1988). *House mouse aggression: A model for understanding the evolution of social behavior.* (In press)

Bronson, F. (1979). Reproduction ecology of the house mouse. *Quarterly Review of Biology, 54,* 265-279.

Brown, J. L. (1975). *The evolution of behavior.* New York: NY: Norton.

Buechner, H. K. (1974). Implications of social behavior in the management of the Uganda kob. In V. Geist & F. Walther (Eds.), *The behavior of ungulates and its relation to management.* Morges, Switzerland: International Union for Conservation of Nature and Natural Resources.

Burhoe, R. W. (1976). The source of civilization in the natural selection of coadapted information in genes and culture. *Zygon, 11,* 263-303.

Cairns, R. B. (1988). Developmental timing and the microevolution of aggression. In P. F. Brain & S. Parmigiani (Eds.), *House mouse aggression: A model for understanding the evolution of social behavior.* (In press)

Campbell, D. T. (1975). On the conflicts between biological and social evolution and between psychology and moral tradition. *American Psychologist, 30* 1103-1126.

Campanella, P. J., & Wolf, L. L. (1974). Temporal leks as a mating system in a temporate zone dragonfly (Odonata, Anisoptera. I. *Plathemis lydia,* Drury). *Behaviour, 51,* 49-87.

Cavalli-Sforza, L. L., & Feldman, M. W. (1981). *Cultural transmission and evolution; a quantitative approach.* Princeton, NJ: Princeton University Press.

Charlesworth, B., & Charnov, E. L. (1981). Kin selection in age-structured populations. *Journal of Theoretical Biology, 88,* 103-119.

Child, C. M. (1921). *The origin and development of the nervous system.* Chicago, IL: University of Chicago Press.

Coleman, D. L. (1962). Effect of genic substitution on the incorporation of tyrosine into the melanin of mouse skin. *Archives Biochemistry and Biophysics, 96,* 562-568.

Corning, P. A. (1983). *The synergism hypothesis: A theory of progressive evolution.* New York, NY: McGraw-Hill.

Corning, W. C., & Ratner, S. C. (Eds.). (1967). *Chemistry of learning: Invertebrate research.* New York, NY: Plenum.

Cottrell, W. F. (1955). *Energy and socity: The relation between energy, social change, and economic development.* New York, NY: McGraw-Hill.

Crane, J. (1975). *Fiddler crabs of the world: Ocypoidae, genus Uca.* Princeton, NJ: Princeton University Press.

Darlington, C. D. (1939). *The evolution of genetic systems.* Cambridge: Cambridge University Press.

Darwin, C. (1859). *The origin of species by means of natural selection, or the preservation of favored races in the struggle for life.* New York, NY: Random House. Modern Library Edition.

Dawkins, R. (1976). *The selfish gene.* Oxford: Oxford University Press.

DeBeer, G. S. (1958). *Embryos and ancestors* (3rd. ed.). Oxford: Clarendon.

Denenberg, V. H. (1959). Learning differences in two separated lines of mice. *Science, 130,* 451-452.

Denenberg, V. H. (1965). Behavioral differences in two closely related lines of mice. *Journal of Genetic Psychology, 106,* 201-205.

DeVore, I. (Ed.). (1965). *Primate behavior.* New York, NY: Holt, Rinehart and Winston.

Dilger, W. (1962). The behavior of love-birds. *Scientific American, 206* (1), 88-98.

Dobzhansky, Th. (1927). Studies on the manifold affects of certain genes in *Drosophila melanogaster. Zeitschrift fur induktiv Abstammungs und Vererbungslehre, 43,* 330-338.

Dobzhansky, Th. (1937). *Genetics and the origin of species.* New York, NY: Columbia University Press.

Dobzhansky, Th. (1960). Evolution and environment. In S. Tax (Ed.), *Evolution after Darwin. The evolution of life* (Vol. I, pp. 403-428). Chicago, IL: University of Chicago Press.

Dobzhansky, Th. (1962). *Mankind evolving.* New Haven, CT: Yale University Press.

Duellman, W. E., & Trueb, L. (1986). *Biology of the amphibians.* New York, NY: McGraw-Hill.

Dunbar, R. I. M. (1986). Demography and reproduction. In B. B. Smuts, D. L. Cheney, R. M. Seyfarth, R. W. Wrangham, & T. T. Struhsaker (Eds.), *Primate societies* (pp. 400-412). Chicago, IL: University of Chicago Press.

Dunn, H. L. (1961). *High-level wellness.* Arlington, VA: R. W. Beatty.

Ebert, P. D. (1983). Selection for aggression in a natural population. In E. C. Simmel, M. E. Hahn, & J.K. Walters (Eds.), *Aggressive behavior: Genetic and neural approaches* (pp. 103-127). Hillsdale, NJ: Erlbaum.

Eibl-Eibesfeldt, I. (1956). Uber die ontogenetische Entwicklung der Technik des Nusseoffnens vom Eichhornchen *Sciurus vulgaris* L. *Zeitschrift fur Saugetierkunde, 21,* 132-134.

Elton, C. S. (1930). *Animal ecology and evolution.* Oxford: Clarendon Press.

Emerson, A. E. (1942). Basic comparisons of human and insect societies. *Biological Symposia, 8,* 163-176.

Emerson, A. E. (1952). The superorganismic aspects of the society. *Colloques internationaux du Centre National de la Recherche Scientific, No. 34* (pp. 333-353). Paris.

Emlen, S. T. (1984). Cooperative breeding in birds and mammals. In J. R. Krebs & N. E. Davies (Eds.), *Behavioral ecology: An evolutionary approach* (pp. 305-339). Sunderland, MA: Sinauer.

Etkin, W. (1985). The evolution of mind and the emergence of tribal culture: A mentalistic approach. (Private communication).

Fisher, R. A. (1930). *The genetical theory of natural selection.* Oxford: Clarendon Press.

Francis, L. (1973a). Clone specific segregation in the sea anemone, *Anthropleura elegantissima. Biological Bulletin, 144,* 64-72.

Francis, L. (1973b). Inotraspecific aggression and its effect on the distribution of *Anthropleura elegantissima* and some related sea anemones. *Biological Bulletin, 144,* 73-92.

Freedman, D. G. (1984). Village fissioning, human diversity and ethnocentrism. *Political Psychology, 5,* 629-634.

Frith, H. J. (1962). *The mallee fowl: The bird that builds an incubator.* Sydney: Angus and Robertson.

Fritts, S. H., & Mech, L. D. (1981). Dynamics, movements and feeding ecology of a newly protected wolf population in Northwestern Minnesota. *Wildlife Monographs, 80,* 1-79.

Fuller, J. L. (1976). Genetics and communication. In M. E. Hahn & E. C. Simmel (Eds.), *Communication, behavior and evolution* (pp. 23-38). New York, NY: Academic Press.

Futuyma, D. J., & Slatkin, M. (1983). *Coevolution.* Sunderland, MA: Sinauer.

Galef, B. C., Jr. (1976). Social transmission of acquired behavior: A discussion of tradition and social learning in vertebrates. In J. S. Rosenblatt, R. A. Hinde, E. Shaw & C. Beer (Eds.), *Advances in the study of behavior* (Vol. 6, pp. 77-100). New York, NY: Academic Press.

Galton, F. (1869). *Hereditary genius: An inquiry into its laws and consequences* (new ed., 1892). New York: NY: Horizon Press.

Geist, V. (1971). *Mountain sheep.* Chicago, IL: University of Chicago Press.

Ginsburg, B. E. (1965). Coaction of genetical and nongenetical factors influencing sexual behavior. In F. A. Beach (Ed.), *Sex and behavior* (pp. 53-75). New York, NY: John Wiley.

Ginsburg, B. E. (1975). Nonverbal communication: the effect of affect on individual and group behavior. In P. Pliner, L. Kramer, & T. Alloway (Eds.), *Nonverbal communication of aggression* (pp. 161-173). New York, NY: Plenum.

Ginsburg, B. E. (1976). Evolution of communication patterns in animals. In M. E. Hahn & E. C. Simmel (Eds.), *Communication, behavior and evolution* (pp. 59-79). New York, NY: Academic Press.

Ginsburg, B. E. (1978). Genetics of social behavior. In P. P. G. Bateson & P. H. Klopfer (Eds.), *Perspectives in ethology* (Vol. 3, pp. 1-15). New York, NY: Plenum.

Ginsburg, B. E., & Moon, A. A. (1983). Regulation of gene expression: Hormonal control of phenotypic thresholds. *Behavior Genetics Association* (Abstract)

Gorovsky, M. A. (1980). Genome organization and reorganization in *Tetrahymena. Annual Review of Genetics, 14,* 203-239.

Gould, S. J., & Eldredge, N. (1977). Punctuated equilibria: the tempo and mode of evolution. *Paleobiology, 3,* 115-151.

Guhl, A. M. (1953). *Social behavior of the domestic fowl.* Mahattan, KA: Kansas Agricultural Experiment Station.

Haldane, J. B. S. (1932). *The causes of evolution.* New York, NY: Longmans Green.

Haldane, J. B. S. (1955). Population genetics. *New Biology, 18,* 34-49.

Hamilton, W. D. (1964). The genetical evolution of social behavior, I & II. *Journal of Theoretical Biology, 7,* 1-16; 17-32.

Hamilton, W. D. (1971). Geometry for the selfish herd. *Journal of Theoretical Biology,31,* 295-311.

Hamilton, W. D. (1975). Innate social aptitudes in man: An approach from evolutionary genetics. In R. Fox (Ed.), *Biosocial anthropology* (pp. 133-155). New York, NY: John Wiley.

Harris, M. (1979). *Cultural materialism: The struggle for a science of culture.* New York, NY: Random House.

Harvey, R. A. (1934). Life history of *Kalotermes (Incisitermes) minor.* In C. A. Kofoid et al. (Eds.), *Termites and termite control* (pp. 217-233). Berkeley, CA: University of California Press.

Hess, E. H. (1973). *Imprinting.* New York, NY: D. Van Nostrand.

Hinde, R. A. (Ed.). (1969). *Bird vocalizations: Their relations to current problems in biology and psychology.* New York, NY: Cambridge University Press.

Hoagland, J. L. (1983). Nepotism and alarm calling in the black-tailed prairie dog (*Cynomys ludovicianus*). *Animal Behaviour, 31,* 472-479.

Honess, R. F., & Frost, N.M. (1942). *A Wyoming bighorn sheep study.* Cheyene, WY: Wyoming Fish and Game Department, Bulletin No. 1.

Howard, E. (1920). *Territory in bird life.* London: John Murray.

Howard, R. D. (1978). The evolution of mating strategies in male bullfrogs, *Rana catesbiana. Evolution, 32,* 850-871.

Hrdy, S. B. (1977). *The langurs of Abu.* Cambridge, MA: Harvard University Press.

Huxley, J. S. (1923). Courtship activities of the red-throated diver (*Colymbus stellatus* Pontopp), together with a discussion of courtship behavior in grebes. *Journal of the Linnaean Society, 35,* 253-293.

Huxley, J. S. (1942). *Evolution, the modern synthesis.* London: Allen & Unwin.

Itani, J. (1982). Intraspecific killing among non-human primates. *Journal of Social Biological Structure, 5,* 361-368.

Jay, P. (1965). The common langur of North India. In I. DeVore (Ed.), *Primate behavior* (pp. 197-249). New York, NY: Holt, Rinehart, and Winston.

Johanson, D. C., & Edey, M. (1981). *Lucy: The beginnings of humankind.* New York, NY: Warner.

Johanson, D. C. & White, T. D. (1979). A systematic assessment of early African hominids. *Science, 203,* 321-330.

Kaplan, S. (1982). Interclonal aggression in *Metridium senile:* Sexual selection in a marine invertebrate. Paper presented at the Northeast Regional Meeting of the Animal Behavior Society, Boston, MA, October, 1982.

Kawai, M. (1965). Newly acquired precultural behavior in a natural group of Japanese monkeys on Koshima Islet. *Primates, 6,* 1-30.

Kellogg, W. N. (1961). *Porpoises and sonar.* Chicago, IL: University of Chicago Press.

Kimura, M. (1982). The neutral theory as a basis for understanding the mechanisms of evolution and variation at the molecular level. In M. Kimura (Ed.), *Molecular evolution, protein polymorphism and the neutral theory* (pp. 3-56). New York, NY: Springer-Verlag.

King, M. C., & Wilson, A. C. (1975). Evolution at two levels in humans and chimpanzees. *Science, 188,* 107-115.

Kislak, J. W., & Beach, F. A. (1955). Inhibition of aggressiveness by ovarian hormones. *Endocrinology, 56,* 684-692.

Kleiman, D. G. (1977). Monogamy in mammals. *Quarterly Review of Biology, 52,* 36-69.

Klinghammer, E. (Ed.). (1979). *The behavior and ecology of wolves.* New York, NY: Garland.

Koehler, W. (1927). *The mentality of apes* (2nd ed.). New York, NY: Harcourt Brace.

Krebs, J. R., & Davies, N. E. (1984). *Behavioral ecology: An evolutionary approach* (2nd ed.). Sunderland, MA: Sinauer.

Kroeber, T. (1961). *Ishi, in two worlds: A biography of the last wild Indian in North America.* Berkeley, CA: University of California Press.

Kropotkin, P. (1902). *Mutual aid: A factor of evolution.* New York, NY: McClure Phillips.

Kruuk, H. (1972). *The spotted hyena: A study of predation and social behavior.* Chicago, IL: University of Chicago Press.

Kullmann, E., Nawabi, S, & Zimmermann, W. (1971-72). Neue Ergebnisse zur Brutbiologie cribellater Spinnen aus Afganistan und der Serengeti. *Zeitschrift des Kollner Zoo, 14,* 87-108.

Lack, D. (1947). *Darwin's finches.* Cambridge: Cambridge University Press.

Lack, D. (1966). *Population studies of birds.* Oxford: Clarendon.

Lacey, R. (1981). *The kingdom.* New York: Harcourt, Brace, and Jovanich.

Layne, J. N. (1954). The biology of the red squirrel, *Tamiasciurus hudsonicus loquax* (Bangs), in Central New York. *Ecological Monographs, 24,* 227-267.

Lazlo, E. (1972). *The systems view of the world.* New York, NY: George Braziller.

Leakey, R. E., & Lewin, R. (1977). *Origins.* New York, NY: E. P. Dutton.

LeBoeuf, B. J. (1974). Male-female competition and reproductive success in elephant seals. *American Zoologist, 14,* 163-176.

Lehrman, D. S. (1965). Interaction between internal and external environment in the regulation of the reproductive cycle of the ring dove. In F. A. Beach (Ed.), *Sex and behavior* (pp. 355-380). New York, NY: John Wiley.

Lerner, I. M. (1954). *Genetic homeostasis.* Edinburgh: Oliver and Boyd.

Lieberman, P. (1975). *On the origins of language: An introduction to the evolution of human speech.* New York, NY: Macmillan.

Lieberman, P. (1984). *The biology and evolution of language.* Cambridge, MA: Harvard University Press.

Livingstone, F. B. (1980). Cultural causes of genetic change. In G. W. Barlow & J.

Silverberg (Eds.), *Sociobiology: Beyond nature-nurture* (pp. 307-329). Boulder, CO: Westview Press.

Lorenz, K. (1935). Der Kumpan in der Umwelt des Vogels. *Journal fur Ornithologie, 83*, 137- ,289.

Lorenz, K. (1941). Vergleichende Bewegungsstudien an Anatiden *Supplement to Journal of Ornithology, 89*, 137-213; 289-413.

Lorenz, K. (1966). *On aggression*. New York, NY: Harcourt, Brace, and World.

Lumsden, C. J., & Wilson, E. O. (1981). *Genes, mind and culture: The co-evolutionary process*. Cambridge, MA: Harvard University Press.

MacArthur, R. H., & Wilson, E. O. (1967). *The theory of island biogeography*. Princeton, NJ: Princeton University Press.

Mainardi, D. (1980). Tradition and the social transmission of behavior in animals. In G. W. Barlow & J. Silverberg (Eds.), *Sociobiology: Beyond nature-nurture* (pp. 227-255). Boulder, CO: Westview Press.

Marler, P. & Mundinger, P. C. (1971). Vocal learning in birds. In H. Moltz (Ed.), *The ontogeny of vertebrate behavior* (pp. 389-450). New York, NY: Academic Press.

Martin, P. S. (1973). The discovery of America. *Science, 179*, 969-974.

Martin, P. S. (1984). Prehistoric overkill: the global model. In P. S. Martin & R. G. Klein (Eds.), *Quarternary extinctions: A prehistoric revolution* (pp. 354-403). Tucson, AZ: University of Arizona Press.

Maxson, S. C. (1981). The genetics of aggression in vertebrates. In P. F. Brain & D. Benton (Eds.), *The biology of aggression* (pp. 69-104). The Netherlands: Sijthoff and Noordhoff.

Maxson, S. C., Ginsburg, B. E., & Trattner, A. (1979). Interaction of Y-chromosomal and autosomal gene(s) in the development of intermale aggression in mice. *Behavior Genetics, 9*, 219-226.

May, R. M., & Anderson, R. M. (1983). Parasite-host coevolution. In D. J. Futuyma & M. Slatkin (Eds.), *Coevolution* (pp. 186-206). Sunderland, MA: Sinauer.

Maynard Smith, J. (1964). Group selection and kin selection. *Nature, 201*, 1145-1147.

Maynard Smith, J. (1977). Parental investment, a prospective analysis. *Animal Behaviour, 25*, 1-9

Maynard Smith, J. (1982). *Evolution and the theory of games*. Cambridge: Cambridge University Press.

Mayr, E. (1963). *Animal species and evolution*. Cambridge: Belknap-Harvard.

Mayr, E. (1970). *Populations, species, and evolution: An abridgement of animal species and evolution*. Cambridge, MA: Belknap-Harvard.

McBride, G. (1964). A general theory of social organization and behavior. *University of Queensland Papers, Faculty Veterinary Science. 1* (2), 75-110.

McClintock, B. (1951). Chromosome organization and genic expression. *Cold Spring Harbor Symposia on Quantitative Biology, 16*, 13-47.

McClintock, B. (1956). Controlling elements and the gene. *Cold Spring Harbor Symposia on Quantitative Biology, 21*, 197-216.

Mead, M. (1939). *From the South Seas: Studies in adolescence and sex in primitive societies*. New York, NY: Morrow.

Mech, L. D. (1966). *The wolves of Isle Royale.* Washington, DC: U. S. National Park Service, Fauna Series No. 7.

Mech, L. D. (1970). *The wolf.* Garden City, NY: Natural History Press.

Mech, L. D. (1977). Productivity, mortality, and population trends of wolves in Northeastern Minnesota. *Journal of Mammalogy, 58,* 559-574.

Meikle, D. B., & Vessey, S. H. (1981). Nepotism among rhesus monkey brothers. *Nature, 294,* 160-161.

Michener, C. D. (1974). *The social behavior of the bees: A comparative study.* Cambridge, MA: Belknap-Harvard.

Miller, J. G. (1978). *Living systems.* New York, NY: McGraw-Hill.

Mills, H. B. (1937). A preliminary study of the bighorn of Yellowstone National Park. *Journal of Mammalogy, 18,* 205-212.

Moehlman, P. D. (1979). Jackal helpers and pup survival. *Nature, 277,* 382-383.

Moon, A. A., & Ginsburg, B. E. (1983). Regulation of gene expression: The lability of innate behavior. *Behavior Genetics Association.* (Abstract)

Moore, J. A. (1985). Science as a way of knowing - human ecology. *American Zoologist, 25,* 483-637.

Moyer, K. E. (1971). A preliminary physiological model of aggressive behavior. In B. E. Eleftheriou & J. P. Scott (Eds.), *The physiology of fighting and defeat.* New York, NY: Plenum.

Mundinger, P. C. (1980). Animal cultures and a general theory of cultural evolution. *Ethology and Sociobiology, 1,* 183-223.

Murie, A. (1944). *The wolves of Mt. McKinley.* Washington, DC: U. S. Government Printing Office. National Park Fauna Series No. 5.

Nitecki, M. H. (Ed.). (1983). *Coevolution.* Chicago, IL: University of Chicago Press.

Odum, E. P. (1969). The strategy of ecosystem development. *Science, 164,* 262-270.

Odum, H. T. (1983). *Systems ecology, an introduction.* New York, NY: Wiley.

Osborn, H. F. (1910). *The age of mammals in Europe, Asia and North America.* New York, NY: Macmillan.

Parker, G. A. (1984). Evolutionarily stable strategies. In J. R. Krebs & N. E. Davies (Eds.), *Behavioral ecology: An evolutionary approach* (pp. 30-61). Sunderland, MA: Sinauer.

Pawlowski, A. A., & Scott, J. P. (1956). Hereditary differences in the development of dominance in litters of puppies. *Journal of Comparative and Physiological Psychology, 49,* 353-358.

Piaget, J. (1970). *Structuralism.* New York, NY: Basic Books.

Pooley, A. C. (1974). Parental care in the Nile crocodile, *Lammergeyer, 21,* 43-45.

Porter, R. H. (1987). Kin recognition: Functions and mediating mechanisms. In C. Crawford, M. Smith & D. Krebs (Eds.), *Sociobiology and psychology: Ideas, issues and applications* (pp. 175-203). Hillsdale, NJ: Erlbaum.

Pugesek, B. H. (1983). The relationship between parental age and reproductive effort in the California gull (*Larus californicus*). *Behavioral Ecology* and Sociobiology, 13, 161-171.

Raff, R. A., & Kaufman, T. C. (1983). *Embryos, genes and evolution: The developmental genetic basis of evolutionary change.* New York, NY: Macmillan.

Reed, S., & Reed, E. W. (1965). *Mental retardation, a family study.* Philadelphia, PA: W. B. Saunders.

Reed, T. E., & Hanna, J. M. (1986). Between and within race variation in acute cardiovascular responses to alcohol: Evidence for genetic variation in normal males in three races. *Behavior Genetics, 16,* 585-596.

Reish, D. J. (1957). The life history of the polychaete annelid *Neanthes caudata* (della Chiaje) including a summary of development in the family Nereidae. *Pacific Science, 11,* 216-228.

Rood, J. P. (1978). Dwarf mongoose helpers at the den. *Zeitschrift fur Tierpsychologie, 48,* 277-287.

Rood, J. P. (1980). Mating relationships and breeding suppression in dwarf mongoose. *Animal Behaviour, 28,* 143-150.

Rubin, G. M. (1983). Dispersed repetitive DNAs in *Drosophila.* In J. A. Shapiro (Ed.), *Mobile genetic elements* (pp. 329-361). New York, NY: Academic Press.

Russell, E. S. (1949a). A quantitative histological study of the pigment found in the coat color mutants of the house mouse. III. Interdependence among the variable granule attributes. *Genetics, 34,* 133-145.

Russell, E. S. (1949b). A quantitative histological study of the pigment found in the coat color mutants of the house mouse. IV. The nature of the effect of genic substitution in five major allelic series. *Genetics, 34,* 146-166.

vom Saal, F. S., & Howard, L. S. (1982). The regulation of infanticide and parental behavior: Implications for reproductive success in male mice. *Science, 215,* 1270-1272.

Saunders, C. D. (1988). *Ecological, social and evolutionary aspects of baboon (Papio cynocephalus) grooming behavior.* Cornell University Ph.D. dissertation.

Schaller, G. B. (1972). *The Serengeti lion.* Chicago, IL: University of Chicago Press.

Schjelderup-Ebbe, T. (1922). Beitrage zur soziol-psychologie des Haushuhns. *Zeitschrift fur Psychologie, 88,* 225-252.

Schneirla, T. C. (1959). An evolutionary and developmental theory of biphasic processes underlying approach and withdrawal. *Nebraska Symposium on Motivation* (pp. 1-42). Lincoln, NE: University of Nebraska Press.

Scott, J. P. (1938). The embryology of the guinea pig. III. Development of the polydactylous monster: A new teras produced by the genes *PxPx. Journal of Morphology, 62,* 299-321.

Scott, J. P. (1943). Effects of single genes on the behavior of *Drosophila. American Naturalist, 77,* 184-190.

Scott, J. P. (1944). An experimental test of the theory that social behavior determines social organization. *Science, 100,* 569-570.

Scott, J. P. (1945). Social behavior, organization and leadership in a small flock of domestic sheep. *Comparative Psychology Monographs. 18* (4), 1-29.

Scott, J. P. (1948). Dominance and the frustration-aggression hypothesis. *Physiological Zoology, 21,* 31-39.

Scott, J. P. (1950). The social behavior of dogs and wolves; an illustration of sociobiological systematics. *Annals of the New York Academy of Science, 51,* 1009-1021.

Scott, J. P. (1953). Implications of infra-human social behavior for problems of human relations. In M. Sherif & M. O. Wilson (Eds.), *Group relations at the crossroads* (pp. 33-73). New York, NY: Harper.

Scott, J. P. (1956). The analysis of social organization in animals. *Ecology, 37,* 213-221.

Scott, J. P. (1957). The genetic and environmental differentiation of behavior. In D. B. Harris (Ed.), *The concept of development* (pp.59-77). Minneapolis, MN: University of Minnesota Press.

Scott, J. P. (1958). *Animal behavior.* Chicago, IL: University of Chicago Press.

Scott, J. P. (1968). Evolution and domestication of the dog. *Evolutionary Biology, 2,* 243-275.

Scott, J. P. (1975). *Aggression* (2nd ed.) Chicago, IL: University of Chicago Press.

Scott, J. P. (1977). Social genetics. *Behavior Genetics, 7,* 327-346.

Scott, J. P. (Ed.). (1978). *Critical periods.* New York, NY: Academic Press.

Scott, J. P. (1981). The evolution of function in agonistic behavior. In P. F. Brain & D. Benton (Eds.) *Multidisciplinary approaches to aggression research* (pp. 129-157). Amsterdam: Elsevier/North Holland.

Scott, J. P. (1982). Biology and political behavior: A systems analysis. *American Political Scientist, 25,* 243-272.

Scott, J. P. (1983). A systems approach to research on aggressive behavior. In E. C. Simmel, M. E. Hahn, & J. K. Walters (Eds.), *Agressive behavior: Genetic and neural approaches* (pp.1-18). Hillsdale, NJ: Erlbaum.

Scott, J. F., & Fuller, J. L. (1965). *Genetics and the social behavior of the dog.* Chicago, IL: University of Chicago Press.

Scott, J. P., & Nagy, M. Z. (1979). Behavioral metamorphosis in mammalian development. In E. C. Simmel (Ed.), *Early experiences and early behavior* (pp. 16-37). New York, NY: Academic Press.

Scott, J. P., & Stewart, J. C. (1947). Lack of correlation between leadership and dominance in a herd of goats. *Journal of Comparative and Physiological Psychology, 40,* 255-264.

Scott, J. W. (1942). Mating behavior of the sage grouse. *Auk, 59,* 477-498.

Scott, J. W. (1950). A study of the phylogenetic or comparative behavior of three species of grouse. *Annals of the New York Academy of Science, 51,* 1062-1073.

Scott, W. E. D. (1901). Data on song in birds. Observations on the song of Baltimore orioles raised in captivity. *Science, 14,* 522-526.

Selander, R. J., & Johnson, W. E. (1973). Genetic variation among vertebrate species. *Annual Reviews of Ecology and Systematics, 4,* 75-91.

Seton, E. T. (1938). *The natural history of the ten commandments.* Santa Fee, NM: Seton Village Press.

Shelford, V. E. (1913). *Animal communities in temperate America, as illustrated in the Chicago region; a study in animal ecology.* Chicago, IL: University of Chicago Press.

Silk, J. B. (1986). Social behavior in evolutionary perspective. In B. B. Smuts, D. L. Cheney, R. M. Seyfarth, R. W. Wrangham, & T. T. Struhsaker (Eds.) *Primate societies* (pp. 318-329). Chicago, IL: University of Chicago Press.

Silvers, W. K. (1979). *The coat colors in mice: A model for mammalian gene action and interaction.* New York, NY: Springer-Verlag.

Simpson, G. G. (1944). *Tempo and mode in evolution.* New York, NY: Columbia University Press.

Simpson, G. G. (1951). *Horses: The story of the horse family in the modern world and through sixty million years of history.* New York, NY: Oxford.

Simpson, G. G. (1953). *The major features of evolution.* New York, NY: Columbia University Press.

Smith, A. (1776). *An inquiry into the nature and causes of the wealth of nations..* Edited by Edwin Cannon. London: Methuen.

Smith, C. C. (1968). Adaptive nature of social organization in the genus of tree squirrels, *Tamiasciurus. Ecological Monographs, 38,* 31-63.

Smuts, B. B. (1986). Gender, aggression, and influence. In B. B. Smuts, D. L. Cheney, R. M. Seyfarth, R. W. Wrangham, & T. T. Struhsaker (Eds.), *Primate societies* (pp. 400-412). Chicago, IL: University of Chicago Press.

Smuts, B. B., Cheney, D. L., Seyfarth, R. M. , Wrangham, R. W., & Struhsaker, T. T. (Eds.). (1986). *Primate societies.* Chicago, IL: University of Chicago Press.

Sommer, J. (1987) Infanticide among free-ranging langurs (*Presbytis entellus* at Jodhpur (Rajasthan, India): Recent observations and a reconsideration of hypotheses. *Primates, 28,* 163-197.

Southwick, C. H. (1972). Aggression among non-human primates. *Anthropology Module 23.* Reading, MA: Addison Wesley.

Spencer, H. (1884). *The man versus the state.* London: Watts.

Stein, D. M. (1984). *The sociobiology of infant and adult male baboons.* Norwood, NJ: Ablex.

Steward, J. H. (1955). *Theory of culture change: The methodology of multilinear evolution.* Urbana, IL: University of Illinois Press.

Struhsaker, T. T., & Leland, L. (1986). Colobines: Infanticide by adult males. In B. B. Smuts, D. L. Cheney, R. M. Seyfarth, R. W. Wrangham, & T. T. Struhsaker (Eds.), *Primate societies* (pp. 83-97). Chicago, IL: University of Chicago Press.

Sumner, W. G. (1883). *What social classes owe each other.* New York, NY: Harpers. Reprinted by Pamphleteers Inc., Los Angeles, CA (1947).

Sutton-Smith, B. (1971). Play, games and controls. In J. P. Scott & S. F. Scott (Eds.), *Social control and social change* (pp. 73-102). Chicago, IL: University of Chicago Press.

Svare, B., & Mann, M. (1981). Infanticide: Genetic, developmental and hormonal influences in mice. *Physiology and Behavior, 27*, 921-927.

Tansley, A. G. (1935). The use and abuse of vegetational concepts and terms. *Ecology, 16*, 284-307.

Tax, S. (Ed.) (1960). *Evolution after Darwin.* Chicago, IL: University of Chicago Press.

Thompson, D. W. (1942). *On growth and form* (new ed.) Cambridge: the University Press.

Tinbergen, N. (1953). *Social behavior in animals.* London: Methuen.

Tomback, D. F. (1983). Nutcrackers and pines – coevolution or coadaptation? In M. H. Nitecki (Ed.), *Coevolution* (pp. 179-223). Chicago, IL: University of Chicago Press.

Tompkins, R. (1978). Genic control of axolotl metamorphosis. *American Zoologist, 18*, 313-319.

Trivers, R. L. (1972a). *Natural selection and social behavior.* Harvard University Thesis.

Trivers, R. L. (1972b). Parental investment and sexual selection. In B. Campbell (Ed.), *Sexual selection and the descent of man* (pp. 136-179). Chicago, IL: Aldine.

Trivers, R. L. (1985). *Social evolution.* Menlo Park, CA: Benjamin/Cummings.

Tyler, M. J., & Carter, D. B. (1981). Oral birth of the young of the gastric brooding frog *Rheobatrachus silus. Animal Behaviour, 29*, 280-282.

Tyler, W. M. (1950). *Cedar waxwing.* Washington, DC: U. S. Government Printing Office. U. S. National Museum, Bulletin No. 197.

Uhrich, J. (1938). The social hierarchy in inbred mice. *Journal of Comparative Psychology, 25*, 373-413.

Vale, J. R. & Ray, D. (1971). A diallel analysis of male mouse sex behavior. *Behavior Genetics, 2*, 199-209.

Varmus, H. E. (1983). Retroviruses. In J. A. Shapiro (Ed.), *Mobile genetic elements.* New York, NY: Academic Press.

Vehrencamp. S. L. (1979). The roles of individual, kin and group selection in the evolution of sociality. In P. Marler & J. G. Vandenbergh (Eds.), *Social behavior and communication* Vol. 3 of F. A. King (Ed.), *Handbook of behavioral neurobiology* (pp. 351-394). New York, NY: Plenum.

Vessey, S. H. (1971). Free-ranging rhesus monkeys: Behavioral effects of removal, separation and reintroduction of group members. *Behaviour, 40*, 216-227.

Waddington, C. H. (1975). *The evolution of an evolutionist.* Ithaca, NY: Cornell University Press.

Wake, D. B., & Larson, A. (1987). Multidimensional analysis of an evolving lineage. *Science, 238*, 42-48.

Walters, J. R., & Seyfarth, R. M. (1986). Conflict and cooperation. In B. B. Smuts, D. L. Cheney, R. M. Seyfarth, R. W. Wrangham, & T. T. Struhsaker (Eds.), *Primate societies* (pp. 306-317). Chicago, IL: University of Chicago Press.

Ward, J. A. & Barlow, G. W. (1967). the maturation and regulation of glancing off the parents of young orange chromids *(Etroplus maculatus*: Pisces-cichlidae). *Behaviour, 29*, 1-56.

Wells, M. J. (1978). *Octopus: Physiology and behavior of an advanced vertebrate.* London: Chapman and Hall.

Wheeler, W. M. (1923). *Social life among the insects.* New York, NY: Harcourt Brace.

White, L. A. (1959). *The evolution of culture.* New York, NY: McGraw-Hill.

Wiley, R. H. (1973). Territoriality and non-random mating in the sage grouse *(Centrocercus urophasianus). Animal Behaviour Monographs, 6* (2), 85-169.

Williams, G. C. (1964). Measurement of consociation among fishes and comments on the evolution of schooling. *Publications Museum of Michigan State University, Biological Series, 2,* 351-382.

Williams, G. C. (1966). *Adaption and natural selection.* Princeton, NJ: Princeton University Press.

Willson, L. (1971). Observations and experiments on the ethology of the European beaver *(Castor fiber* L.). A study in the development of phylogenetically adapted behavior in a highly specialized mammal. *Viltrevy: Swedish Wildlife, 8,* 115-226.

Wilson, E. O. (1971). *The insect societies.* Cambridge, MA: Belknap-Harvard.

Wilson, E. O. (1975). *Sociobiology: the new synthesis.* Cambridge, MA: Belknap-Harvard.

Winslow, J. T. & Miczek, K. A. (1985). Social status as determinant of alcohol effects on aggressive behavior in squirrel monkeys *(Saimiri sciureus). Psychopharmacology, 85,* 167-172.

Wolfe, H. G., & Coleman, D. L. (1966). Pigmentation. In E. L. Green (Ed.), *Biology of the laboratory mouse* (2nd ed., pp. 405-425). New York, NY: McGraw-Hill.

Wolpy, J. H. (1967). *Socially controlled systems of mating among wolves and other gregarious mammals.* Ph.D. Disseration, University of Chicago.

Wright, S. (1922). The effects of inbreeding and crossbreeding on guinea pigs. II. Differentiation among inbred families. Washington, DC: U. S. Department of Agriculture. *Bulletin 1090.*

Wright, S. (1931). Evolution in Mendelian populations. *Genetics, 16,* 97-159.

Wright, S. (1932). The roles of mutation, inbreeding, crossbreeding and selection in evolution. *Proceedings 6th International Congress of Genetics, 1,* 356-366.

Wright, S. (1935). Evolution in populations in approximate equilibrium. *Journal of Genetics, 30,* 257-266.

Wright, S. (1945). Tempo and mode in evolution: a critical review. *Ecology, 26,* 415-419.

Wright, S. (1968). *Evolution and the genetics of populations.* Volume I, *Genetic and biometric foundations.* Chicago, IL: University of Chicago Press.

Wright, S. (1977). *Evolution and the genetics of populations.* Volume III, *Experimental results and evolutionary deductions.* Chicago, IL: University of Chicago Press.

Wright, S. (1978). The relation of livestock breeding to theories of evolution. *Journal of Animal Science, 46,* 1192-1200.

Wright, S. (1980). Genic and organismic selection. *Evolution, 34,* 825-843.

Wynne-Edwards, V. C. (1962). *Animal dispersion in relation to social behavior.* Edinburgh: Oliver & Boyd.
Wynne-Edwards, V. C. (1968). The regulation of animal populations. *International Encyclopedia of the Social Sciences* (Vol. 14, pp. 360-365). New York, NY: Macmillan.

Author Index

Subject Index

Adaptation
   active and passive, 76–78
   and Differential Survival, 40
   and systems theory, 88
Adaptive radiation, 85–86
Adaptivity
   of genotype, 26
   and systems theory, 7
Adoption, across and within species,
   141
Africa, human origins in, 239–240
Aggregations, 207
Agonistic behavior, 104–105
   dispersive effect, 208
   evolution of function, 182–193, 320
   evolutionary pathways, 194–196
   expressed in social relationships,
   199
   patterns of, 108
   regulates competition, 173
   and social organization, 196–197
Agriculture and ecosystems, 289–291,
   299
Agricultural revolution, 253–254,
   266–267
Allelomimetic behavior, 104–105
   in fish, 222–223
   provides mutual protection, 175
Allelomimetic groups, 146–148, 208
Allometry, explains orthogenesis, 87
Allotetraploidy, and speciation, 92
   See also hybridization
Altruism, 216
Altruistic behavior, 128, 130, 165
   evolution of, 142, 320
Amphibia
   agonistic behavior, 184–185

   caregiving, 136
Anatomical defenses, 178–179
Animal Behavior Society, 151
Annelida, agonistic behavior, 183
Approach-withdrawal, 103
Armor, correlated with immobility,
   179
Arthropoda
   caregiving, 135–136
   external armor, 177–178
   shelter-building, 180
Asexual reproduction
   and evolutionary change processes,
   28
   and Two-Process Theory, 62
Attachment
   in primates, 192
   and social organization, 207
Australopithecus, 241, 242
Avoidance behavior, evolution of,
   179–180

Baboon, *Papio cynocephalus*, mating
   system, 139
Bacteria, and Two-Process evolutionary theory, 62
Baldwin effect, 98–99, 112–113, 316
Beaver, *Castor sp.*,
   shelter building, 181
   social organization, 138
Bees, *Apis mellifica*
   altruism, 133
   caregiving, 135
   genic correlations, 133
   inbreeding, 220, 222
Behavior
   and Differential Survival, 118–119